Reporting Religion

Reporting Religion

Facts & Faith

edited by
Benjamin J. Hubbard

POLEBRIDGE PRESS

SONOMA, CALIFORNIA

Design & composition: Polebridge Press, Sonoma, California

Printing & binding: McNaughton & Gunn, Inc., Saline, Michigan

Display type: ITC American Typewriter Medium

Text type: Times Roman

Library of Congress Cataloging-in-Publication Data
Reporting religion : facts and faith / edited by Benjamin J. Hubbard.
    p. cm. — (Eagle books)
  Includes bibliographical references.
  ISBN 0-944344-10-0 : $17.95
  1. Journalism, Religious—United States—History—20th century.
2. Religious newspapers and periodicals—United States—Social
aspects. 3. Journalistic ethics—United States. 4. Social ethics.
5. Religion and sociology—United States. 6. n-us. I. Hubbard,
Benjamin Jerome. II. Series: Eagle books (Sonoma, Calif.)
PN4888.R4R47 1989
070.4'49200'973—dc20   89-29051
                                                 CIP

Printed in the United States of America

Contents

PART III   Ethical Issues   143

Preface

This collection of essays is an attempt to explore a subject—the inter-action of the media and religion—which has been largely ignored by scholars and practitioners in both the communications and religious studies fields. Part I (chapters 1 through 4) focuses on the special role of the religion writer in the secular press and the problems connected with this beat. Part II (chapters 5 through 9) looks at the way the media are used by the principal religious traditions in this country (Catholic, Protestant, and Jewish) and with the uniquely American and currently very troubled phenomenon of TV evangelism. Part III (chapters 10 through 12) takes up ethical issues surrounding the media: religion's role in the media reform movement; the question of whether the press is capable of fairness and objectivity (i.e., of being ethical) in its work; and a case study of media ethics, whether it is right for the press to muzzle a religious bigot, as it did with Gerald L. K. Smith.

I am grateful to all the contributors to this volume for accepting their assignments and completing them in a very short time frame. I wish to thank one contributor in particular, Professor William Thorn, my former mentor at Marquette University, for his encouragement and advice at every stage of this project. I am also grateful to the Office of Faculty Research at California State University, Fullerton, for providing me with a grant in the summer of 1987 to pursue this study and to my student Tom Wright who provided research assistance. And I want to thank Judy Hubbard for suggesting the title of the book, for making several sugges-tions for improving my own chapter, for preparing the Index, and for making me smell the roses and plant the pansies when it seemed the project itself wasn't going to bloom.

Benjamin J. Hubbard, editor

Foreword

This book represents a point of transition. For years advocates of better coverage of religion in the press had to spend all their energies providing apologiae, defenses of their enterprise. Now that religion coverage is more established, more secure, they can put those energies to work trying to improve that coverage. Many of these essays look back to and through the long years when they had to make a case. Many of them look forward to the time when they can put all energies into improving the product.

This Foreword will have something of that Janus-character, as well. Invite a historian to introduce journalists and you cannot help evoking a backward glance. Invite a historian who is also a journalist and you cannot help provoking a contemporary analysis. I accept the urge to do both.

In the nineteenth century, the prehistoric era so far as this book is concerned, the daily press covered religion as a matter of course, not in segregated fashion in "religion pages." That was easy to do, since the culture in most places was so dominated by a single ethos: call it evangelical Protestant of the white man mainstream sort. Protestants of this sort, in easy alliance with secular-minded folk of a certain sort, went about their business. That business usually included responsible participation in, say, Episcopal, Presbyterian, or Congregational churches.

The people in these churches ran the downtown business, the corporations, the voluntary associations. A sense of noblesse oblige (or, some of their critics would say, guilt) led Vanderbilts and Goulds, Fisks and Rockefellers, McCormicks and Drews, to build seminaries and universities. Naturally, such actions made Page One. And the daughters of these folks at the center of the culture would marry, and their grandparents would die, and their offspring would be christened—all events whose rites were covered in the press. Many papers covered Sunday sermons of the prominent. What the Episcopal bishop did, or the Presbyterian Stated Clerk said, or the Congregationalist theologian thought, had cultural import. One did not need a "religion page" or a "religion editor," so taken for granted was reportage on all this.

In the twentieth century there was a new situation. During the last half of the nineteenth, Catholics came to run northern cities, and what the

archbishop said mattered. As blacks moved north, their churches complicated the scene, as did synagogues and churches of newly arriving Eastern
and Southern Europeans. Pluralism bewildered editors: how is it possible
to cover all these groups? Which Episcopalian cared about what the Naza-
renes did? Did Baptist news interest Presbyterians any longer, especially
when those Baptists were of the no-count, no-class Southern sort?

What should the press do when there was conflict in religion? The
churches did not like to publicize their problems. They wanted the press to
do public relations, to cover smorgasbords and ordinations, suppers and
stewardship drives. But in the twenties and thirties religious people did
things that made Page One, often in embarrassing ways. Fundamentalists
fought modernists; news reporters, not religion writers, covered William
Jennings Bryan versus Clarence Darrow in the Scopes Trial. Aimee
Semple McPherson made the front page when she "disappeared." Father
Coughlin stirred the masses; his clerical collar appeared on pictures next
to those covering the Roosevelt administration. One kind of religion was
news; the other kind of religion was segregated into Saturday's black-
bordered religion columns.

At mid-century it was clear that religion, church-and-synagogue religion, was "reviving." But editors had a hard time spotting this. George
Cornell here reviews some of the work of pioneers, people who accepted
the marginal status of religion writing and helped bring it back to the front
page. This new group needed more ability, more grit, more steadfastness,
than did their nineteenth-century predecessors. They had to deal with
subcultures and show how they affected whole cultures. They had to show
that religiously pluralist America was producing news that concerned
more than the people in the denomination or sect on which a particular
story concentrated.

If I read these essays right, and properly recall many late-night rump
sessions of the Religion Newswriters Association—they let me in to their
beery wind-down parties, but one's memory is naturally a bit blurry in the
morning after, a third of a century later—one of the big problems was the
shortsightedness of editorial management. If editors were responsible,
they were suspicious, a bit cynical, wary of piety, dismissive of churchly
self-advertising. So they set up high hurdles for religion writers, and
remained unimpressible.

At the same time, many were irresponsibly unaware of the religious
dimension of life around them, as some of these essays point out. Why?
Some studies suggest that the cohort of people who make up media management tends to be drawn from an unrepresentative sample of the population. Many of them went to colleges and universities where religion

courses were nonexistent; there was a kind of hostility to religion among the professors. A good editor had probably left old First Church behind, because it was boring or repressive. With it went everything that religion had ever represented. Gradually, otherwise farseeing people were blinded.

One might say that most of the time "everyone" knew that religion was important except the two sets of people who were supposed to monitor the culture: academicians and media people.

Today things have changed. If World War III starts, it could well have its beginning in the Middle East, over typographical errors or blundering interpretations of the book of Ezekiel, or Revelation, or the Qur'an. More people kill each other in the name of religion than of anything else, in the tribal wars of today. Modernisms jar churches and fundamentalisms jolt cultures. People heal in the name of religion: most medical ethical stories have a religious tie. In today's world 1.4 billion people are called Christian, and for the first time more than half of them are in the southern, or poor, world. They are restless, and will make news. Theologians discuss changes in meaning systems, as John Dart here points out; and moralists are in the forefront of controversy in times of sudden change. Churches are busy dealing with change in sexual ethos. The women's movement has many religious overtones. Abortion is the most controversial political issue around, and it is religious. Pope John Paul II makes news as he travels, cracks the whip on dissent, and intervenes in Latin American politics. This book shows again and again how vital religion is.

Print media have chances to cover religion better than television does. Television cannot deal well with the abstract, as Robert Abernethy is herein quoted as remarking, and not all religious trends are concrete, hard news. So the public press's religious dimension is of great importance. (Some essays in this book deal with Catholic, Jewish, and Protestant press; this form of communication has some different ground rules but is relevant in the same world of change.) Some of the essayists are optimistic, and spend their time pointing out how to capitalize on the movement and do even better.

So we are at the point where religion coverage is more secure, its writers more experienced, its readership expanding. It may still have a long way to go, but the beginnings are here. Serious writers, teachers, editors, critics, public philosophers, and theologians, some of whom wrote essays in this book, have now begun to point to ways to advance the cause further.

The basic theme: while awareness grows, so must competence. Some metro and city desk editors still send general assignment reporters to cover papal travels; they do well on crowd size and decor but miss the spiritual themes that underlie such occasions. It is easier to deal with conflict than with healing, so unrepresentative reporting occurs. Church public relations agents often want to have churches exempt from scrutiny. How can we break the barriers? How can we eliminate trivia, or know what trivia is, to make room for the significant? You may find more questions than answers in essays on these themes, but the fact that such questions can now be pushed forward is a sign of the maturation of a profession within a profession. Which means that the writers in this book can speak for themselves. Having set some context for them, I now have the pleasure of stepping aside so the reader can read what they have to say. I hope the reader includes newspaper editors as well as secular and religious people who depend upon their sense of what is news and why, what to feature and how to do it. We can all benefit.

Martin E. Marty

Part I

Reporting on Religion in the Secular Press

1

The Importance of the Religion Angle in Reporting on Current Events

Benjamin J. Hubbard

NEGLECTING THE RELIGION ANGLE: THREE CASE STUDIES

There is a curious irony about the juxtaposition of the guarantee of the freedom of the press and the separation of church and state in the first amendment. The intention of the framers of the Constitution was to ensure that neither the press nor religion would be under the state's thumb, and also that there would be no official, state-sponsored church. But one has the feeling that the press considers itself liberated from religion by the first amendment and free to report on the business of the nation without bothering about irrelevant religion business. Religion, so this theory goes, is in the private sphere of faith, not the public domain of facts. Yet facts are what journalism is all about.

Though the generalization is less true now than it was twenty years ago, the journalistic community is not very comfortable with religion. Editors view religion stories as soft, irrelevant, and non-objective. Benjamin C. Bradlee, executive editor of the *Washington Post*, admitted in a *Los Angeles Times* interview that religion doesn't interest him as much as most other journalistic beats, and said he has "never sat down and thought about religion coverage."[1] "The verities involved in religion are eternal and unchanging," Bradlee commented. "Why should we cover the president going to church . . . What's so big about that?" The case studies presented below attempt to answer Bradlee's question.

Jimmy Carter's evangelical Humanism

President Carter went to church regularly and sometimes taught Sunday school classes. What was "so big about that?" UPI reporter Wesley G.

1. Shaw, "Religion Writers Way Objectivity." *Los Angeles Times*, 29 December 1983.

Pippert considers it "astounding" that one of the most powerful persons in the world would stand in front of a small group, without benefit of research and speech writer, and reflect on his values.[2] Yet most reporters viewed Carter's Sunday school comments as irrelevant. Pippert questioned one reporter about a Carter Sunday school remark in print concerning the SALT II Treaty. Had the President said anything else? Pippert asked. "Oh, no," the reporter replied, "that was just a sentence or two he [Carter] said. The rest was about kings and prophets and things like that."[3] Carter probably drew some parallels between war and peace in ancient Israel and in modern America, and about the ideal of peace set down by the prophets. If the reporter had possessed even a modest comprehension of the biblical material, he might have been able to understand the mind of Carter on the disarmament issue—and the public would have been better informed as a result.

Carter said as much in an 1983 interview. He spoke of "the irresponsibility of the press" in failing to explain how his religious views affected his actions on controversial issues such as the Iranian hostage crisis, the Panama Canal Treaty, his defense of former Budget Director Bert Lance, and his widely publicized remarks to Playboy Magazine about having "committed adultery in my heart many times." The press had "no desire to explain my faith or understand it," Carter said, despite his having made clear early in his presidential campaign that "there is no way to understand me and my political philosophy without understanding my faith."[4]

In a little-reported speech to the general council of the World Jewish Council in 1977 (which parallels the disregarded Sunday school lessons), Carter provided the rationale for his emphasis on human rights issues:

> I've been steeped in the Bible since early childhood, and I believe that anyone who reads the ancient words of the Old Testament with both sensitivity and care will find there the idea of government as something based on a voluntary covenant rather than force—the idea of equality before the law over the whim of any ruler; the idea of the dignity of the individual human being and also of the individual conscience; the idea of service to the poor and to the oppressed; the idea of self-government and tolerance and of nations living together in peace, despite differences of belief.[5]

2. "Moral Considerations," 20. See also Pippert's *The Spiritual Journey of Jimmy Carter (In His Own Words)*.
3. Pippert, "Moral Considerations," 20.
4. Shaw, "Jimmy Carter's Rise Brought Evangelicalism to Front Pages." *Los Angeles Times*, 28 December 1983.
5. Quoted in Pippert, "Moral Considerations," 21.

Because most members of the Washington press corps weren't familiar with the material Carter was referring to, they gave the speech short shrift. If they had possessed even a basic understanding of the Pentateuch (the first five books of the Hebrew scriptures) and the writings of the prophets, they might have viewed Carter's concern for human rights issues in a different light.

Finally, Carter's most memorable achievement, the 1979 Egyptian-Israeli peace treaty, was viewed primarily in political terms by most diplomatic reporters. But the three leaders, Begin of Israel, Sadat of Egypt and Carter, saw a religious motivation for the negotiations: the common monotheistic heritage of Jew, Christian and Muslim—the People of the Book. Carter concludes his 1985 book, *The Blood of Abraham*, with words mirroring the religious motivations which impelled him to keep negotiating during the bleakest moments at Camp David:

> The Blood of Abraham, God's father of the chosen, still flows in the veins of Arab, Jew, and Christian, and too much of it has been spilled in grasping for the inheritance of the revered patriarch in the Middle East. The spilled blood in the Holy Land still cries out to God—an anguished cry for peace.[6]

In sum, Jimmy Carter's evangelical heritage drove his political agenda to an extent largely unrecognized by the legion of journalists who hung on his every word—except when those words struck a religious note.

Ronald Reagan's christian militarism

President Reagan became the hero of the New Christian Right—largely populated with evangelicals—by supporting school prayer and opposing abortion. Political writers have correctly analyzed his position as stemming from his conservative political philosophy and indirectly from his personal religious convictions. But the press didn't take seriously the impact of the apocalyptic writings of the Bible on his thinking about war and peace. Drawing principally upon the books of Ezekiel and Daniel in the Hebrew scriptures and of Revelation in the Christian, fundamentalists over the past 150 years have spun elaborate theories about the nearness of the end time and the inevitability of a final, cosmic conflict. Most of them espouse Dispensationalism, the idea that the Bible divides history into distinct eras or dispensations. The last of these will involve a struggle between good and evil, Christ and anti-Christ at Armaggedon, the mount (in Hebrew, *Har*) of Meggido in northern Israel.

6. Carter, *Blood of Abraham*, 208.

In *Prophecy and Politics* Grace Halsell documents President Reagan's lifelong interest in the dispensationalist view of biblical prophecy.[7] His mother was a devout member of the Disciples of Christ (Christian Church) and he taught Sunday school classes at the First Christian Church in Dixon, Illinois. He was strongly influenced by Hal Lindsey's immensely popular *The Late Great Planet Earth* with its vivid scenario of supposedly now-unfolding events leading to Armageddon.[8] In 1971, then-Governor Reagan, in a dinner conversation, told James Mills, president pro-tem of the California State Senate:

> In the 38th Chapter of Ezekiel it says God will take the children of Israel from among the heathen, where they'd been scattered and will gather them again in the promised land. That has finally come about after 2,000 years. For the first time ever, everything is in place for the battle of Armageddon and the second coming of Christ.[9]

Mills countered that what Reagan said was true enough, but "the one thing the Bible says most clearly about the second coming is that no one can know when it will happen." Reagan responded intensely, "Everything is falling into place. It can't be long now. Ezekiel says that fire and brimstone will be rained upon the enemies of God's people. That must mean that they'll be destroyed by nuclear weapons. They exist now, and they never did in the past." Reagan went on to equate Gog, the mythical prince described in Ezekiel 38 and 39 as attacking Israel from the north, with the Soviet Union. This didn't make sense before the Russian Revolution, Reagan explained, but "now it does, now that Russia has become communistic and atheistic, now that Russia has set itself against God."[10]

In 1980, presidential candidate Reagan told TV evangelist Jim Bakker in a PTL Club interview, "We may be the generation that sees Armageddon." In 1983, President Reagan told Tom Dine, director of the American-Israel Public Affairs Committee, "You know, I turn back to your ancient prophets in the Old Testament and the signs foretelling Armageddon, and I find myself wondering if we are the generation that's going to see that come about."[11] Although the President's remarks were widely reported in the press, few editorialists or columnists seem to have taken them as significant for the nation's foreign policy. Yet, earlier that year (1983), Reagan had told the National Association of Evangelicals that the

7. Halsell, *Prophecy and Politics*, 40–50.
8. It is estimated the book has sold 18 million copies.
9. Mills, "Conversation with Reagan," 141.
10. Mills, "Conversation with Reagan," 141.
11. Quoted in Halsell, *Prophecy and Politics*, 48.

Soviet Union was "the focus of evil in the modern world." The remark itself has become famous, but its background in the militant anti-communism of Dispensationalism went largely unreported.

In the article about his 1971 conversation with Reagan, Mills notes that the victory of Israel and its allies over the powers of darkness was prophesied by Ezekiel. But he adds that conservative Christians, including Reagan, "are not allowed the spiritual luxury of taking that victory for granted. Making the forces of righteousness strong to win that all-important conflict is . . . acting in fulfillment of God's prophecies and in accordance with His divine will . . ." Mills sees Reagan's policy decisions as influenced by these apocalyptic perceptions: "Certainly his attitudes relative to military spending, and his coolness to all proposals for nuclear disarmament, are consistent with such apocalyptic views. Armageddon . . . cannot take place in world that has been disarmed."[12]

In his second term especially, Mr. Reagan has listened to voices other than the prophet Ezekiel. His "evil empire" rhetoric was absent at the Moscow summit where the Intermediate Nuclear Forces Treaty was signed in May 1988, and "good chemistry" prevailed between himself and General Secretary Gorbachev. Nonetheless, President Reagan's understanding of biblical prophecy, which had a considerable influence on his basic thinking about communism, relations with the Soviets, military preparedness, and nuclear disarmament, was overlooked by the press. With little understanding of the uniquely American phenomenon of fundamentalism and of the biblical corpus from which it derives, journalists tended to sidestep the whole issue. We were thereby deprived of a full understanding of the underlying philosophy of the nation's chief executive and the leader of the Western Alliance.

The Ayatollah Khomeini's Islamic reformation

While under house arrest in 1963, Ayatollah Ruhollah Khomeini was visited by the head of SAVAK (Iran's secret police), General Hasan Pakravan. The general tried to persuade the Ayatollah to abandon his campaign against the Shah, Mohammed Reza Pahlavi. "Politics is lies, deception, shame and meanness," said Pakarvan. "Leave politics to us." Khomeini replied, "All of Islam is politics."[13]

This cardinal principle, Islam is politics, was unknown or unappre-

---

12. Mills, "Conversation with Ronald Reagan," 141.
13. Bakhash, *Reign of the Ayatollahs*, 32. Though political orientations differ from country to country (left wing, right wing, "establishment," etc.), the common thread in movements as diverse as Shiite Islam, liberation theology and the New Christian Right is the conviction that society must conform to religious convictions.

ciated not only by the press but by the U.S. State Department as well. The Iranian debacle—which eventually stung the Reagan administration in the Iran-Contra scandal as it had the Carter in the hostage crisis—has complex origins going back at least to the reinstatement of the Shah in 1953 by the CIA. The aim here is not to analyze that debacle as such[14] but to examine how the press's ignorance of Islam contributed to our national misunderstanding of the Iranian Revolution and to a negative assessment of Islam by Americans. What follows is a brief review of the principal mistakes made by the media in its coverage of the Revolution.

Misunderstanding of Islam

In covering the Iranian Revolution, most reporters had only a rudimentary understanding of Islam and its history. On the 21 November 1978, CBS Evening News, Randy Daniels spoke of Muharram, the Muslim month in which Shiites commemorate the martyrdoms of Hussein and Hassan. These grandsons of Muhammad are believed by Shiites to be in the direct line of prophetic succession from him. Daniels described Muharram as the period when Shiites "celebrate Muhammad's challenge to world leaders." The statement was completely inaccurate. The events of that month have nothing directly to do with Muhammad, nor did Muhammad ever challenge world leaders.

As already noted, the intimate connection between religion and politics, especially for Shiite Muslims, was either missed or negatively evaluated by the press. In a 6 November 1978, *Washington Post* news analysis, Jay Ross—who, to his credit, recognized that it was not unusual for Shiite clergy to get involved in politics—wrote: "Shiites do not accept the notion of separation of church and state and Iranian governments long before the Shah have been plagued by difficult relations with the mosque."[15] Ross implies that church-state separation is good for all nations at all times and that the mosque and its mullahs should stay out of politics.

Underestimation of Islam's influence on its adherents

Typically, editors and reporters underestimate religion's impact in all cultures. This was certainly true about estimations of Islam's influence at the time of the Iranian Revolution. For example, Flora Lewis, a *New York Times* European correspondent, wrote in the Times in November of 1978:

14. For an excellent summary, see Smith, *Morality, Reason and Power.*
15. Ross, "In Iran: Modernization, Repression and Now." *Washington Post,* 6 November 1978.

> Many of these people [elements of the anti-Shah forces] are opposed to any suggestion of theocratic rule or an imposition of Islamic orthodoxy on a Moslem country where most of the people have traditionally taken a relaxed view of the scriptures of their faith.[16]

Although she was correct that not everyone who wanted the Shah out wanted Khomeini in, she underestimated the strength of Islam.

Disdain for Islam

Disdain for Islam, particularly for its Shiite branch, was widespread in the media at the time of the Revolution and has helped promote prejudicial attitudes toward Muslims ever since.[17] Ray Moseley of the *Chicago Tribune* wrote in a 25 November 1978 article:

> People who consider dying to be an honor are, by definition, fanatics. Vengeful blood lust and a yearning for martyrdom seem especially pronounced among the Shiites Moslems of Iran. This is what impelled thousands of citizens to stand unarmed and defiant against troops with automatic weapons during the revolution.[18]

If one were to apply Moseley's criteria to the American Revolution, then Nathan Hale who said, "I only regret that I have but one life to lose for my country," would have been a "fanatic"; a whole cadre of Minutemen would have been filled with "vengeful blood lust" against the British; and Washington's men at Valley Forge might be thought to have "yearned for martyrdom." This is not to deny that martyrdom has been prized historically in Shiite Islam (as the Iran-Iraq war has poignantly demonstrated). But millions of young men of many faiths have died on thousands of battlefields thinking they were fighting for God.

An earlier story was equally simplistic regarding Islam's role in Iran:

> Much of the recent rioting has grown from demonstrations called by religious extremists opposed to the Shah's attempt to westernize this oil-rich, anti-communist nation and to loosen the traditionally firm grip of the Moslem clergy.[19]

It is unlikely that the same writer would have described the civil rights or anti-war activists of the sixties and seventies who were often motivated by

16. Lewis, *New York Times*, 6 November 1978.
17. See Said, "Iran," 22–33, and Dorman and Omeed, "Reporting Iran the Shah's Way," 27–33.
18. Moseley, "Conformity, Intolerance Grip Revolution." *Chicago Tribune*, 25 November 1978.
19. *Los Angeles Times*, 10 September 1978.

deep religious convictions, as "religious extremists." However, because
Islam is religiously foreign it was viewed by the press during the Iranian
Revolution as fanatical, fundamentalist, and intolerant. The point is not
to justify the human rights abuses that have occurred under Khomeini,
but only to emphasize that different—and biased—norms have been
applied in Iran. South Africa, for example, is predominantly Christian, yet
its sad human rights record is seldom attributed to Christian intransi-
gence.

An editorial in the 10 November 1978 *San Francisco Chronicle*
opined that:

> It would be hard to convince us that any modern state as large and
> economically advanced as Iran could conceivably be ruled successfully or
> for long by the kind of fanatic priesthood that Khomeini symbolizes.[20]

It has been ten years since Khomeini's "fanatic priesthood" came to
power. As Shaul Bakhash in *Iran and the Islamic Revolution* demonstrates, the mullahs have consolidated power during those years and may
be more difficult to dislodge than their various opponents ever expected.[21]

In short, the religious dimension of the Iranian revolution was mis-
understood, underestimated and scorned by the press to the detriment of a
full understanding by Americans of what was happening there. Had Iranian history and Shiite Islamic teachings been better grasped by the press,
the American public and perhaps the American government might have
responded differently to events.

A word about television coverage of religion

During a six-week span in the spring of 1988, Axel Kyster, as part of a
research project for my course "Religion and the Mass Media" at California State University, Fullerton, watched 75 hours of national and local
television news which included 650 distinct items. Only ten (about 1.5%)
dealt with religion, and six of these were about Jimmy Swaggart's fall from
grace. Other than papal visits and preacher scandals, TV usually ignores
the sphere of religion—an unfortunate situation in a world which gets
more and more of its information from the tube.

In a two-part 1985 series in *TV Guide Magazine*, Joanmarie Kalter
documented the major networks' lack of attention to religion and lack of
sophistication in the religion stories they did cover.[22] In particular, she
focused on coverage of the abortion controversy, where TV journalists

20. *San Francisco Chronicle*, 10 November 1978.
21. Bakhash, *Iran and the Islamic Revolution*. See also Mehr, "Impact of Religion."
22. Kalter, "Abortion Bias," 5–17, and "Greatest Stories Never Told," 14–22.

admitted they softened their professional standards to give right-to-lifers their due, and of the school prayer amendment, where they greatly over-estimated the strength of the pro-amendment forces in the Senate.

Despite these inadequacies, some fine work has been done, especially on the Public Broadcasting System. The 1986 documentary "Holy War, Holy Terror" in PBS's "Frontline" series won an Emmy for its lucid analysis of the link between religious fanaticism and political extremism in Iran. Bill Moyers' three-part 1987 series "God and Politics" explored the ongoing rift between moderates and conservatives in the Southern Baptist Convention over interpretation of the Bible, and between liberal and conservative Methodists over U.S. policy in Nicaragua. Finally, two 1988 ABC pieces were first-rate: Ted Koppel's on the TV evangelist scandals and the "20/20" report by Stone Phillips, "Journey to Faith," which fairly and sensitively examined the claims of appearances by the Virgin Mary to several children in the Yugoslav village of Medjugorje. If this kind of work were done consistently, the religious illiteracy of most Americans about faith communities other than their own might be alleviated.

These case studies indicate that to disregard religion's power in the lives of leaders and peoples is to risk misunderstanding its power to motivate and activate. It is necessary next to look at religion newswriters, that cadre of specialists who do comprehend the religion factor in current events and yet are not always consulted by their editors.

EXPLORING THE RELIGION ANGLE:
THE CHALLENGE FACED BY RELIGION NEWSWRITERS

Why has religion been neglected by so many newspapers, and why is the religion beat considered a difficult assignment? William Simbro, religion writer for the *Des Moines Register and Tribune*, provides a succinct analysis:

> To take a thorny theological problem and do a story with enough zip to get it past an editor, enough simplicity that the average reader will want to read it and will understand it, and enough intellectual integrity that an expert in the field believes you have enlightened and explained rather than trivialized, is an enormous challenge.[23]

Despite the problems Simbro summarized, there has been a trend in the 1980s toward more media coverage of religion's activities and role in American life, and more respect for religion newswriters.

23. Simbro, "Unheralded Religion News," 23.

To assess the challenges faced by this growing guild of specialists, I interviewed thirteen of them from around the country. They are:

Robert Abernethy, NBC-TV, Washington, D.C.
Bruce Buursma, *Chicago Tribune*[24]
Russell Chandler, *Los Angeles Times*
Virginia Culver, *Denver Post*
Jim Franklin, *Boston Globe*
Ari Goldman, *New York Times*
Marjorie Hyer, *Washington Post*
Don Lattin, *San Francisco Examiner*
Clark Morphew, *St. Paul Pioneer Press*
Ron Morris, *Riverside (Calif.) Press-Enterprise*
Gustav Niebuhr, *Atlanta Journal and Constitution*
Helen Parmley, *Dallas Morning News*
Adon Taft, *Miami Herald*

Religion newswriters: backgrounds, frustrations, satisfactions

Religion newswriters have varied backgrounds and seniority. Gus Niebuhr has been at it for about two years, Adon Taft for 36 years. Two of the interviewees earned seminary degrees: Russell Chandler and Clark Morphew. Three others took leaves from their news organizations to study religion: Robert Abernethy at Yale, Ari Goldman at Harvard, and Don Lattin at the Program in Religious Studies for Journalists, University of North Carolina. The rest learned the field on the job. All, however, consider their religion assignment challenging and complex. Goldman had covered various beats for the *New York Times* (including the subway system) and felt that, "In a brief time you can get the general picture. But covering religion—it was a shock!" That shock was what prompted him to request his study leave.

Several of the writers said that stories which cause embarrassment to a religious group are hard to do. According to Virginia Culver, religion officials are "unwilling to talk about things that are unflattering." Ron Morris mentioned a series that *Press-Enterprise* had published about an ex-convict who bilked a Catholic diocese. "For a time this caused me some problems with diocesan officials who thought the stories were anti-Catholic."

Adon Taft said that many groups at one time or another "are gun shy, wary of the press" for bad reasons and even sometimes for good ones. This used to be true of Pentecostals until they gained more respectability, Taft said. He noted the difficultly of writing about a controversial group: the

24. Buursma recently left the religion beat and is now a *Tribune* sportswriter.

temptation is either to glamorize or condemn, as with a guru: "We do some things out of perspective because the sensational gets noticed."

Two writers commented on the difficulty of reporting about Catholicism because of its hierarchical and centralized structure. Clark Morphew mentioned Catholic teaching on abortion and surrogate motherhood: "Catholics on the local level can't do anything about what the global Roman Catholic Church does and teaches, but Protestants and society in general don't understand this." Ron Morris observed that Catholic groups are not independent, as in much of Protestantism: "Somebody up there is pulling the strings and people [at the local level] have to be careful what they say." Despite this, as earlier studies and several of the interviewees' comments indicate, Catholicism is the most amply covered denomination.

The interviewees said their editors were open to most of their story ideas but were sometimes hard to convince when the subject was more abstract and theological. As Bruce Buursma put it, "Medical writers have no problem with any new breakthrough even if it's complete bullshit. But if it's a religion writer doing a new discovery or a theological breakthrough, it's looked upon with a yawn and glazed eyes by the editor—or he might tell you to take the day off!" One of Ari Goldman's *New York Times* editors told him recently he wanted more conflict and controversy in religion stories. Goldman admitted to a church official that his denomination should get more coverage but didn't because it lacked these elements. In a similar vein, Russell Chandler said editors are hard to sell on religion stories with "long-range implications but no immediate bang."

According to Robert Abernethy, one of the very few television journalists covering religion, "In TV everything abstract is difficult." Yet, he has reported on meetings of Catholic bishops and Southern Baptists, done special segments on U.S. Catholics and fundamentalists, and does yearly specials at Easter, Passover and other religious holidays.

The consensus of the religion writers was that mainline Protestant denominations were underreported because their activities lacked pizzazz. As Adon Taft said, "Plodding churches who do a steady good job in the community—feed the poor, run Sunday schools—can be interesting, but it's a real challenge and takes good reporting." Jim Franklin said the Massachusetts Conference of the United Church of Christ was unhappy with him for not doing a story on a stand it took opposing the Reagan Administration's policies in Nicaragua. Franklin's editors just didn't see this as very newsworthy. Similarly, Marjorie Hyer said, "I don't think any of us do a good job on *why* people go to church, but it's the most widely attended activity in the country." She added that it is hard to convey to readers what religion means to "the average communicant." Yet she would like to spend some time with a congregation and find out what it is doing on a daily basis. Ron Morris did just that in a highly informative series, "Religion in Riverside County," which ran on consecutive Sundays between 30 March and 11 May 1986. He profiled the congregational life of Catholics, mainline Protestants, evangelicals, a black Pentecostal church, Mormons, Seventh Day Adventists, Jews, and Muslims. Included were summaries of the principal beliefs of each group. It was a difficult assignment, according to Morris, but responses from the denominations covered were "very positive . . . nobody was offended." And many people purchased tabloid copies of the entire series, which were so informative that a religious studies professor found it valuable. Such profiles of religion in a particular metropolitan area not only educate the readership about what is going on religiously but are an antidote to prejudice.

There was considerable unanimity among the writers about which denominations are the most poorly covered: mainline Protestants, Black churches, Mormons, Pentecostals (though the Bakker and Swaggert scandals have made them very visible recently), and smaller independent (usually fundamentalist) churches. The problem with the mainline denominations, according to Jim Franklin, is that, "We tend to take them for granted because they're there. But, in fact, they may not always be there." He added he was not happy with his own coverage of the mainliners. Adon Taft noted that traditional Hindu and Buddhist groups—as opposed to "flashy gurus"—get little coverage. Bruce Buursma thinks coverage depends on locale: "Mormons get ink in Salt Lake City, the New Thought movement in Southern California."

Despite the problems of reporting about religion, those surveyed expressed a high degree of job satisfaction and felt that the position of the religion newswriter had improved in the past six or seven years. They attributed this to a heightened awareness by editors and the public of religion's impact on current affairs. Examples cited included: the Roman Catholic Church's visibility because of the U.S. bishops' letters on peace and the economy and the controversies surrounding Archbishop Raymond Hunthausen of Seattle and Father Charles Curran of Catholic University; the liberation theology movement in Latin America; the continuing influence of the New Christian Right, including Pat Robertson's presidential bid and the recent notoriety of tv evangelists, especially Jim and Tammy Bakker, Oral Roberts and Jimmy Swaggert.

Several writers attributed the increased respect given them to the growing quality of those in the field. Bruce Buursma noted that "highly qualified, intelligent people are now applying for the religion job. That wasn't true in 1980. Things are better because we are better." Helen Parmley, who was serving as president of the Religion Newswriters Association when contacted, said that papers with a religion opening often call her for a recommendation of a religion specialist, "whereas before 1980 a paper was more apt just to take its youngest writer."

Most of the religion writers thought that the people they report about are a great source of the satisfaction they experience. As Robert Abernethy put it: "Here are people who believe in God and it affects their lives—and they're not kooks or thieves." As an example he cited a small Episcopal order, the Fisher Folk, who moved into a Pennsylvania town with high unemployment to buoy peoples' spirits with their music. "You get to meet fascinating people with fascinating insights into life," said Marjorie Heyer. Adon Taft drew inspiration from meeting spiritual giants such as Mother Theresa of Calcutta and Frank Charles Laubach (founder of the international literacy program bearing his name). Virginia Culver, who did a major profile of evangelist Billy Graham in April of 1987, said she is pleased when people read such a story and remark, "Boy, I really know that person now."

Several religion writers got satisfaction from informing people about an area where there is much misinformation. Jim Franklin said he is pleased when he teaches his readers something new, as he did in a series on prayer. This was a notion some people had "previously dismissed. But they said they had gotten new insights—a window was opened." Similarly, Russell Chandler derives satisfaction from making a contribution to the body of knowledge about a religious personality, movement or concept. "Thus, I serve the public and can aid people as they consider ultimate issues."

Clark Morphew's principal fulfillment comes from being able to expose religious groups which control peoples' thoughts and abuse them spiritually and physically. Yet, he added, "You meet a very thoughtful, gentle group of people for the most part, not charlatans and liars."

Helen Parmley, who has covered religion news for twenty years, says that the longer she does the job the more she realizes that "religion is the most powerful force in peoples' lives." She came to this conclusion partly by observing how religion interrelated with other facets of life—the environment, the arts, etc.—and affected them. This has been a rewarding insight for her.

Regarding specific college courses that would help prepare aspiring religion reporters, nearly all the interviewees (nine of thirteen) recommended world religions. Almost as many (eight of thirteen) mentioned church history or the history of religion in America. Gus Niebuhr (grandnephew of the late Reinhold Niebuhr, the distinguished Christian ethicist) stressed the importance of political science and general history, along with "a thorough grounding in the Bible, especially as it relates to evangelicals." Several others mentioned biblical studies, as well as theology and contemporary American religious movements. Bruce Buursma thinks a course on "fundamentalism of all shapes and backgrounds" would be valuable because "we tend to label someone a 'fundamentalist' whom we don't like . . . Jerry Falwell is glad to be called a fundamentalist but he uses [the term] in a different sense than reporters do."

Taking account of religion in political reporting

The interviewees thought that editors and political and foreign correspondents had begun to take the religion dimension more seriously in recent years. But there is considerable room for improvement in the view of many of the religion specialists. This is particulary true of Islam where, Marjorie Heyer said, there is "massive ignorance" among journalists.

Clark Morphew recalled that he had put a foreign correspondent covering the 1984–85 Ethiopian famine in touch with church personnel who had done relief work there for years. However, the correspondent stuck to her political contacts and produced a story that was "thin and had no substance."

Gus Niebuhr considers foreign correspondents "utterly blind to religion" and thinks major stories have been missed as a result. By contrast, Bruce Buursma mentioned that his paper, the *Chicago Tribune*, improved its coverage of the Pope's 1987 visit to Poland by sending him there to collaborate with its Warsaw correspondent. "Almost every story around the world has a religion sub-plot," said Buursma. He was the most positive in his appraisal of how seriously journalists at home and abroad now regard the role of religion.

Both Don Lattin and Jim Franklin thought their papers were doing a better job of taking account of religion in international news coverage. Lattin added, however, "If political writers did more on world religions, we'd have a better sense of the context in which stories develop." Franklin mentioned a fine series by his *Boston Globe* on Islamic culture in several Asian countries.

Several writers spoke of the frequent "intersection" of religion with politics, medicine, the law, and the arts. Their observations parallel an insight of historian-of-religion Ninian Smart that religious studies is a species of a larger genus which he calls "worldview analysis." He defines it as "the task of describing and trying to understand belief-systems and practical orientations to life."²⁵ Such analysis may blend motifs from a traditional religion with those of a modern ideology, such as nationalism or Marxist-Leninism. Examples are numerous: the *Mujahedeen* ("holy warriors") in Afghanistan who waged a guerrilla war against the Soviets under the aegis of Islam; the *Gush Emunim* ("block of the faithful") who consider the occupied West Bank part of Israel by biblical mandate; the militant Sikhs of India's Punjab state who desire a separate nation in the name of religious freedom.

Smart maintains that in academe worldview analysis gets artificially segmented among several fields: anthropology, philosophy, political science, religious studies, etc. In a corresponding way, many media professionals tend to see a story as primarily political, financial, medical, legal—or religious. What religion reporters realize—and keep trying to convince their bosses and colleagues—is that religion often "intersects" a story that has political, social, or ethical lines. What they seem to be pressing for is even greater participation in the job of analyzing these intersecting stories and more recognition from their editors and peers that the religion angle ought not to be overlooked.

Kenneth Woodward, religion editor of *Newsweek Magazine*, has proposed an approach comparable to Smart's. Drawing upon several experiences from his own career at *Newsweek*—including the civil rights march on Selma, Billy Graham's influence on Richard Nixon, and post-Vatican II Catholicism—Woodward maintains that "reporting religion inherently involves cultural analysis, often of a very complicated kind."²⁶ Woodward's underlying assumption is that religion affects culture significantly and is an aspect of culture. He cites a comment by Jimmy Carter's sister, Ruth Carter Stapleton, in a 1978 interview: "I believe that when Jesus was in the Garden of Gethsemane what he willingly took upon himself was the subconscious of the whole human race."²⁷ To Woodward the remark expressed the coming together—in Stapleton's "inner healing" ministry—of two previously hostile movements in America's sub-culture, "the evangelical and the pop-therapeutic."²⁸

There are numerous instances of other convergences between religious and secular culture since Stapleton made her comment ten years ago: (1) fundamentalist Christianity with political activism, as first signaled in

---

25. Smart, *Religion and the Western Mind*, 82–83.
26. Woodward, "Roots and Horizons," 49.
27. "Sister Ruth," *Newsweek*, 17 July 1978, cited in Woodward, "Roots and Horizons," 65.
28. Woodward, "Roots and Horizons," 49.

the founding of the Moral Majority by Jerry Falwell in 1979, and as crystallized by Pat Robertson's quest for the 1988 Republican presidential nomination; (2) the U.S. Conference of Catholic Bishops with the nuclear arms debate through the publication in 1983 of its pastoral letter, "The Challenge to Peace: God's Promise and Our Response"; and (3) American Jews with evangelical Christians on the issue of support for Israel.[29]

Religion, as these examples show, does make a difference to American culture and the national ethos. The challenge for religion writers and the media in general is to make the implicit religious dimension in American life more explicit.

Smart, then, thinks religion analysis is part of worldview analysis, the effort made by scholars, politicians, and the press to understand the social and political changes, the economic developments, and the ideological conflicts affecting nations. Similarly, reporter Woodward is arguing for religion analysis as part of cultural analysis, the effort to detect trends in the way Americans live, work, create, spend leisure time, view the world, and even worship. Both view religion as a key factor in contemporary life which helps shape our overall outlook. It is important, however, to avoid two extremes in assessing religion's significance: (1) that it is peripheral for most people and important only for a minority—the faithful remnant, or (2) that it is the most important single factor in understanding human behavior. The importance will vary from situation to situation, but its seriousness and its subtleties need the attention of professionals.

29. The seeds of this convergence were planted in 1967 when mainline Protestants were unsupportive of Israel during the Six-Day War, and came into bloom after the Israelis launched their controversial incursion into Lebanon, Operation Peace for Galilee, in 1982.

BIBLIOGRAPHY

Bakhash, Shaul, *Iran and the Islamic Revolution*. New York: Basic Books, 1986.
Carter, Jimmy, *The Blood of Abraham*. Boston: Houghton Mifflin Co., 1985.
Dormant, William and Ehsan Omeed, "Reporting Iran the Shah's Way." *Columbia Journalism Review*, Jan./Feb. (1979): 27–33.
Halsell, Grace, *Prophecy and Politics: Militant Evangelists on the Road to Nuclear War*. Westport, CT: Lawrence Hill & Co., 1986.
Kalter, Joanmarie, "Abortion Bias: How Network Coverage Has Tilted to the Pro-Lifers." *TV Guide*, 9 Nov. (1985): 5–17.
——, "The Greatest Stories Never Told . . . Right." *TV Guide* 16 Nov. (1985): 14–22.
Lindsey, Hal, *The Late Great Planet Earth*. Grand Rapids: Zondervan, 1970.

Mehr, Farhang, "The Impact of Religion on Contemporary Politics: The Case of Iran." Pp. 124–73 in *Spirit Matters: The Worldwide Impact of Religion on Contemporary Politics*. Ed. Richard L. Rubenstein. New York: Paragon House, 1987.

Mills, James, "The Serious Implications of a 1971 Conversation with Ronald Reagan." *San Diego Magazine*, Aug. (1985): 140–44, 258.

Pippert, Wesley G., *The Spiritual Journey of Jimmy Carter: In His Own Words*. New York: Macmillan, 1978.

⸻, "Moral Considerations." *The Quill*, 67 (Dec. 1979): 20.

Said, Edward, "Iran." *Columbia Journalism Review*, Mar./Apr. (1980): 23–33.

Simbro, William, "Unheralded Religious News." *The Quill*, Dec. (1979): 23.

Smart, Ninian, *Religion and the Western Mind*. Albany: State University of New York Press, 1987.

Smith, Gaddis, *Morality, Reason and Power: American Diplomacy in the Carter Years*. New York: Hill & Wang, 1986.

Woodward, Kenneth, "Roots and Horizons: Does Religion Make a Difference?" Pp. 48–54 in *The Religion Beat: The Reporting of Religion in the Media*. Published privately by the Rockefeller Foundation, 1981.

SUGGESTIONS FOR FURTHER READING

Hadden, Jeffrey K. and Anson Shupe, eds., *Prophetic Religions and Politics: Religion and the Political Order*. New York: Paragon House, 1986.

A collection of essays by sociologists of religion indicating that the world is involved in a new religious upsurge, contrary to the secularization theory of religion.

Rubenstein, Richard L., ed., *Spirit Matters: The Worldwide Impact of Religion on Contemporary Politics*. New York: Paragon House, 1987.

Parallel in scope to Hadden and Shupe's book, *Spirit Matters* presents a global view of the interplay of religion and politics from a religious studies perspective.

Shaw, David, "Media View Religion in a News Light," *Los Angeles Times*, 28 Dec. 1983; "Religion Writers Weight Objectivity," *Los Angeles Times*, 29 Dec. 1983.

A comprehensive look at religion coverage and its evolution into a respected specialty beat on major American newspapers.

2

The Evolution of
the Religion Beat

George W. Cornell

At the General Assembly of the United Presbyterian Church in Buffalo, New York, in June of 1961, the "commissioners," as delegates are called, launched an attack on the press. They charged it had misreported an action of the previous day. An outrage, they termed it, a blatant example of the irresponsibility of the secular media. Reporters there at the Kleinhans Music Hall had been allocated seats in the orchestra pit. As the denunciations rolled on from a succession of delegates, the press section slowly began sinking until it had disappeared from sight.

At that point the church's then-stated clerk, its chief executive, the late Rev. Eugene Carson Blake, intervened from the podium. Notes in hand, he pointed out that the news reporters actually had been correct, that the assembly by a fluke of procedural maneuvers, had in fact taken the action that the news accounts described. As he spoke, the press section inexplicably began rising, gradually bringing it back toward the normally visible level. In the quiet that settled over the subdued, somewhat chastened assembly, Blake remarked: "We are now witnessing the resurrection of the press."[1] That, of course, defused the entire affair and turned it into appreciative laughter. The episode has become part of the cherished lore among religion reporters, along with many other such oddly memorable events of the last forty years of gradually-increasing coverage of the religion scene in America.

If not exactly a "resurrection," there has been a genuine enlivening of journalistic efforts on the religion front. They are larger and better. The upward trend has had its pauses, hesitations, and even scattered setbacks

---

1. The time and place of this incident were confirmed in recent telephone conversations with William Folger, an old-time Buffalo religion reporter and by Otto Finkbeinder, a long-time aide to Rev. Blake.

along the way. It still has some long strides to take to become adequate in relation to religion's impact on society and the turns of history. Nevertheless, religion reporting in the secular media has grown immensely in my thirty-eight years of experience, both in quality and quantity. From a state of inertia, it has, indeed, come alive.

The transition has come under the propulsion of a demanding chain of events: the rise in the late forties and early fifties of the ecumenical movement, the Roman Catholic reforms of the 1962–65 Second Vatican Council, the civil rights movement in which religion played such a decisive role, the upheavals abroad generated by religious passions, the emergence of religious right-wingers into the political arena which they had so long disdained, and the latter-day TV preacher scandals. These and numerous other occurrences—such as when a "born again" president, Jimmy Carter, utterly baffled a religiously illiterate White House press corps—insisted on attention to the religious factor. It started coming out of the woods.

There it had been in the shadows, potent, lurking, an underlying drive, yet generally disregarded, sidelined, considered a personal, overly touchy and controversial zone, a private matter, a separate, ecclesiastically-feuding turf, unfit for socially informative journalism or worth the energies of any hard-probing reporter. Coverage on religion reflected that exclusion from legitimate news. Dealings with it were generally of the kid-gloves, superficial, offhand type. The task often was shunted to obituary desks, implying its morbidity.

To a substantial degree, that was religion's newsroom status, dead. Although stirring bothersomely, and beginning to be noticed by some major news outlets, coverage for the most part was abysmal back in those beginning days of the 1950s. Except in a few rare cases, in a few enterprising niches of a few gradually awakening news publications, authentic coverage of religion scarcely existed. The subject, when treated at all, was mostly ghettoized, trivialized, boxed off in an innocuous corner.

Editors, by habit and engrained traditions of their craft, just didn't see religion as a news staple. Cover the courthouse, the legislature, the police blotter, accidents, political contests, the chamber of commerce, doll things up with an occasional feature about some eccentric's hobby. Religion just didn't fit the package. Habit, and perhaps the imitative frailty of any occupation, imposes a strong grip. Religion hadn't belong before, so it didn't belong.

Instead, religion was sidelined as pap, superfluous filler, and puffery, equated with advertising and relegated to an inconspicuous Saturday "church page" whose contents generally matched the insipid category to which religion had been consigned. It was awful: Ministerial appointments, sermon topics, church picnics, visiting choirs, fund-raising drives, building plans, revival campaigns, holiday programs, and bake sales.

Little or nothing appeared about the content of faith or its implications for the community or wider environment. Only the thin and superficial got noted, usually accompanied by an appropriately paid ad. Coverage was, in a sense, a caricature of the inherent dynamism and pervasive impact of religion, as disparaging and misrepresentative of it, as some contemporary aberrations on television.

However, the news approach to the subject has changed phenomenally. Several factors have figured in the transformation. Both events and the caliber of journalists going into religion reporting have forged the difference. In my estimation, the change has come primarily from the force of events, the virtual compulsion of the modern tromp of history. Pressured stemmed both from the churnings in the religion world itself and from events that commonly had been assumed to be of only secular concern. Yet many events loomed as inherently religious occurrences, impelled by religion.

As just one example here, consider the fall of the Shah of Iran in 1979 and the subsequent imprisonment for 440 days of the U.S. embassy hostages. The events shocked the U.S. government and the American public, largely because the festering resentments of a Shiite Moslem population had not been adequately assessed.

Neither the press nor U.S. intelligence services had recognized the might of that religious upheaval. Morehead Kennedy, a chief embassy officer among the hostages, later told me that disregard for religion has been the blinding gap in U.S. intelligence, a gap prevailing in many sectors of the world. He has sought to sensitize the State Department to the importance of religion in any informed analysis of national moods and potentialities, a key element that too often has been missing both in government and news interpretations.

Yet the consequence of religion has shown up repeatedly in modern times, a provocative sway demonstrated in the falls of dictators in the Philippines and Haiti; in the human rights struggles in Latin America, South Africa and elsewhere; in conflicts in Afghanistan, the Middle East, Northern Ireland, Tibet, and India and in the ongoing friction between the U.S. and the Soviet Union. The governments and press have had to take more notice of the religious current, mainly because it has been thrust upon them simply by the clout of events.

My longtime lament has been that we generally fail to seek views of religious leaders and theologians on social, political, and economic conditions and issues. Numerous studies have found that the clergy sense best the pulse of a people and are the most trusted of any institutional representatives.[2] It thus seems that if the press is going to convey the sense and directions of a people, reporters need to lend an attentive ear to the religious domain, to a sector that is tuned to attitudes of the public and has its confidence.

The realization has flowered among perceptive religion reporters that religion is not an enclosed arena, that it has ramifications for virtually every area of life. Misleadingly, the term's Latin root, *religio*, implies something confined reverentially, fenced about, reserved to holy preoccupations. News desks often have brushed religion off as a soft, intimate irrelevance, something as one wag put it, that consenting adults do behind the closed doors of their churches and synagogues.

But it isn't so understood by competent religion journalists who spot religion's imprint, directly or indirectly, in nearly every area of human concern—social, economic, political, familial, and personal. A central issue in all these categories is whether conduct, policy, law, or a course of action is right or wrong, good or bad. And for most people, that question throbs with religious-moral content.

The religious factor impinges on the public business and trends far beyond what some consider the enclosed, delimited religious sphere. Research by the Center for the Study of Beliefs and Values at the Search Center in Minneapolis brings out this interplay vividly. It found that religious beliefs and political decisions are closely and actively connected. On the basis of extensive interviews establishing religious profiles of a cross-section of the U.S. Congress, votes could be predicted in eight key legislative areas ranging from military expenditures to civil liberties, health, and agriculture.[3]

The findings shatter common assumptions—resulting from latter-day elaborations of the church-state separation principle and echoes in textbooks and sometimes court briefs—that religious motivations must not be reflected in laws or public policies. In fact they are, and quite closely, the research revealed: "We found that religious beliefs and values are strongly related to voting behavior in each of the eight legislative areas," says psychologist Peter Benson, who directed the study. "Both social scientists

2. "The Connecticut Mutual Life Report on American Values in the '80s: The Impact of Belief," Hartford, 1981; also "Emerging Trends," Princeton Religion Research Center, Nov. 1984, and other years.
3. Benson, *Religion on Capitol Hill*. Oxford University Press, New York, 1986.

and the public have been rather naive about the religious dimensions of human life generally and of politics in particular."[4]

Whatever the issue—whether foreign aid, crime and punishment, taxes, genetic engineering, abortion, money, racial equity, labor rights, business ethics, war, or peace—religion and its moral premises have definite implications. Recognizing those connections has done much to lift religion reporting out of its past compartmentalization and toward treating it as a relevant ingredient of the whole.

Accomplishing that integrating purpose remains a principal challenge to good religion journalism. Failures to pursue such fully orbed reporting remain a crippling flaw. Remedial efforts are going on in some news quarters against obstacles of entrenched patterns and the necessary working time and resources. Integration is developing slowly, sporadically, as able reporters tackle it as a necessary objective. That, in itself, offers promise.

However, I'm outpacing my story. The nub of it is that both events and a growing cadre of capable reporters alert to the influence of religion and the amount of interest in it have greatly magnified coverage in the last four decades. The people involved initially were a tiny band, back in the early 1950s. It was a field scantily regarded, even scorned, by most reporters and editors.

Only a handful of major newspapers, perhaps a score of them, had staffers assigned to the field full-time. The Associated Press had none until I began working there in 1951, and the other major wire service, United Press (now UPI) had no specialist until 1953, when the late Louis Cassels plowed into it with verve. Our regular reporting on religion—spot news, features, and columns—soon became regular fixtures in many newspapers across the country. This has continued to be so through my work and that of Cassels's successor at UPI, David Anderson, along with increasing syndicated religion news from major newspapers.

BLAZING THE TRAIL

The wire service workhorses were not the pioneers of the trade. That spadework belongs to a small forerunner crew, a contingent of crusty, top-flight journalists who, as if by some bolt out of the blue, spied religion as a fertile field, an untapped mother lode of provocative material and activity needing to be watched, examined, and reported. To them it was essential,

4. Associated Press, 5 March 1982.

and it remains so, if journalism is to tell the whole story and not ignore a basically influential part of it, as generally had occurred in the time before. The early venturers into that religion zone were a salty lot, straight, hard-facts reporters, not pundits or opinion dispensers, but of the old and still best school of objective, impartisan journalism, neither drummers for religion nor debunkers but chroniclers. They discerned in this field both substance and drama of real news appeal, and of significance and power. It was an anomaly in news rooms then, but destined for greater stature and respectability.

I knew most of all those early trail-blazers and became their friend as the new kid in the territory. A sinewy lot they were, keen of ear and intellect, questioning, probing, clarifying in common English the some-times murky, oracular jargon of religion.

There was the breezy, bantering George Dugan of the *New York Times*, who pondered using a middle initial, "O," in notes to his editor pressing for attention to various religious matters, his urgings thus carry-ing the weight of "GOD." George had a jovial, cynical exterior, but also such a caring streak that he once stayed brooding all day in his hotel room after the *Times* had spiked a key story he had filed on a religious conven-tion.

Others among that early band included the courtly John T. Stewart of the *Saint Louis Dispatch*; the brainy, vibrant Terry Ferrer of *Newsweek*; the intensely driven Caspar Nannes of the *Washington Star*; the serious, magisterial Harrison Fry of the *Philadelphia Bulletin* (now defunct); the Bible-quoting Lance Savitz of the *Buffalo Evening News*; the blunt, pep-pery Margaret Vance of the *Newark News*; the jolly, pungent Jo Ann Price of the *Milwaukee Journal* and later the *New York Herald Tribune* who always gleefully conveyed the insider religious gossip. There was the calm, cool Robert Whitaker of the *Providence Journal*; the whimsical Ora Spaid of the *Louisville Courier Journal*, who interspersed religion reporting with interviewing a horse being groomed for the Derby; the astute, diplomatic Dan Thrapp of the *Los Angeles Times*, who spent vacations with pack and horse in the New Mexico mountains and published numerous books about the old West.

Many of these early explorers of religion news are now gone, but they helped cut a path for the rest of us. In 1949 some of them founded the Religion Newswriters Association, an outfit made up of those who regu-larly report religion for the secular press and dedicated to raising the

5. Dugan, *History of the Religion Newswriters Association*.

standards of religion reporting. The RNA's membership had grown from 33 to 73 by 1959.[5] It climbed to close to 100 through the seventies then spurted to 149 in1982 and 225 in 1988. A recent check by Edward Briggs of the *Richmond News and Courier*, found that more than 500 newspapers in *Editor and Publisher* list religion editors or writers.[6]

These statistics show the expansion of religious newswriting in the numbers of specialists. Their quality today makes this old heart pound with admiration and delight. Many of them are very, very good. They not only are good, reliable reporters, grasping the nub and implications of issues, but casting them into their inter-religious perspective and broader social framework. They vary, of course, some better than others, some harder diggers, cleaner writers. But as an old tiller in this vineyard, I must say I am wholly optimistic about the future of religion coverage as indicated by the general quality of today's reporters.

Religion coverage has become far better, more comprehensive, expository. Other veterans in the field attest to the change. "It's more extensive, and more competent people are doing a better job of it," says William Thorkelson, religion editors from 1942 to 1982 of the *Minneapolis Star* and now correspondent for Religious News Service and a string of dailies and weeklies. William Folger, who covered religion for the *Buffalo Courier-Express* from 1948 to 1973, says it's now handled with "more depth and as it happens," rather than being shunted into a weekend dumping ground.[7] Virginia Culver, for twenty years religion reporter for the *Denver Post* says "I see it expanding." The *Post* wants "everything I can dig up"; in other papers, "what I see looks good and varied and broad." John Dart of the *Los Angeles Times*, on the beat for twenty-one years, says attention to religious news has grown steadily and "has become especially competitive with other news" from 1985 to 1988.[8]

IMPACT OF THE ECUMENICAL MOVEMENT

The forces that produced this broad, deeper coverage of religion were not just the people at work but also a most unusual, cumulative flow of events that simply could not be ignored. The early catalyzing development, the ecumenical movement, took off strongly shortly after World War II with the 1948 founding of the World Council of Churches in Amsterdam. It was highlighted by a struggle over the moral aspects of

6. Figures provided by RNA president Edward Briggs in May, 1988.
7. Telephone interviews with Thorkelson and Folger on 25 May 1988.
8. Written replies to a questionnaire circulated among members of RNA at its May, 1988 annual convention in Saint Louis.

capitalism and communism in the then-raging cold war between East and West, a clash personified by two Presbyterians, the West's late roving diplomat John Foster Dulles, later U.S. Secretary of State, and the East's late Hungarian churchman Josef Hromadka.

The council finally went down the middle, saying neither system met divine ideals, seeing sin in them both and opting only for biblical principles. This rankled Western civil religionists, who considered American policies God's will.

Then came the founding in 1950 of the National Council of Churches, forging working ties between most of the country's mainline Protestant and Eastern Orthodox bodies. The domestic ecumenical surge, along with a series of church mergers, generated a combined, more muscular religious thrust on various social fronts. A new thing then, firing criticism and controversy, ecumenism made news.

So did the early national assemblies and ground-breaking world assemblies. The second one—the *Evanston Assembly* in 1955—drew more than six hundred American and foreign reporters. The radically different atmosphere of that time was demonstrated by a ban issued by Chicago's then-Cardinal Samuel Stritch against any Catholic visiting, associating with, or heeding the non-Roman global gathering of Christians.

In those days you had to nurture carefully the rare Catholic sources who would even talk with reporters. One of mine, the late Rev. John Kelly, information officer of the Catholic church's social-affairs agency, eventually was ousted for his openness with the press. How drastically different the atmosphere became. In 1972 Catholic bishops even opened their meetings to the press after some RNA nudging and negotiating. So did the Methodist bishops two years later.

A landmark in the ecumenical revolution came at the 1961 World Council of Churches' assembly in New Delhi. There, the vast Eastern bloc of Christianity, cut off from the West for one thousand years, entered the council. These ancient Eastern churches included the Russian Orthodox and other Orthodox strongholds in the communist orbit, sparking new drama as the religious realm faced up to demands of a technologically and economically shrinking, interdependent earth.

As with the United Nations, the ecumenical forums at Sweden in 1968, Kenya in 1975, and British Columbia in 1982 saw Africans and Asians gradually assume a more powerful role. No longer was world Christianity dominated by the Protestant industrial West.

Ambling into the shifting picture, the beaming, spontaneous old Pope John XXIII, signalled a transformation of Catholicism and its relations with others. In 1959 he summoned the Second Vatican Council, which from 1962 to 1965 turned insular, "fortress" Catholicism inside out, plunging it into the modern world, consulting official Protestant and Orthodox observer-delegates in the process.

Vatican II espoused religious liberty, put the Latin liturgy into the vernacular, instituted "collegially" shared church governance to balance past monarchical papal rule, and vigorously embraced ecumenism with other Christians and Jews. Under Vatican II the church abandoned its rigid insistence on "return to Rome" in favor of mutual approaches toward one another, and stressed the Bible and encouraged popular study of it, a pursuit previously reserved for scholars. "La Biblie Torne a Roma," headlined an Italian newspaper: "The Bible Returns to Rome."[9]

Until that council, coverage out of Rome was almost totally, ceremonially superficial, with decorously polite descriptions of the pomp and ceremony. Vatican II changed that completely, permanently and for the good. The late Bishop Fulton Sheen once lectured reporters there to keep in mind that we were dealing with "sacred matters" and must limit our stories only to what served "holy mother church." That didn't impede the upwelling of straight, open reporting from the Eternal City and the journalistic candor initiated there has continued, a lasting gift to the public's knowing.

In about the same period the U.S. elected its first Roman Catholic president, John F. Kennedy, in a religious-political transition that mirrored the reforming impulses of Rome. Kennedy had to validate himself in a confrontation with Baptists in Texas. Nowadays, a candidate's Catholicism gets no more notice than if he were a Presbyterian.

Vatican II launched the church-at-large on a tumultuous shakedown cruise. All the adjustments, overhaulings, and revampings on the national and local scenes, along with the attendant conflict and turmoil, yielded a steady spinoff of news which still sizzles.

The reforms of Vatican II unleashed a wave of resignations by Catholic priests, and continued pressure for dropping the rule of priestly celibacy. Women demanded a fuller voice, including ordination, a right they gradually had won by the mid seventies in most all major Protestant bodies, as well and Reform and Conservative Judaism, but not yet in Catholicism or Eastern Orthodoxy. These reforms and the maturing of others, along with current Vatican efforts to throttle them, furnished a continuing story.

Massive participation in the civil rights drive of the 1960s also spurred press attention to the religion sector. It was a pastor in Little Rock who won the 1954 Supreme Court decision desegregating public schools.

9. Cornell, *Voyage of Faith*, 152.

There were the later clergy-led "freedom riders"; the Rev. Martin Luther King, Jr.; that giant Christian-Jewish rally in Washington in 1963; the 1965 Selma march of nuns, pastors, and prelates, whites and blacks, broken up by sheriffs' clubs at the Pettus bridge; and the clergy jailings and slayings, including the 1968 assassination of King.

Symbolizing Rome's emergence from its guarded enclave, the "prisoner of the Vatican" began traveling here, there, and about everywhere. Papal travels started with Paul VI's 1964 trip to Jerusalem. There, in one of the most electric moments of my career, under the flickering, smelly flares of oil torches on the Mount of Olives, the five-foot-eight, white-robed Paul VI embraced the six-foot-four, black-clad chieftain of Eastern Orthodoxy, Patriarch Athenagorus of Constantinople.[10] For more than five centuries the Western and Eastern church heads had not spoken to each other, and then only in circumstances too strained to budge the bitter rift between them since 1054 A.D. In the warming glow of that Jerusalem encounter, the two men promptly rescinded the old anathemas and excommunications that had lasted for a millennium.

Papal travels since have become standard news fare, especially that by the current peripatetic John Paul II. A Pole, his 1978 election to the papacy had been the first of a non-Italian in four centuries, another break-out into the wider reaches of life and grapplings with it. I had tried to move a story—based on reckonings of some sapient Vatican veterans—that a non-Italian would get it, but our Rome bureau wouldn't use it, pointing to unanimous predictions of the Italian press that it would go to another Italian. Anyone from the communist East was considered especially "non-papabile," the prevailing wisdom went.

RECENT DEVELOPMENTS

In recent times, numerous other unforeseen and somewhat incongruous developments have spotlighted the religion sector. The religious right, which had long belabored mainstream churches for meddling in politics suddenly in 1979–80 began its own vehement political meddling. The Rev. Jerry Falwell, Moral Majority, and numerous kindred organizations swept into mass mailings and the precincts, pushing causes and candidates. A similar power shift was blazed in the 1980s by the fundamentalist takeover of the Southern Baptist Convention. Movements of the religious right have left mainline churchmanship a bit stunned and deflated.

Lately came the more sensational twists in 1987–88 of TV preachers

10. See Cornell, *Voyage of Faith*, 140.

Jim Bakker and Jimmy Swaggert, fervent denouncers of sexual lapses, disclosed as involved in sex scandals themselves. These, too, fed journalistic appetites for religion news.

So did the 1970s phenomenon of the cults, those tightly indoctrinated and disciplined, mostly insular groups dominated by authoritarian figures. Groups such as the Hare Krishnas, "Moonies," and Children of God triggered a torrent of religion stories about their systems, "brainwashing" charges and kidnap "deprogrammings."

A much more significant story, of long-range implications, is simmering in the persistent friction, in courts and outside them, over the relationships between religion and public law and policy. An accumulation of court decisions, beginning in 1947, has progressively squeezed religion further out of public affairs, based on interpretations of the Constitution's "non-establishment" clause. The trend has virtually imposed non-religion or an absence of religion on public institutions, including the schools.

However, the presumed danger of a state-established religion in this highly diverse society seems totally unrealistic, a straw man. At the same time, it hardly makes sense for people to cancel their strongest convictions at the gate of public life, officially sanctioned or not. The struggle continues between strict "separationist" and "accommodationist" approaches, with the eventual outcome unclear but of pivotal consequence.

Another struggle, over abortion—too shallowly, scantily, and nervously reported—smoulders in the body politic, with obvious religious ramifications.

Under the long hammering of events, however, religion coverage has improved. But it has not yet matured sufficiently, compared to the strong influence it has on society. An extensive 1981 study of American motivations, involving lengthy responses from 3,780 persons, found that religion is the most decisive factor in people's drives and judgments, the "strongest determinant" of values among all other factors such as age, sex, economic status, race, or liberal or conservative sway.[11] The researchers didn't even intend to examine religion. it simply leapt out of the data, "so startling, so compelling," says project director John C. Pollack. "We weren't hunting for religion. But there it was, showing up in every statistical analysis."[12] A yawning gap also showed up between the public and professional leaders (except for the clergy), with public leaders being much more religiously committed. That commitment was gravely underestimated by leaders in

11. "The Connecticut Mutual Life Report on American Values in the '80s: The Impact of Belief," Hartford, 1981.
12. Associated Press, 31 March 1981.

various professions. This included journalism, which apparently still misgauges the public pulse and thus partly misses its story.

Comparing news coverage of sports and religion, and their relative interest to the public, religion news is a small fraction of what it ought to be. The stark imbalance showed up in statistical comparisons I did in 1974 and 1980, only slightly moderated in the latter year and still hugely lopsided. Sports attendance in 1980 totalled 356 million. That included professional and college football, basketball, hockey, major and minor league baseball, auto racing, soccer, tennis, boxing, flat and harness racing, even dog racing. Yet attendance at churches and synagogues for the year was thirteen times greater, totalling 4.7 billion. Gate receipts of professional football, baseball, and basketball totalled $423 million. In contract, religious contributions totalled 22.1 billion, fifty-one times more than people put into the three biggest sports. Yet in terms of news space devoted to the two areas, the figures were almost opposite.

A classical yardstick of where people's interests lie is where they put their time and money. They invested thirteen times more of their hours and fifty-one times more of their money in religion than sports, but the news media gave religion only a tiny sliver of the coverage lavished on sports.

Nevertheless, religion reporting is gaining. A recent survey conducted by Ernest C. Hynds, a University of Georgia journalism professor, indicated that many newspapers feel religion coverage is (and needs to continue) advancing both in quality and quantity.[13] A 1982 survey by the mass communications department of Middle Tennessee State University found that, of the thirty newspapers polled, the number devoting more than one hundred column inches to religion news each week had gone from twenty-seven to fifty-nine percent in the last decade.[14]

Rich Oppel, editor of the *Charleston (N.C.) Observer* writes that his paper covers religion intensively: "That's what our readers want. They care about religion, so religion sells newspapers." It's the "stuff of Page One, day by day," consuming a "prime news beat and then some."[15] Not many papers have indicated that sort of unreserved zest for religion news, but an increasing proportion of them are waking up to its potential, colleagues say.

13. Hynds, "Large Daily Newspapers Have Improved Coverage of Religion." Fifty-five newspapers across the country participated in the 1987 survey. A survey by Hinds ten years ago yielded similar results.
14. Shaw, "Media View Religion in a News Light." Los Angeles Times, 28 Dec. 1983.
15. Oppel, *The Bulletin*, American Society of Newspaper Editors, Washington, D.C., January, 1988.

"At many newspapers the church page has evolved into the religion news page and sermon summaries have changed to news roundups," writes Terry Mattingly of the *Rocky Mountain News* in Denver. "At some papers, religion editors are now allowed to write for the regular news page, seven days a week. Religion has begun to overlap with politics, science and other traditional 'news' topics."[16]

Others affirm the development while indicating its insufficiency. It is "significantly expanding," says David Crum of the *Detroit Free Press*, but he adds: "It continues to be difficult for religion stories to compete head to head with other hard news." His comments, recognizing gains but also persistent obstacles, generally paralleled those of a score of other religion specialists responding to a questionnaire about the status of religion coverage.

"It is expanding, but on a quirky, uneven sort of basis," says Ann Rogers-Melnick, on the beat for eight years. Rogers-Melnick joined the *Pittsburgh Press* in 1988 after covering religion for the *News-Press* in Fort Myers, Florida. "So much still depends on the personal inclinations of individual editors and publishers."[17]

Richard Ostling of *Time* magazine says, "Newspapers in the United States are generally giving more and better attention to religion, with some notable exceptions." He observed that *Time* shifted in the mid seventies from weekly religion sections, which it had pioneered at its founding in 1923, to less frequent but larger projects on religion.[18]

Bill Higgins of *The State* in Columbia, South Carolina, said his paper's religion coverage has "expanded exponentially" in his six years there, along with a "growing understanding" of its value. Russell Chandler of the *Los Angeles Times*, paired with John Dart in one of the best religion reporting teams in the country, says: "It's a funny thing—the religion beat seems to expand and shrink at the same time. While some papers make new and solid commitments to coverage of religion, others are cutting back."[19]

However, occasional, scattered cutbacks, in which papers lose religion specialists without immediately replacing them, generally have turned out to be temporary. The beat revives after a lapse, often under pressure of events and public demand.

John De Mott of Memphis State University, a one-time staffer of the *Kansas City Star and Times* and since then a journalism professor for a

16. Mattingly, "The Religion Beat," 14.
17. Replies to questionnaires May, 1988 RNA convention.
18. Personal interview, May, 1988.
19. Replies to questionnaire, May, 1988 RNA convention.

quarter century, has taken a special interest in religion coverage. De Mott maintains archives on the subject for the RNA and keeps a close academic watch on it. Of the evolution of religion coverage in the U.S. he says:

"The emergence of objective religion news reporting as a challenge befitting our profession's finest, is itself one of the great news stories of the 1970 and 80s. In only a generation or so, religion news has evolved from church press release rewrites . . . into an exciting daily adventure in the exploration of moral issues that go to the heart of modern society and its spirit . . .
Today's religion news specialists, more and more often exceptionally well educated and experienced as investigative reporters . . . are ranging far afield beyond the comfortable pews catering to society's establishment . . . Today's religion news reporters . . . have "hit the streets."
They're in the ghetto. On the farm. In hospitals and hospices. At a narcotics treatment center in South America. In the jungles of Nicaragua. Inspecting the concentration camps of Palestine/Israel's West Bank and Gaza strip. Behind the "iron curtain," interviewing Jewish refuseniks. They're everywhere, it seems nowadays. Wherever there exists a true test of modern society's morality.
Within only a generation or so, we have expanded the definition of "religion news" enormously. And justifiably. For there is a religion "angle" or aspect of almost every news event or development.[20]

Bruce Buursma of the *Chicago Tribune*, who in 1988 quit what he calls the "God beat" after thirteen years to move to the "jock beat," says: "I really think the battle's been won" in putting religion coverage on the map. "There has been a steady incremental improvement both in the quality of religion writing in the American press and also in the status given religion writers by their peers in the world of journalism and by readers as well. Even the most hard-boiled anti-religious editor pays a kind of grudging recognition to the role religion plays in society. Religion stories have become far more numerous and the style of reporting is increasingly sophisticated, with increasing appreciation of the significance of religion in American public life. I think we can be justifiably proud of what has happened."[21]
Better religion coverage has helped fill an educational gap between the faiths. Public schools avoid teaching the subject. Hearsay and mutual

20. De Mott, John, Memphis State University, "Perspectives on Religious News." Unpublished paper provided to the author at 1988 RNA convention. De Mott several times has served as one of the judges of the annual RNA religion reporting contests, and thus is highly familiar with the kind of work being turned out by religion specialists on many newspapers.
21. Telephone conversation, May, 1988.

misconceptions from behind denominational walls have resulted in damaging social mischief and prejudices. I think fuller religion reporting, providing a cross-pollinizing of accurate information among believers of different stripes, has helped heal an old sore. For that, religion specialists can indeed take some pride.

The Overseas Press Club once carried out a fascinating inquiry among seasoned top American foreign correspondents, asking their selections of the greatest news happenings of all times. The list gradually was honed down to twenty-three events of all history. Eight were of a religious nature, making the subject loom larger than any other over the long stretch of time.[22] "It came as a great surprise," said the late Will H. Yolen, editor of the study. "All through the turning points of civilized life, we came on the religious element, not only in thought, but in action, in art, music, education, government." Yolen suggested that this might give newspapers and journalism schools something to think about.[23]

Hindsight always puts reality in perspective. People often wonder why they hadn't seen the importance of something when it happened. But this usually takes time. Any reading of history makes it resoundingly clear that religion is not just a private sideline, but a crucial stuff of human annals. It has moved armies, determined boundaries, toppled and made rulers, and planted rudimentary issues in the world today.

Religion is a determining element in the human story, a powerful ingredient of the social mix. To disregard religion in chronicling that story prevents any intelligent perspective on conditions in this society or any other. Certainly no one can understand America, its history and present forces without understanding the nature and history of its religious life. After all, that was mainly what brought settlers here in the first place.

The news media have begun, slowly but surely, to record this provocative dimension of American life more completely and competently. Without the religion angle, they can't tell the story straight or even truly.

22. Yolen, *Newsbreak.*
23. Associated Press, 31 May 1974.

BIBLIOGRAPHY

Benson, Peter, *Religion on Capitol Hill.* New York: Oxford University Press, 1986.
Cornell, George, *Voyage of Faith.* New York: Odyssey Books, 1966.
Dugan, George, *History of the Religious Newswriters Association, 1949–59.*
Hynds, Ernest, "Large Daily Newspapers Have Improved Coverage Of Religion." *Journalism Quarterly* 64, 2 and 3 (1987): 444–48.

Mattingly, Terry, "The Religion Beat: Out of the Ghetto into the Mainsheets." *The Quill*, Jan. (1983): 14.
Oppel, Rich, "We Don't Need a Scandal to Make Religion an Important Newsbeat." *The Bulletin*, Jan. (1988): 4–10.
Yolen, Will, *Newsbreak*. Harrisburg, PA: Stackpole Books, 1974.

SUGGESTIONS FOR FURTHER READING

MacDougall, A. and Curtis D. and Reid, Robert D., *Interpretive Reporting*. New York: Macmillan, 1987.
Meston, Edward L., *The Press and Vatican II*. South Bend, In.: University of Notre Dame Press, 1967.
Ostling, Richard N., *Secrecy in the Church: A Reporter's Case for the Christian's Right to Know*. New York: Harper & Row, 1974.

3

Religion News in the Secular Press: Moving Beyond Naivete

John Dart

FROM CHURCH EDITOR TO RELIGION WRITER

Religion news reporters in today's secular press generally have shed the "church editor" image of years ago. The label had not been entirely out of place in the 1950s, when churchgoing was fashionable and local preachers were counted either as civic leaders or as the in-principle gad-flies. But in the 1960s, as revolutions of conscience swept nationwide, both organized religion and journalism seemed to broaden their perspectives, recognizing that they too were involved in society's biases against minorities. News coverage was urged to become less superficial and to exhibit greater fairness. Good coverage of major religion news—as with other beats—now called for more detail with multiple points of view and a heightened sense of context. Today's religion-reporting corps has shown remarkable ability to sort out the evangelical, charismatic, and funda-mentalist frictions within Protestantism that otherwise might be dismissed as just a clash of personalities. Likewise, tangled church-state conflicts as well as overlapping sources of tension and revitalization in Roman Catholicism have received sophisticated treatment from religion news specialists.

What next? It always depends, of course, on individual editors, reporters, and the particular limits established at each newspaper. But pacesetting news organizations and imaginative reporters must continue to keep an eye out for ways to chronicle a growing Muslim and Buddhist presence in the United States and, perhaps at some point, coalitions of nonbelievers and the areligious. Political editors must be convinced that religion specialists should share in reporting the religious side of politics, if they don't already. On the other hand, news stories on ethics controversies are probably best handled by specialists in whichever field demands the greatest expertise, whether it is business, medicine, politics, or religion, and so on.

NEGLECT OF ACADEMIC RESEARCH IN RELIGION NEWS

A glaring weakness in religion news coverage is one that has existed far too long—the paucity of stories drawn from academic research. Not that university sources haven't been increasingly valued lately. Journalists sought out analysts on the 1987–88 upheaval among television evangelists and, before that, on the rise of the Religious Right. Vatican policies in sexual matters have also sent reporters off to expert professors for commentary. Certainly the news value of scientific surveys on religious beliefs and practice has been recognized in the newsroom. Responses to religious questions in Gallup polls have been widely quoted in the 1980s.

Yet religion scholars and their knowledge have usually been tapped only for quotes and background to give greater insight into current events. Relatively few stories arise strictly out of the research done in religious studies. This is the case in spite of rather provocative and productive work in critical biblical scholarship and revealing studies in the sociology and psychology of religion. The field of theology has been somewhat moribund of late, but more than liberation and feminist theologies could be reported on.

The magnitude of this neglect is not too evident unless we look at the work of science and medical writers in the press (i.e., newspapers, wire services, and news magazines). Scientific discoveries, new theories, and medical advances represent a heavy proportion of the news served up by science and medical reporters. These stories tend to be the most fascinating on their beat, often getting prominent play. Medical findings, of course, offer the possibility of eventual relief or cure for hundreds of thousands of victims. But a great deal of scientific news has no obvious practical application—a new most-distant object in the observable universe or the oldest-yet evidence of human life, for instance.

I suspect that science and medical news—regardless of any pragmatic relevance—is appealing because it deals in the thrill of discovery and unraveled mysteries. Even when it is made clear (by both scientists and journalists) that initial findings will be held in abeyance until confirmation, there is the sense of being on the threshold of knowledge. This coincides nicely with the natural desire of serious consumers of news to update, enrich, and correct their understanding of the world. Those readers want to keep up with events, emerging issues, and the rise and fall of influential ideas. Are the readers of religion news, either habitual or potential readers, any less interested in keeping up, learning more, and sharing the adventure of new findings?

Comparisons of science and religion sometimes appear ill-founded: religion is a matter of opinion bound by varying degree to tradition,

whereas science works with objective data unfettered by past concepts—
or so it might be said. It may be true that religion honors faith and science
seeks facts, but the journalistic standard for the two fields has been
unnecessarily disparate. Medical and scientific discoveries rarely purport
to be conclusive or unalterable. Some science stories chronicle the ups and
downs of theories—such as whether or not the dinosaurs became extinct
because a giant meteor filled the atmosphere with dust, disturbing the
climate and conditions for survival. A science reporter—indeed, any
reporter—is obliged to develop a news story if new research or theories are
distinctive and timely, presented and/or accepted by credible scholars,
and significant. The same journalistic criteria should be applied in assessing religious research.

Why the resistance to theoretical stories in the religion field? First of
all, the religion beat has to overcome its own history. Having evolved out
of the so-called church beat, the religion beat at times still gives the
impression that it seeks to bolster faith.[1] Articles about new biblical
interpretations and social science analyses often challenge prevailing
assumptions about Bible history, or about reasons behind belief in supernatural phenomena such as apparitions of the Virgin Mary and tongues-
speaking. But these often skeptical studies can be reported without implying that belief in the phenomena is necessarily misplaced or discrediting
faith. Just as news reporters on Marian apparitions could include some
critical analysis for balance, a story focusing on new psychological
research on that recurring phenomena could incorporate the responses of
thoughtful believers.

We have yet to realize fully what it means to write for the *secular*
press—namely, for media outlets whose neutral stance toward religion
should translate into let-the-chips-fall-where-they-may attitude. Contemporary religion research itself tends to take this approach. Many
professors in religious studies now teach at state universities or other
institutions which cherish research unfettered by creedal restrictions.
Their findings might be stated in ways that would shock the religiously
unsophisticated. However, the results are usually couched in technical
jargon and evasive conclusions, and safely ensconced in academic journals as if to avoid the feared misinterpretation by journalists and
churches, because readers of a religion naturally do not want to feel

1. The *Los Angeles Times*, for instance, continued into the 1970s its practice of
writing a news story about a Sunday sermon for the Monday paper. Also, on Easter
and Christmas the appropriate gospel narrative was substituted for the newspaper's
lead editorial, inviting the reader to infer that the *Times*, in the last analysis, was
Christian after all.

assaulted repeatedly by faith-disturbing news.[2] But a caveat is required. Journalistic principles prohibit the press from avoiding newsworthy occurrences, and the religion pages will get their share of "negative stories" (to use the parlance of the person unhappy about conflict and misfortune in organized religion). No major newspaper, to my knowledge, sheds all objectivity in favor of turning the Saturday religion pages into a cheering section. Besides, my experience indicates that readers of the religion section range from the devout to the devoid of faith.

Another reason why writers and editors overlook the research side of religion may be their perception that religious institutions tend to ignore new theories or conclusions. Academic research, for the most part, is designed to serve the career of a scholar, not to benefit houses of worship and the clergy. "If the churches don't care," one could then ask, "what does it matter?" Granted, every news story must answer the question "So what?"; nevertheless, indifference from religious bodies does not excuse overlooking a thesis with compelling features of its own. What if the study contradicts what we always thought was the case about a prominent figure in the Bible or about why churchgoing differs by geographical regions? Unexpected or unprecedented findings can be newsworthy. So can those which run against current church policies; such was the news appeal of studies showing that North American Catholics are increasingly receptive to the idea of women and married men being ordained as priests regardless of the Vatican's steadfast opposition. The long-term power of ideas—enhanced by the availability of news and opinion today—has surely been demonstrated in religion.

BIBLICAL SCHOLARSHIP AND THE CHURCHES

Critical biblical scholarship ranks as the scholarly pursuit in religion most seriously neglected by the press—despite the fact that our perception of the spiritual past impinges on contemporary issues. Christianity, and to some extent Judaism, consults its religious history and tradition to argue the pros and cons of women's ordination and benevolence toward homosexuals. Avowed non-believers see certain biblical images as harmful to intellectual progress—such as the "creationist" views of human origins,

---

2. This commonsense guideline ought not to rule out critical editorial opinion on decisions and pronouncements by influential elements in organized religion. Newspapers, especially editorial cartoonists, already feel free to criticize the actions of such public figures as the pope and right-wing preachers. The liberal or moderate mainline church leaders get less commentary because, for one reason, they are not making much news and are seen as less powerful.

and the heavy masculine cast to deity and the related exercise of spiritual authority. Even when the Bible is quoted only to defend positions previously shaped by economic, political, or social factors, it remains an important reference point for western civilization.

Differences between what people have been told and what is likely true are the raw stuff of many news stories. Such is the case when reporters cover government, science, education, and other fields. If the disparity is quite large—and deceit, fear, or negligence has been the reason—the story's importance grows accordingly. Such a disparity, in fact an enormous gap, exists between mainstream biblical scholarship and the understanding of the Bible in most churches.[3]

Before discussing biblical research, however, we must distinguish between two camps—liberal and conservative scholarship. Conservative churches find no significant gap between their position and that of scholars in the same tradition. Bible professors at theologically conservative institutions are expected to conform to what is regarded as an orthodox, understanding of Christianity taught through the ages, and to affirm unhesitantly the Bible's reliability and consistency in matters of faith—if not in every respect. Conservative studies tend to accept every purported author in the Bible as the actual author despite evidence of inconsistent vocabulary and theology. The conservative biblical commentaries may also discuss the differences in, say, gospel accounts, but the apparent contradictions tend to be "resolved" into a harmonious whole. Inherent in conservative scholarship is the assumption that God is the ultimate inspiration for what is said in the Bible; and because God is not inconsistent, problems of interpretation are the result of limited human understanding.

The purpose of Bible teaching in this case is to provide insights into God's purposes—with the understanding that the Bible addresses the faithful today, sometimes specifically on matters of today. Newsworthy findings and theories from this milieu tend to be limited to the implications of biblical interpretation for conservative theology. One such story is the impact, so far relatively minor, of "kingdom now" theology in Pente-

3. By mainstream scholarship I mean that typical of the Society of Biblical Literature, the large, principal professional organization for biblical scholars. Its members teach at places like the divinity schools of Harvard, Yale, and the University of Chicago; the University of California campuses, Claremont Graduate School, and other universities; and many seminaries run by liberal-to-moderate denominations. The interpretations these scholars present in books, articles, and papers for academic conferences usually try to settle unresolved questions or refine the working premises that most future priests and Protestant ministers learn in seminary.

costal circles and its roots in the radical Reconstructionist thinking, which foresees a gradual "restoration" of dominion in the world by true Christian believers. The theology, in all its variations, has influenced a number of Christian Right leaders. Some research within moderate evangelical faculties on what the Bible says about women, sexuality, peace, and justice may be progressive in that context, though perhaps old news in the light of mainstream biblical studies.

The line of demarcation between liberal and conservative scholarship is usually determined by a scholar's use of historical-literary critical method. Generally speaking, conservatives oppose this analytic method because they say it leads down the slippery slope of unbelief. Both conservative Protestant and Catholic leaders also contend that in dissecting biblical narratives for evidence of earlier sources and later additions, scholars reduce the texts to religiously meaningless writings.[4] Those charges sound reasonable among people who share the opinion that scholarship should defend doctrine, since "history" as the Bible presents it cannot be misleading or erroneous. There are scholars, however, whose methods incorporate both evangelical principles and historical-critical approaches; they do not fit easily onto either pole of biblical studies.

A great many biblical scholars who are Christian are convinced that faith and intellectual integrity are compatible, and that inconsistencies in the Bible are not detrimental. One example of the liberal approach to biblical texts will illustrate a different way of understanding inconsistencies: In the Gospel of Mark, Jesus' mother and family are depicted rather harshly, most scholars agree. How could Mark have done this to Mary, the virgin mother of Jesus? Part of the answer is that the author of the oldest New Testament gospel probably had no knowledge of stories later told by Luke and Matthew of a miraculous, angel-foretold birth. The nativity stories in Luke and Matthew reflect what the gospel writers emphasized in their own expansions of Mark's narrative. Luke shows sympathy for women and the poor (thus Mary is highly praised and shepherds come to honor the babe); Matthew wants to present a kingly messiah who fulfills Jewish scripture (thus a star shows the way and three magi from the East present expensive gifts to the newborn). Along with other authors of their era who described exemplary men, Luke and Matthew wrote birth stories that signaled greatness and divine qualities.

Unfortunately, the press has frequently accepted speculations from Bible specialists who treat scripture as literal history. Every season religion writers expose how little we know about the state of research on the

---

4. Cardinal Joseph Ratzinger of the Vatican is such a conservative Catholic.

nativity stories and Jesus' Passion. One favorite Christmastime news story is a new calculation of Jesus' birthdate tied to Matthew's star, and a discussion of the possible conjunction of two planets or the appearance of a supernova or comet. Matthew's gospel is treated as basically accurate, and it is assumed that indeed there must have been a bright object in the sky at that time, otherwise Matthew or his sources would not have said so. But a number of contemporary scholars have noted the similarity of Matthew's story about the star and magi to the story of Moses in the book of Numbers. A foreign sorcerer, Balaam "from the East" (Num 23:7), refuses to deliver a curse on Moses as ordered by a king, and instead gives a blessing. A reference in his blessing to a "star" (Num 24:17) was taken by later Jewish tradition to refer to the Messiah, according to Donald Senior.[5] In other words, the star and other features of the nativity stories may very well be literary-theological inventions for suggesting an auspicious moment. That argument should at least be pointed out in any story attempting to identify the Bethlehem star or the magi from the East. Better yet, how about a moratorium on Bethlehem star stories?

BASIC BIBLICAL LITERACY

Imagery from the Hebrew scriptures was used repeatedly by gospel authors to dramatize the religious significance of Jesus' life—especially of his trial and crucifixion. Details of his punishment recall the "suffering servant" from Isaiah, and his words on the cross echo lines from Psalms. From a devout point of view, it might be argued that the Old Testament foreshadows Jesus' coming and Jesus said godly things as death approached. There are numerous pitfalls in this apologetic point of view, and the news writer must beware of describing a Christian interpretation of the Hebrew scriptures that Jewish and mainstream biblical scholars dismiss.

Most critical scholars are convinced that, more often than not, the early church put words on Jesus' lips and punishment on his body in order to create a convincing case for his divine nature. The argument for first-hand recollections in the gospels grows weaker by the decade. Yet the *Journal of the American Medical Association* recently published a highly uncritical article which sought to explain the precise cause of Jesus' death.[6] Every detail mentioned in the gospel accounts of Jesus' punish-

5. *Invitation to Matthew*, 34.
6. W. D. Edwards, W. J. Gabel, and F. E. Hosmer, "On the Physical Death of Jesus Christ." *Journal of the American Medical Association* 255:11 (1986): 1455–63. The article's principal authors were a pastor and a Mayo Clinic pathologist.

ment and crucifixion, along with supposedly pertinent data from the image of a bloodied man on the Shroud of Turin, was summoned. Passages about Jesus sweating blood, which are found only in some (not the best) manuscripts of Luke, were accepted as historically reliable by the authors. Unfortunately, because of the credibility of the journal—despite its editor's biblical naivete—some news media carried stories on the conclusions.

Religion news writers should be familiar enough with the prevailing interpretations of the most famous biblical scenes to warn editors away from such stories. (It is not easy; I was unable to convince a writer and editor in another department of the *Los Angeles Times* to reject JAMA's story.) Unfortunately, the New Testament accounts are so often accepted as basically historical that journalists are confident they won't shock the readers by printing a little pious speculation. In addition, these stories have a strong news appeal because they can be released a little before Christmas or Easter.

THE JESUS SEMINAR

An ongoing event that has challenged journalists and churches to take critical biblical scholarship seriously is the Jesus Seminar, a group of more than one hundred biblical scholars who are systematically studying and voting on the likeliest authentic sayings of Jesus. Meeting twice a year since 1985 and averaging about thirty scholars at each balloting session, the Seminar meets in a different city every time. Religion news writers thus have a geographical justification for doing a story—in other words, it's happening in or near our city. Furthermore, by bringing scholars together to work, the seminar overcomes another excuse for not covering developments in biblical research, namely the difficulty of knowing whether the provocative work of one scholar is considered credible by his or her peers.

The voting results from the Seminar have been significant. One session found, to some of its members' surprise, that few scholars believe the historical Jesus predicted a calamitous end of the world in his lifetime, or that he predicted an Armageddon at all. A subsequent session confirmed, in the Seminar's view, that Jesus' sayings about the Son of Man returning in the clouds to install the kingdom on earth did not derive from Jesus but rather from the apocalyptic hopes of some early Christians. These votes challenge the underpinnings of orthodox Christian teaching.

Reflecting what many other colleagues have decided, the Seminar declared that little is known about the final days of Jesus other than that he was crucified in Jerusalem around Passover under the reign of Pontius Pilate. Members voted overwhelmingly that "there was no Jewish trial of Jesus before the Roman authority executed him and there was no Jewish crowd involved in this condemnation."[7] Among the reasons for doubting the trial's historical basis was that the charge of blasphemy as defined in Jewish law does not fit the sayings attributed to Jesus.

Even if other scholars might disagree with these conclusions, it is difficult to deny the newsworthiness of so many biblical experts concurring that the New Testament misrepresents Jesus. Religion news writers are willing to report the most dismaying failings of preachers and churches—legitimate news because everyone accepts the idea that humans and human institutions, however religious, are imperfect. If, then, the Bible, so influential in western culture, is not all that tradition has told us, then are we writers hesitating because we think we are tampering with the sacred? Are we favoring a literalist view of scripture and an anti-intellectual assumption that advances in biblical scholarship are illusory or impossible? Or are we just lazy and uninformed?

Nobody can do it all on the religion beat. Even with a religion-writing colleague to share the work, and general assignment writers who fill in some gaps and come up with their own enterprising stories, the *Los Angeles Times* will miss or be late on some news developments. Demands and expectations on the religion beat vary according to region and circumstances.

But I think we have an obligation to be familiar with biblical exegesis—much in the same way science and medical writers are aware of the state of things in their fields. Only then do we have some idea of what is new, plausible, and thus possible material for a story. Religion reporters also have to judge whether the same weight must be given to creedal-regulated, apologetics-oriented scholarship and to the research done in mainstream academic circles.

Jargon, unexplained premises, and technical details in any field of scholarship are daunting. To overcome these, religion news writers could use some help from scholars. The Jesus Seminar is attentive to outsiders. Organized by Robert W. Funk, the Seminar designates two scholar-participants as spokesmen to inquiring reporters. Background information is made available for non-members attending the meetings. But writers have not found any such assistance at the annual meetings of the Society of Biblical Literature. No news release ever accompanies an issue of the Society's *Journal of Biblical Literature* or of other journals.

7. Borg, "The Jesus Seminar and the Passion Sayings," 86.

HUNTING FOR GEMS AT ACADEMIC GATHERINGS

The large annual meeting of the Society of Biblical Literature and the American Academy of Religion, joined by the leading biblical archeological society, holds promise as a news-making source.[8] The overwhelming majority of papers and lectures there are not newsworthy, but the sheer number makes it possible to find a few stories. What is needed is a press room with someone to assist in acquiring texts and arranging interviews. This has been rare at past meetings, and woefully inadequate when tried. Yet a whole range of religious research is represented here and at the smaller annual meeting of the Society for Scientific Study of Religion. At these gatherings a religion writer can pluck out some gems of news stories. To lighten the inevitable overload of material at the meetings themselves, the writer needs advance copies of the programs and abstracts for meetings of the AAR–SBL and the Society for Scientific Study of Religion. Without attending academic meetings, the religion writers can still be alerted to new work at a local university or research on a topic pertinent to the news writer. For example, *Religious Studies News* listed a paper by a Brite Seminary professor on Pat Robertson's end-times views scheduled to be read at a regional AAR meeting. When I followed up by phone, the scholar gave me some information vital to my story on how the presidential aspirant's self-perceived role as God's choice to "usher the coming of my Son" may have played a role in his political candidacy.

Some of the gaps in religion coverage might be bridged through study fellowships, one-day seminars, better public relations by academic societies, and greater efforts by religion writers to establish contacts in academe. I think the first step, however, is to examine how far beyond the church beat we've really advanced. If we traded places with the medical writer at our news organization, would we concentrate on hospital and health care stories to the exclusion of articles about new findings in medical research? If we swapped jobs with the science writer, would we focus on new technology, funding problems, and aerospace projects while bypassing work on the frontiers of scientific knowledge? The religion news corps may not only be missing a lot of exciting stories, but doing a disservice to the American public.

8. The meeting drew five thousand scholar registrants in 1987.

BIBLIOGRAPHY

Borg, Marcus J., "The Jesus Seminar and the Passion Sayings." *Forum* 3,2 (1987): 81–95.
Senior, Donald, *Invitation to Matthew*. Garden City, NY: Image Books, 1977.

SUGGESTIONS FOR FURTHER READING

Achetemeir, Paul, ed. *Harper's Bible Dictionary.* San Francisco: Harper & Row, 1985.
Brown, Raymond E., *The Birth of the Messiah.* Garden City, NY: Doubleday & Co., 1977.
Dart, John, *The Jesus of Heresy and History.* San Francisco: Harper & Row, 1988.
Kelber, Werner H., *Mark's Story of Jesus.* Philadelphia: Fortress Press, 1979.

4

Why Editors Miss
Important Religion Stories

Kenneth A. Briggs

The memory of when there was practically no authentic coverage of religion in our newspapers and magazines is distinct in the minds of many reporters who now till that field for a full-time living. Except for some perfunctory, polite, attention given to major churches and the rarest of synagogues, usually done out of patronizing or honorific motives, there was until quite recently nothing in the papers about religion save for the occasional account of the berserk evangelist rampaging naked through the streets of a sleepy, conversion-saturated town, or some such bizarre or innocuous thing.

This was true for the most part even through the biggest church bonanza in the nation's history, the 1950s, when the Gross National Product and parish membership rolls soared in happy conjunction. Some publications did monitor the boom in very respectful fashion, recording the official pronouncements of church leaders who, like their political and corporate counterparts, sported three-piece names. But there was little stomach for taking a hard look at those religious institutions. They were part of the success story, fixtures in our cultural heritage, therefore sacrosanctly good. No need to probe them or doubt their word or see what role they played in the larger cultural picture.

It is now widely agreed that two events changed all that. One was the civil rights upheaval, which enlisted many religious leaders on the side of protest and dissent. This radical break with the overall conformist attitudes that prevailed during the fifties lent a sudden new image to much of the religious establishment. News organizations, being what they are, quickly took note. The other seismic development was the Second Vatican Council, an event so astounding and baffling that many editors, generally as ill-equipped to make sense of the goings-on as anyone else at the time, went scurrying about to find writers who could read obscure ecclesiastical tea leaves. What was happening was no less than an attempt to move a huge medieval institution into the twentieth century. Most Catholics, including many bishops at the Council who hadn't the faintest grasp of Vatican machinations, were equally at a loss. Pope John XXIII alone seemed to know the story line.

Those seminal events helped spawn a new kind of religion writer—variously called religion "editor," "specialist," and "reporter," in addition to the time-honored newsroom "hey you"—and ushered in a time when the breadth of coverage expanded to include analysis of ethical issues and arcane theological matters as well as features, profiles, magazine pieces, and so on. Since about 1960, religion stories started landing on Page One by virtue of their own newsworthy merits.

I recite that capsule history in order to declare categorically that in the past two decades or so, religion reporting has never been better. That claim is intended to knock down the curiously widespread notion that religion has lost its foothold in American journalism. No doubt things could be much better, and there are some grievous lapses, but on the whole there are more highly qualified people now writing about religion than ever before—many of them with a solid education in the fine points of religion—and they are writing with intelligence, perception, and often with wide latitude from their editors. I have been honored to work with some of the best. Their skill, knowledge, and integrity are exemplary. They have opened up a new avenue for reportorial energies and creativity. For that we should be grateful even while acknowledging their human limitations and the imperfect world they live in. At the very least, their examples have engendered a modest crisis of rising expectations. Many readers have come to expect more from the religion coverage in their newspapers than they once did and are more critical if the reporting falls short of their standards.

Given the economics of newspapering, the situation just described obtains mostly among the largest dailies and weeklies which can afford the luxury of specialization. But there are stunning exceptions. Some of the largest dailies have failed to provide good coverage, while many small-to-medium newspapers have performed superbly. Here I should mention the role of dumb luck in determining the outcome. Those who imagine the news business as a finely tuned conspiracy obviously know nothing about such matters. Newspapers may strive to look like well-honed instruments for the sake of public credibility, but the truth is that they are as much the creatures of chance, chaos, and whim as any other human undertaking, perhaps more than most. This means that happenstance and accident are much more likely to govern affairs of the newsroom than blueprints and carefully designed policies. What it comes down to is this: *The Daily*

Horizon may have sparkling religion coverage because by sheer chance a certain reporter with sufficient interest, background, and spunk took up the beat; *The Evening Sunset* may not because, when the last religion reporter left to join a think tank, nobody with those abilities just happened to be there to pick up the ball and run with it. Inertia took over, and the crush of daily events kept editors frazzled and distracted until, before you knew it, religion coverage has been neglected for as long as anyone could remember.

Religion is hardly singled out for special neglect in this regard. Qualities of randomness and dumb luck are in evidence across the newsroom. Newspapers use the talent they have: if a terrific medical writer crops up, so much the better, at least until the person goes elsewhere. Then, who knows? The wheel of fortune will spin all over again.

Editors are accustomed to adapting to a constantly shifting team of reporters, deploying available personnel in response to the demands of the hour. There is certainly much more planning than there used to be since the days when practically everyone was a general assignment reporter. Big newspapers, in particular, increasingly adopt the look and feel of the corporations in which they subsist, hiring "experts" within special departments and relying more on computers to do the reporting by delivering information from data banks to the reporter's desk. But chance still intrudes in the grandest of designs and most sophisticated organizational charts. Happenstance remains a mischievous factor in whether your favorite daily is doing a good or bad job of religion coverage.

Quality and quantity are also contingent on the will and disposition of management teams. Everyone in the field has known how the warm breezes of encouragement from one set of editors can shift suddenly to ice blasts from their replacements. Sometimes it amounts to the smile of favor or the frown of disfavor from a single editor. Individual likes and dislikes sometimes count more heavily when it comes to religion because of the intensely emotional and personal nature of the subject. There is nothing more agonizing for a religion reporter than to become innocently embroiled in an editor's unresolved religious conflict. Neurotic preoccupations with the perceived traumas of parochial school or burning resentment at forced Sunday school attendance, among many other real or imagined grievances, can haunt the unsuspecting reporter and pose a huge roadblock to effective reporting. At the other extreme, the newly-baptized convert with strong evangelistic or messianic leanings can be a nemesis of quite a different order.

With the passing of time fewer editors seem ostensibly to know or think very much about religion, a commentary perhaps on the rise of biblical and theological illiteracy. For reasons that may not bode well for religion, the beat is less an emotional-religious litmus test and more an accepted, rather objective area that needs coverage because it's part of the American scene.

It seems clearer all the time that religious education is usually among the weakest components in the training of the sort of "informed" person who winds up in a position of authority in our society in general, and for purposes of our discussion, in the press in particular. That this gap exists among newspaper editors accounts for at least two very distinct situations. One is that those whose instruction stopped at the elementary level tend to reflect simplistic, childish notions of religion. The other is that the growing ranks of the totally uninformed, though perhaps a bit too susceptible to exotic strains of hybrid religion, very often display a lively, unbiased curiosity about all religion that some religion reporters do well to cultivate. Such interest is more likely to be objective and formal than personal, viewing religion as a branch of social studies.

Before looking more closely at the obstacles to good religion coverage, I would like to briefly outline my understanding of the basic rationale for the dissemination of news. As I grasp its function, the newspaper serves the crucial interests of a democracy by providing information by which democratic decisions that affect the general welfare are rendered. An informed electorate is, presumably, a wiser electorate. At any rate, under its voluntary mandate, the press becomes primarily oriented to two kinds of activities, the ways that public officials exercise power and the manner in which public monies are spent. Upholding the public trust relative to the use and abuse of power and money is the single greatest responsibility of the newspaper. It is its raison d'etre. All else is more or less peripheral to this central purpose, though market demands for all sorts of other kinds of coverage quickly change the focus of energies in the real world of the metropolitan daily.

By this definition of what is essential, religion becomes an elective. But, increasingly, newspapers have assumed a much wider scope of responsibility: the need to explain the workings of a complex society as a means of promoting the general welfare. This wider interpretation of the public's need to know provides ample justification for thorough religion coverage. For any accurate reading of a society necessarily entails a comprehension of its religious character.

RELIGION'S PLACE IN THE LARGER SCENE

Fortunately for religion coverage, the course of events has rendered benefits. The primary sources have been the sudden explosion of political religion on the world scene. The overthrow of the Shah of Iran by Aya-tollah Khomeini was the most startling event in this panoply but hardly the only one. News moguls, like most government officials and political experts, were totally taken aback by the power and passion of funda-mentalist religion, Christian, Islamic, and Jewish. Just when religion had become interpolated out of most political coverage, there was again a need to factor it in somehow. Almost nobody had seen it coming, which meant that eyes and ears had often not been trained in the proper direction.

The upshot of this set of conditions was that more journalists became interested in those often subtle interstices between politics and religion and culture and religion. The traditional symbols and language of faith could no longer be quickly dismissed as anachronistic vestiges or nostalgic longings. As their bold initiatives demonstrated, the fundamentalists could become the galvanizing core of political movements and rallying points for outrage against the pretensions of the modern world. The Aya-tollah's strength arose from rejection of the Shah's flirtation with Western "progress." Journalists needed to catch on to those movements before they erupted into full-scale revolutions.

As everyone who reads the papers knows, the same sort of dynamic process was observable in this country with the rise of the Religious Right, though its complexities and contradictions were seldom grasped. The press most often portrayed the march of the Moral Majority as the old challenging the new, but it was more complicated than that. The leaders of the old were greatly enamored of the free enterprise spirit and the con-sumer proclivities of the new. Their fight was very selective, and the issues chosen to fight about sometimes only populist means to political ends. At any rate, the links between an all-but-forgotten American revivalism and mainstream politics awoke reporters and editors to the constant interplay between religious legacies and cultural forces.

The overall result was, at least for the short run, a greater openness and alertness to religious elements creeping into the areas of political coverage newspapers considered most important. Correspondingly, the attention given to religion for its own sake suffered in some quarters. Religion sometimes became a piece of the story rather than the story itself.

Meanwhile, attitudes about the place of religion in American life were changing so as to further influence the direction of religion reporting. Robert Bellah's research team has brilliantly documented the drift toward the privatization of religion in *Habits of the Heart*. Though homage is still paid to the clout that religious institutions are believed to have (such as the Catholic bishops' influence on abortion politics) there is scant evi-dence of any such power residing in ecclesiastical headquarters of any kind. If a person's spiritual life has, indeed, become generally even more sacrosanct than sex it raises profound questions about what is worth covering. There is, to be sure, a good deal of "public religion," the denominational confabs and so on, and that will suffice to some degree, but how then does the reporter get at the more difficult challenge of detecting where religion as a broader phenomenon actually makes its impact? Is religion, after all, only a supporting actor? A philosopher writing recently in the *New York Review of Books* answered that question in the affirmative, albeit in extreme and reductionistic fashion. In America, he said, both religion and politics are merely "business by other names."

Religious groups themselves are not sure how to approach that question. Most can cite the superficial indices of religiosity such as belief in God or confidence in religion, but they usually cannot begin to describe what religion really has to do with what makes this society tick. We do know that the religious establishment is in serious decline; but where exactly does that leave religion if not, to return to Bellah's analysis, behind closed doors where, presumably, it is inaccessible to the press?

If religion is increasingly a subjective experience, effable, private, and non-translatable, than how is it to be captured by the busy reporter? If religion no longer provides the paradigms for understanding the meaning of life, than how important can it be? It becomes a secondary effect rather than a primary cause. These are questions which indirectly underlie the conscious grappling that goes on in the newsroom. We cannot figure out where religion belongs in a world in which the religious metaphors have been displaced at the center of public life, not by conspiratorial forces, as some would have us believe, but through the momentum of the secular mentality. The religion reporter and the city editor cannot be expected to make up for this loss or to be less confused than anyone else who stops to think about the issue for a moment or two. Reporting does reflect the widespread quandary about the place of religion. It cannot by itself either put Humpty Dumpty back together again or pretend he never slipped off the wall in the first place.

Shifting sands on the religious landscape do not imply a loss of sand, many have argued. Religion might be less detectable but still there in some form. The post-death-of-God sages often made this point: after all the talk about the disappearance of religion, they said, it had crept back around the fingers to tell us that seeking after God (or gods) is congenitally human. Push it away in one guise and it will re-emerge in another.

Apart from the truth or falsehood of that claim, one undeniable fact is that much of the action in religion has erupted far from the mainline churches at the edges of the known religious world. Curiosity about the spiritual life was sparked more by gurus than by the trusty local clergy association. The shamans and monks and mullahs were able to raise the religious question in a way that the Christian establishment, taken for granted as it was, could not. People were trying things, perhaps searching for meaning, perhaps just extending the dimensions of their consumer sampling, but in any event the doors of American religion were thrown open to a huge flea-market of exotic offerings that were news. For the religion writer, this bustling marketplace was sometimes less than a thrilling shopping basket of delectables. The problem was how to sort out all the unknown quantities in order to know which to write about and how. Hybrid groups, cults, sects, ashrams, or whatever kept cropping up, vying for attention. The public needs to be warned about some like the Children of God or the Bhagwan, but many stories like that led up blind alleys; at the very least they take loads of time that one could use on other topics. And, to be fair, the public also needs to know about the relatively unknown legitimate religious traditions that are, after all, what's "new" as in "newspaper."

To put it mildly, the field of religion reporting has broadened immensely just at the time when religion's place in society has become more enigmatic. In many ways, religion has become whatever the religion writer says it is, and she can feel torn in many directions by a vaguely-felt responsibility to the ever-increasing number of constituencies. A religious establishment is still honored in some parts of the country: Catholics evoke homage in the Northeast and urban Midwest, Southern Baptists get that attention in much of the South, and Lutherans are accorded top-dog status in parts of Wisconsin and Minnesota. But the grip of even these churches on the press has been considerably weakened relative to their diminution in the wider public sphere. Aside from that remaining dutiful coverage, everything else is pretty much hodge podge, nothing commanding that much more of a reporter's time than anything else. It is all increasingly relative.

THE TWO SIDES OF THE RELIGION/PRESS FENCE

Given the plethora of possibilities for religion reporting, many religious groups are likely to feel slighted or overlooked. There are lots of potentially terrific stories with a limited audience. Stories of a broad interest to a highly pluralistic audience are, by contrast, rather few in number. For years, many religion writers have struggled mightily to surmount "ghetto" treatment of religion and are understandably loathe to retreat again into that restricted function. Like a great many other people, religious groups enjoy publicity and often hope it will generate a kind of

evangelistic promotion. But for newspapers to lapse back into safe, bulle-
tin-board coverage that publicizes religious groups irrespective of their
news value or general interest is a giant step backward. Neither newspapers nor the cause of religion in the media is well served.

In the competition for press attention, there is bound to be a kind of
"whose ox is fed?" syndrome. Moreover, at a time when many large
church groups are losing members and support, pressure understandably
mounts for "good" publicity. Accordingly, the definition of what constitutes a solid piece of religious reporting differs greatly. Many religious
leaders who complain the most about the lack of religion coverage may
actually be saying they don't like the kind of stories that are appearing.
Gripes that some groups receive better or favored coverage generate
chronic resentments, jealousies, and bitterness.

Having worked for the *New York Times* for many years, I can attest to
a fairly widespread assumption that a mention in that newspaper is
counted more precious than gold, except, of course, if the attention is
grossly unflattering. (Many do not seem to mind even that.) This may be a
fact of life in public relations, but it saddens me. It's as if religious groups
cannot believe in their own legitimacy apart from confirmation by a press
vehicle deemed "important," a sort of secular blessing on their mission. A
couple of years ago, for example, the United Methodist Church, which has
a very capable news staff, hired a New York public relations firm to promote the Methodist bishops' statement on nuclear weapons. The moved
"worked" in that the adoption of the letter received wide attention, but
whether the device made any real difference in achieving the more substantive aims of the church remains very uncertain. Like many churches,
the United Methodists are feeling pressure to move away from news to
public relations, a direction I can only interpret as a desire to manage the
news and tout "image making" (as if capturing that spotlight is a supreme
good in and of itself). It is, in my view, an ominous drift that can only
complicate sound religious journalism.

Certainly religion deserves space in newspapers and time on television, and it's perfectly natural for groups to want to put their best feet
forward in hopes of capturing the spotlight. But the stakes can become so
high as to defeat more significant purposes. Conspiracy theories concocted
to explain "failure" to "impact the media" are mostly or totally
unfounded. A complex set of circumstances, rather than deliberate exclusion or inclusion, usually accounts for the admittedly uneven distribution
of coverage.

The question of why good stories get missed, then, is contingent on
several factors, the most important of them often having to do with the
perspective from which the judgment of "good" is made. Opposing views

arise as to what "valid" stories get left out. Religious groups have their idea of what should be covered as do editors. Many candidates I might submit as "good" for the news could presumably be considered "bad" by the groups being covered.

For example, the collapse of effective youth programming, educational or otherwise, among Catholics and Protestants strikes me as a woefully neglected story that would have broad appeal. So would, it seems to me, some further digging into religious television. While non-fundamentalists scamper around looking for an alternative to the televangelists, scarcely anybody notices that there has never been, so far as I know, a solid rationale behind these efforts. Some churches have been willing to sink a pretty sum of money into television studios and uplink satellite devices without a credible programming concept that would demonstrably help the church achieve its ends. Let's assume that the goal is evangelism, a fair guess because most of the groups going into the TV business are fighting a war of attrition. A reporter might ask two questions: (1) where is the format that will deliver effective non-fundamentalistic television (is TV capable of handling anything other than simple appeals to the already converted?); and (2) who knows whether television, even if it turns out to the satisfaction of the churches, does anything at all to promote the desired end?

Those are only some examples of a type of story that might face tough going, not within my newspaper but among the churches whose projects are open to question. Perhaps it would go the other way; church people with integrity would welcome a hard look at the issue, while I'd have trouble selling it to my editors. But that possibility does seem less likely. Good reporting involves digging and unpleasant revelations. Religious groups have a duty to present themselves as they would prefer to be perceived. News gathering operations are, by their very nature, adversarial. The two sides will disagree, sometimes painfully, even under the best conditions. When newspapers began taking religion seriously, that meant forsaking an attitude of patronizing tolerance for the same skeptical posture taken toward any other institutions. That is a big adjustment for some religious groups to go through, particularly those which have been coddled and protected.

For the religion writer in the foxhole, the problems involved in trying to do a respectable job can be daunting. So much the more, then, is the need for "sources" who can be relied upon to provide a trustworthy perspective on the fast-changing scene. My work has been assisted invaluably by people who acted as analysts and interpreters from a somewhat detached point of view. They have been wonderful sounding boards, catalysts for worthwhile stories and dumping grounds for bad ones. Religion reporters need to be cultivated by people in religion who know how to make suggestions in a non-coercive manner. The process is, after all, one of human relations rather than public relations. Reporters usually bristle when they're "told" what a good story is or lectured to about the obvious. They are, likewise, grateful to those who avoid attempts at manipulation and offer possibilities which the reporter can feel free to accept or reject. The cause of good religion coverage depends considerably on the fostering of decency, helpfulness, and respect across the religion/press divide.

For most of this discussion, I have taken a benign look at newspapers in particular and the media in general. The problem of the considerable gaps in religion coverage has been traced primarily to other factors largely beyond either religion or the press. They are functions of cultural shifts. But lest I be accused of letting the news organization off the hook, let me add some critical comments. Many newspaper editors and reporters cast jaundiced or blind eyes toward religion. The cause may stem from unresolved personal conflicts about religion, alluded to earlier, from a mentality wholly wedded to an empirical outlook, from sheer ignorance, or any number of other factors. But such aversion does exist, of course, and can make the job of covering religion very difficult. Another problem has to do with stereotyping. News operations are basically conservative institutions watching the world whirl by. It is difficult for them to comprehend the roots of substantive change until the process has already been certified a hundred times over. A running joke within the field is that by the time trends appear in feature articles they are already on their way out. Reporters may themselves be fairly liberal in some ways, which usually means they see enough intractable problems to make them open to change, but the institutions they work for are generally very cautious. The nuances have a way of getting lost, and old concepts and images stick long after they are any longer appropriate. This hampers religion coverage, for many religious institutions have been, it seems, wrongly sized up forever. News operations are conventional and move very slowly.

The reluctance to challenge conventional wisdom results in a disservice to much more than religion. Sheer lack of this kind of ambition kept newspapers from uncovering the recent New York City political scandals (and before then the city's financial collapse). Space reporters basked long in the reflected glory of the space program as privileged insiders, yet they and their editors were somehow remiss in failing to report the mess behind the glamorous facades. It took the Challenger disaster for newspapers to bring NASA into some perspective. The Islamic revolution was another major "surprise" that might have been anticipated as was the "sudden" drug crisis. There is plenty of neglect and lethargy to go around; reporters should not excuse what happens in religion news but give events some context. In one sense it all comes down to motives. If there is sufficient incentive for reporters to push ahead, which usually entails strong enough interest among editors and a plausible outcome to the effort involved, the story has a much greater chance of getting done. No matter how intriguing or meaningful something else might be, if it doesn't have the constituency within the newspaper, then chances are it won't see the black and white of a newspaper column.

Beyond those limitations, there are restrictions related to the readership. A public that grows less theologically and scripturally literate with every passing year simply cannot handle some stories that should be told about religion. The language and conceptual framework of the social sciences, the lingua franca of our age, have come to substitute as medium of common communication. Much religion reporting therefore gets reduced to religious sociology (a category that permits surveys and psycho-religious movements ample room), ecclesiastical politics (either bishops knocking heads or tackling social problems like nuclear war) or entertainment (Jim and Tammy Bakker). The subject of ethics is another presumed avenue for discussions of religion, but in practical terms the focus is almost always removed from ideas about transcendent or traditional religious reasoning. At best, the end result is a kind of unintended natural theology.

Two other characteristics, one on each side of the religion/press fence, play into each other somewhat neurotically. Earlier I mentioned a certain crisis of rising expectations stemming from the vast improvements in religion reporting. Closely related to that mood, it seems to me, is what happened with the demise of so much of the "religious press." For financial reasons, church groups have had to discontinue dozens of publications that once were used to report regularly on in-house issues. With the death of those vehicles, secular news outlets have been expected to fill some of the resulting gap. Sometimes those hopes cannot realistically be fulfilled. Then, on the press side, the problem is compounded by the built-in hesitancy to follow-up stories. Some of the best undone pieces are of that variety. Because the press is so present-time oriented, the what-happened-after-the-floodwaters-receded stories get left on the pile of good ideas. A year after the Vatican dropped its major opus on reproductive technology on the world, there was hardly any comment on what difference this document had made, on, say, Catholic hospitals. Long after the Vatican's crackdown on liberal theologians, far too little had been said about how the actual work of theologians might have changed as a result; if a chill had set in, that would have been news. As a working journalist for years, I know how difficult it is to squeeze in time for those kinds of stories. There are constant brushfires to attend.

Despite the problems, there is in my estimation no better beat at a newspaper, none that affords such a multi-faceted look at belief, behavior, history, theology, institutional politics, and intimate personal struggle. And within the limits and frustrations of the press, lots of informative and otherwise helpful material does get reported. There is the "hard" news that elbows its way in because it intersects with the urgent concerns of the day. Churches confront sexism, parishes organize sanctuary movements, a bishop refuses to pay a portion of income tax as an anti-nuclear protest, and so on. Then there are the thematic or feature stories, perhaps familiar to those inside churches but fascinating to outsiders: teaching business executives to pray, establishing hospices for AIDS patients under church auspices, a cathedral looking back at 175 years of existence, a synagogue assisting in refugee resettlement, the challenge of teaching sex to church young people—these suggest the breadth. The analysis and interpretation of big religious events is another function performed by some religion writers to great effect.

Then there are the terrific ones that got away. The press was either asleep at the switch or didn't understand or just plain didn't care. And that's a shame, but not a calamity because there are grounds for hope. Religion reporting has come a long way and is in flux. Nothing is fixed forever within the workings of the press. There is room for further development. One thing that is good to keep in mind, it seems to me, is that the press is an approximate reflection of our own mentality. We get what we want in a larger collective sense. If the reporters and editors suffer gaps in perception, or don't seem to grasp what is important to some of us, it is probably because the distortions belong somehow to the wider society. The wheel constantly turns and delivers surprises. I have a hunch that with a little flair a good story on just how many angels might be able to dance on the head of a pin, given the evidence of holography, could very well end up on Page One.

SUGGESTIONS FOR FURTHER READING

Bellah, Robert N. et al., *Habits of the Heart: Individualism and Commitment in American Life*. Berkeley and Los Angeles: University of California Press, 1985.

Dupre, Louis, "Spiritual Life in a Secular Age." *Daedalus* Winter (1982): 21–33.

Herberg, Will, *Protestant, Catholic, Jew*. Garden City, NY: Doubleday & Co., 1955.

Part II

The Use of the Media by Organized Religion

5

What Makes the
Televangelists Tick?

Peter Elvy

"Without doubt it is a delightful harmony when doing and saying go together."

Montaigne[1]

A GATHERING OF RELIGIOUS BROADCASTERS

It happens every year in Washington and I still do not know quite what it is. At one level it is the annual jamboree of America's burgeoning religious broadcasting industry. It is more than that. Beneath the sea of stalls and the exhibitions there flows an ideological current. To me, it seemed to be a tribal gathering: patriotic, masculine, defensive, and hierarchical. A large part of its creed is free enterprise but it marches to a well-orchestrated, silent tune. There are seminars and superstars. Visiting politicians come to worship and be worshipped. Great chieftains stalk the halls surrounded by their minions and their acolytes. Alliances are forged between sober-suited, Bible-believing capitalists, sipping soft drinks. Other transactions are blatantly less decorous. Hard-bitten agents jostle for the payphones to fix deals in fifty states. So much that goes on in the Sheraton during this convention of religious broadcasters is totally irreligious. But that can be said of consistories in Rome or pilgrimages to Mecca. Most of all, it is a yearly gathering of a very special clan. Some are millionaires and world famous. Most are little, local heroes, earning a less than spectacular living from their calling. These are the born-again, paid-up members of National Religious Broadcasters (NRB), the trade association of America's "electronic church."

Of course, I am an outsider at this gathering of televangelists, a very

1. C'est sans doute, une belle harmonie, quand le faire et le dire vont ensemble. *Essais*, Book 2, Ch. 31.

minor curiosity with an Old World accent. I had not grown up with religious broadcasters like these. I had read about them and heard about them and listened to recordings. Only the pirate radio ships in the North Sea have carried their heavily accented message. For most of my life, it has been illegal to solicit funds on the airwaves of my part of the European continent. Indeed, this youthful deprivation gave me much sympathy and many conversation starters as I queued for lunches in the Sheraton. ("Meet Peter from England. Religious broadcasting is illegal there. Everything is state controlled.") Even when I met a representative of the BBC, I soon realized that I was not on home ground, for this particular one worked for the *Bott* Broadcasting Corporation.

For many weeks, I had traveled the United States in search of the species *televangelist Americanus*. But I had taken in too much, and only some of my memories remained vivid. I love fountains and canaries, and so I had no problems reflecting on the sunny humanism of Robert Schuller's Crystal Cathedral. Like a spy in Jericho, I had given many a surreptitious look into the megalithic follies of Oral Roberts. For these confidences that I was not supposed to know, I hardly needed a notebook. Naturally, my photographs were fixed in my mind's eye long before my films were processed. I can still see every wheel of Paul Crouch's "Holy Beamer"—a mighty mobile satellite uplink. For some strange and quirkish reason, my visual memories of the Pat Robertson estate in Virginia focus on some primitive metal sculptures of the twelve apostles. They are on the first floor of the main building. The reproduction colonial architecture impressed me less than my gracious and expensive executive lunch.

In the end, the furious pace confused my recollection processes, and it took some weeks of thinking and writing to disentangle the threads of memory. Triumphantly but tiredly, I looked back on visits to twenty states of the Union and I had to consult my notebooks to see whom I had met and where I had been. Before my journeyings, I had heard many generalizations about the TV preachers. Most of them had been totally negative and hostile and therefore have to be (to my mind) suspect. My own generalizations come from the conflation of very many introductions and experiences. I think that I now know something about "The Televangelist, Great and Small," but the danger in making judgments about him from the perspective of a tourist is that he is not a single flesh-and-blood person. He is many different people rolled into one, according to my personal roller coaster ride through some parts of his world.

But the Sheraton Hotel was different. Every self-respecting televangelist belongs to NRB. The convention is in town again and, for me, acts as a mental fixative. The televangelists are no longer dotted across the continent. Here they are, more or less together under one roof. And so, on this particular early morning, I took my reserved twenty-dollar place. A few feet away, at the top table, sat the cardinals of the electronic church. This was the annual Prayer Breakfast in honor of the State of Israel. Pat Robertson, Oral Roberts, Jimmy Swaggart, and a cohort of lesser luminaries sat side by side. This time, there were no cameras, make-up girls, or offstage choirs. The big guns had come down from their suites in the Sheraton to affirm one of their most serious theological positions. It is also a political position, and Senator Albert Gore and Ambassador Jeanne Kirkpatrick were at the top table also to emphasize bipartisan support—at least for the political reality of Israel. This is serious theological politics and it is breakfast. Televangelists, rabbis, ambassadors, and politicians munch contentedly and unitedly. The meaning of Israel is self-evident. These are the end times and the remaining time is short. The Bible is coming true. God still has a purpose for his people the Jews. Armageddon is just round the corner.

Whether the Israeli ambassador and the rabbis and the congressmen really believe that the world is about to end with a great battle in the dried up bed of the River Euphrates is open to question. But, whoever it was who said of the United States that foreign policy is an unknown science would, this morning, feel mightily reinforced. The televangelists really do believe that Israel's establishment is the most decisive of the signs of the times. A great many other groups, for very different reasons, purport to lend them their support. But I digress. I had visited most of the studios and I had watched most of the major televangelists in action. But still the lingering doubts persisted. Even here, before this galaxy of stars of David, I wondered . . . "Are they just showmen? Where is Elmer Gantry this morning?"

A CONVERSION EXPERIENCE

The speeches droned on. The many rabbis at the tables were clearly bored stiff by all the talk of the Rapture and the Second Coming. The man from the Israeli airline El Al (trying to catch the mood of the moment) made a moving plea for more tourism to the Holy Land. The Israeli ambassador (quite the cleverest man present) managed to sound like a Christian fundamentalist while saying almost nothing. The curiously characterless face of Pat Robertson twisted unconvincingly as he spoke of the misfortunes that his own broadcasting equipment had suffered in the Middle East. And then it happened. It was, for me, a bolt from the blue—a Damascus Road experience. Something occurred that had the nature of a conversion. From that moment on, I knew that, as with most of us, there is within The Televangelist, Great and Small a core of genuine conviction.

It is an almost impossible event to describe but I will have to try. It went like this. In the middle of the speeches, a Christian saxophone player was introduced. I had never heard of him and cannot even remember his name, although he was greeted with a warm and knowing burst of applause. Now the most obvious thing to say about saxophony is that not much else can be done at the same time. Your hands hold nothing but the saxophone and your mouth is also fully occupied. He played for a few minutes and then his tempo quickened. There seemed to be a general audience response to the music and then it happened. He was standing among the tables and suddenly his left hand left the saxophone and went skywards in something like a Black Power salute. Ever the reporter, I scribbled "charismatic saxophonist" in my notebook. But the televangelists were not writing. They were on their feet. Oral Roberts was clapping heartily and Jimmy Swaggart, his eyes alight, would have played along too if he had been able to. For me, it was a convincing insight. I had seen a great deal to disillusion me, shock me, and even sicken me. But I now knew something else. Televangelism is not just showmanship and commercialism.

CONFESSIONS OF A RELIGIOUS BROADCASTER

My friends tell me that I am always too kind about the televangelists. They may be right and, if they are, I think I know the person. I am myself a religious broadcaster. I have spent many hundreds of hours in studios, and I have had time to think about my trade. For six long years, I co-hosted a Sunday morning radio show on a British commercial station. My program was the company's contribution to the faith of the county. Nine short bursts of religion were laced into three hours of pop music and quizzes. The bursts were never longer than three minutes—not because the radio company had anything against religion. If they did have a grudge, it was against the spoken word for (according to the gospel of the audience measurers) speech loses listeners. It did not take me long to realize that I was working with a group of good-natured but inflexible audio-fundamentalists. Once I had been out and about with my tape recorder and I returned (like some kilted Highlander who has landed the biggest salmon of the season) with a punchy interview with our former Prime Minister Edward Heath. "How long is he?" asked the Australian Program Controller. "Five minutes forty," was my defensive reply. "But it is Edward Heath." The reply was instant and instinctive. "Sorry, mate. You will just have to cut him in half and play something in the middle." Broadcasting is all about winning viewers and listeners and that means understanding who they are and what they want. Modern broadcasting owes very little to the parable of the sower. Words and music are no longer simply scattered into the ether in the hope that not all will land among the tares or on the stony ground. Sowing seeds has changed since the time of Jesus. The farmer of the Western world knows just where he is going to sow his seed. He knows the optimum depth in the soil and he anticipates the humidity. In the same way, professional broadcasting is not the haphazard business of the parable. The modern broadcaster spends a great deal of time and money targeting his unseen audience.

So the televangelist has first of all to know his business. He has to be a broadcaster before he is anything else, and this is not to assault his integrity. It is a simple fact of communication. It is something I have learned about myself over and over again. Sometimes people are inquisitive about my motives for deserting my parishioners for radio and TV studios. On very many occasions, evangelicals have fixed me a firm gaze and asked me a straight question. Their slight anxiety is always discernible, and I think they are seeking reassurance. The sense of their questions is always the same: "When you sit down at the microphone and you think about all those people out there, what is it that you are really trying to do?"

I have long since given up tailoring my answer. I now give it to them straight. I readily admit to the most awful secret. When I sit down in a radio or TV studio, my first priority is to be a performer: to survive, to project myself, and to entertain. I want people to like me and to listen to me and to stay with me. I do not want people to turn me off or switch to the BBC. But then, of course, I am not the kind of Christian who has an inner voice driving me to preach the word of repentance at every possible opportunity. To survive, I have to be a rather tentative evangelist. First of all (and this is a crucially important difference between me and a real televangelist), I am using someone else's broadcasting studio. I can be dismissed, sent into outer darkness by the general manager to be seen no more. Then too, I have to remember that I am an uninvited guest in someone's home. My listener (there is only one to the true radio man!) is probably in bed or in the bath or reading the Sunday morning paper. He could be a Catholic or a Jew or a Sikh. Or she may be mumbling dark threats about her husband's reluctance to make the early morning tea.

When I broadcast, I am merely a blind fly on the listener's wall—a disembodied voice beneath an automobile dashboard. With every passing second, a hundred fingers touch a hundred buttons. I am either consigned to oblivion or I crackle into life. Occasionally (in mid-sentence), I am

resurrected. I am switched off and on again but my re-entry is often
mutilated. I am left senseless and verbless in an unappreciative world. The
word for all this coming and going is communication. Of course, it is no
such thing. It is a one-way street—a peculiar non-return valve down which
I must squeeze my persona. This is followed, at a safe distance, by my
convictions. Furthermore, despite all the electronic projection, unless I
can firmly grab my listener's intellect or emotions, I am rarely honored
with his or her undivided attention. More often than not (and this applies
to both radio and television) I am simply the familiar background noise,
or wallpaper.

THE REALITIES OF TELEVANGELISM

The televangelist has to find his way through this complicated broadcasting world. To survive, he himself has to be a broadcaster. Of course, he
can do something that, in my own wildest dreams, I have never con-
templated doing. He can buy the station. This may relieve him of the
sensitive, subtle, and sometimes tiresome task of working within someone
else's overall philosophy and style. But it will most certainly not let him
escape from the inexorable and primary law of audience satisfaction. A
televangelist has to have an audience, for, as his audience grows, so does
his star rise and his power and wealth increase. But it is in his sometimes
frenetic efforts to build his audience that he makes his most serious compromises with the world, the flesh, and the devil.

But there are further extenuating circumstances, and other reasons
why the televangelists are not totally responsible for their own actions. For
instance, Jim Bakker and Jimmy Swaggart will go down in broadcasting
history as the terrible twins whose sexual sins found them out. We all
enjoy seeing hypocrisy exposed. The whole world laughs when the game-
keeper is found to be a poacher after all. But I am not quite sure if it is right
or wise to laugh too loudly. Perhaps, for a moment, we should forget the
flesh and even the devil and begin to study the world. Both Swaggart and
Bakker are bizarre symptoms of an unhealthy system that was created not
by any particular televangelist nor by a conspiracy of televangelists. The
North American electronic church was created by nothing less than an
agency of the U.S. government. A broadcasting environment has been
formed in which, if the Swaggarts and Bakkers and Oral Robertses and
Robert Schullers did not exist, it would be necessary to invent them.
Televangelists evolve inevitably and only the fittest survive. Swaggart and
Bakker may diminish, but as they do, newer and rising stars will move
forward and take their places.

It is easy to trace the cause of this continual process of evolution which favors the entrepreneurial TV preacher and which has almost obliterated the mainline churches from the screens. The primary cause is a broadcasting policy shared by successive American governments. Seemingly matter-of-fact directives from the Federal Communications Commission have had a shattering influence on broadcasting history. Vital bricks have been dislodged and a whole building has come tumbling down. The FCC simply ordered that religious broadcasting would still be required on American screens but that, henceforth, this religious airtime could be *paid for*. Two spectacular results followed. Religious broadcasting almost immediately became a big business. The nationally-known televangelists have to spend enormous sums on airtime. The preaching politician, Pat Robertson, has to find more than $220,000,000 to buy time on five thousand cable systems. The only people who can provide this money are the viewers themselves. The main preoccupation of the televangelist continues to be audience-building, but he has first of all to be an entertainer . . . in order to build up a big enough audience . . . in order to receive enough financial support . . . to stay on air . . . as an entertainer of his growing audience.

The televangelist is a prisoner in a commercial treadmill. His appearances as a free spirit are pure illusion. He has to be both the star of the show and the chairman of the board. Above all, his ministry has to grow and be ever more successful. Ratings are all-important. God's blessings have to be more apparent each month. It is no wonder that these men crack up. It is no surprise that Oral Roberts took to his Prayer Tower and told his followers that God would kill him if they did not come up with eight million dollars. Oral has a wife to support . . . and a son and heir to the business . . . and a university . . . and the biggest sports hall in Oklahoma . . . and a hospital . . . and a TV complex.

The other side of the coin is equally visible. As a result of the deregulation of religious broadcasting, the churches have been knocked from their privileged perch. They cannot take the heat of free-market competition. Catholics and Lutherans and Methodists have been all but banished from the screen. There are no more Archbishop Fulton Sheens with their own advertisement-supported programs. By Western European standards, the American churches are packed to overflowing. There are more Catholics in the U.S. than there are Britons in Britain. There are more Southern Baptists than there are Dutch in Holland. But the churches cannot cope with buying airtime. Nor can they afford to buy time. So despite Swaggart and Bakker and Roberts, the show will go on. The electronic church will continue. It will do so until the American government realizes that there may be a better way to manage religious broadcasting than to put it up for sale.

American broadcasting scandals are not new. Global television itself has amplified their impact. Aimee Semple McPherson was a controversial broadcaster if ever there was one. Most of the U.S.'s religious radio and television is now in the hands of independent preachers. Only a very few of them are multi-millionaires or superstars. Oral Roberts, Jim Bakker, Pat Robertson, Jimmy Swaggart, Robert Schuller, and Jerry Falwell are the names that hit the headlines. But these are just the front row in a "church" which seats tens of thousands of lesser mortals. Compared with the big fish, most radio and TV preachers are small fry. They may have a half-hour spot on local radio or enjoy a regional following in a small chain of television stations. Many are honorable men with their backgrounds in missionary radio. Some (a smaller number) preach an eccentric personalized religion which the battle-hardened early Christians would have wasted no time in condemning as heresy. The airwaves of America are crowded with religious messages of one kind or another. Some cities have a dozen or more all-religious radio stations. Most (but not all) of those who occupy these pulpits of the air would think of themselves as the purveyors of a traditional, Bible-based gospel.

Scandals notwithstanding, it is both unfair and fatuitous to dismiss all this activity as so much cynical money-grubbing. Of the thousands who earn their living in the religious broadcasting industry, only the biggest stars can command earnings that are spectacularly high. At the heart of this electronic church there is considerable religious idealism. It would be surprising to find a complete unanimity of belief among so many prima donnas, but there are a number of clearly marked strands of belief. Most of the TV preachers would gather around one or the other of two clearly identified totem poles. One group would call themselves "fundamentalists." Their standard-bearer is Jerry Falwell. They represent a long-established tradition in American religion. Belief in the inerrancy of scripture is paramount. They would draw much of their strength from the conservative wing of the mighty Baptist tradition.

Much more important in the highest echelons of the electronic church are "charismatics" who, as well as stressing the gifts of the Spirit and free expression in their worship, emphasize the fulfillment of prophecy and the imminent end of the world. Armageddon is hardly entertaining, and there is a considerable difference between the broadcast and written messages of an Oral Roberts or a Paul Crouch. But only a little way beneath the show biz surface is the sometimes subliminal message that the end is at hand. The new generation of broadcast satellites are themselves God's messengers that will preach the gospel to every creature. The satellites are, in fact, the angels in the sky foretold in the Book of Revelation! The secular state of Israel is a fulfillment of Bible prophecies and a sure sign of the coming conflict.

Biblically-based politics is only one of the perils of televangelism. First of all, the whole system stands on a most dangerous (assuming that temptation is a danger!) financial basis. Religious broadcasters great and small rely on the cash offerings of the listeners and viewers. Preachers cannot simply proclaim their message. Somehow or another, they have to attract donations. Second, the mainline American churches are now more or less excluded from the airwaves. If the role of broadcasting in a civilized state is to reflect the cultural mix of the country, then the U.S.'s liberal Protestant denominations and its mighty Catholic population are therefore seriously deprived and under-represented. Third, and less important, is the "star-factor" which has excited so much publicity. The electronic church has thrown up half a dozen preaching superstars whose power and property set them far apart from America's local Christianity. This is but the tip of the iceberg. It is not the most crucial problem, but it is the best known and the most talked about.

A TOUR OF THE BROADCASTING EMPIRES

Robert Schuller

Every Sunday morning, from his Crystal Cathedral in California, Dr. Robert Schuller transmits an "Hour of Power." It is a glittering show from a truly wonderful building. The message, based on Norman Vincent Peale's "power of positive thinking," is upbeat. The stress is on patriotism and personal potential. Interestingly, in the terms of the sixteenth century Reformation, this is a startlingly un-evangelical theology. The emphasis is on good works, mind-over-matter, and just about everything that Luther condemned. Be that as it may, the Crystal Cathedral has nine choirs, fountains, canaries, a superb organ, and the largest television screen in the world upon which the engaging Dr. Robert twinkles and extols his be-happy-attitudes.

Oral Roberts

The earthly empire of Oral Roberts can be fully appreciated only from the air. He is just about as famous as his "good friend" Billy Graham. Roberts started out as a tent crusader. He went from town to town with a big top and held evangelistic rallies. He became an important name among itinerant preachers. Then he made the transition to radio and, later, the change to television. He became a star, but he hung on to the old method of fund-raising. In the old days in the preaching tent, he had to pass round the hat. When it came to TV, Oral Roberts continued to plead for financial support. By this time, he had entered a new universe of financial scale. Now he had to ask not just for money, but for a king's ransom. In order to stay on the screens, he had to ask his viewers for tens, hundreds of millions of dollars—and the money came in. With his profits, this proud, magnetic, brilliant, mercurial, and dictatorial man built his own city.

The Roberts complex in Tulsa, Oklahoma, is truly a wonder. There is a huge hospital—a trio of medical skyscrapers—which Roberts has named the City of Faith Healing Center. There is a sports astrodome—the biggest in the state. There is a university with five thousand students, producing doctors, preachers, and teachers. The students at the Oral Roberts University call it "the campus that landed." Needless to say, the heart of the Roberts city-state is a complete satellite TV complex whence Oral pumps out his entertaining mix of Good Morning America and Old Time Religion. There are retirement villages for the older fans. There are libraries and buildings full of accountants. And in the middle of it all stands a rather odd, futuristic shape like a tall child's top. It is the now world-famous prayer tower, air-conditioned and staffed night and day by teams of volunteers who pray for causes that are free-phoned in from all over America.

Four years ago, Oral Roberts's good fortune began to run out. His position in the ratings began to slip. The multi-million piles of money needed to drive his empire began to shrink, and so he sat atop his prayer tower like some latter-day Simon Stylites and issued an amazing threat to his followers. Send me eight million dollars or God will call me home. The money came in. God left Oral in Oklahoma. But one of the buildings in Roberts's complex depends little on supernatural signs. Without it he would perish. Inside this solid structure are the whirring word processors and computers that write Roberts's letters for him. There are signature machines that sign his personalized appeals and acknowledgements. Drawers contain the precious software that presents him as caring and friendly and concerned for the individual donor. Needless to say, the Roberts word processors send sensitive replies and draw on a bank of the televangelist's most personal and original phrases.

Jerry Falwell

Most of the front-rank televangelists are as renowned for their real estate as for their broadcasts. In Lynchburg, Virginia, the politically powerful Jerry Falwell ministers to the third biggest Southern Baptist Church in the U.S. To be fair, the growth of his church congregation, and not just his television audience, has been phenomenal; Falwell's Thomas Road Baptist Church is now in its third building. Falwell is the Mr. Clean of the front-rank televangelists. For a time (after the Bakker debacle), he tried to hold together the PTL empire. It was not an easy task. Falwell is proud to call himself a fundamentalist and represents a different type of Protestant evangelicalism. Robertson, Bakker, Roberts, and Swaggart would all call themselves charismatic Christians.

Pat Robertson

Not too far away (in American terms), in Virginia Beach, another political TV preacher, Pat Robertson, presides over yet another familiar mix of broadcasting studios and a university. Robertson is one of the most visible Christians in history. Starting with a run-down TV station, he built it into the Christian Broadcasting Network—the U.S.'s biggest religious broadcasting network. His flagship program is the "700 Club"—a glittering mix of current affairs and spiritual healing. He served in the U.S. Marine Corps and has a law degree from Yale. His father was a U.S. Senator, and one of his ancestors was the Reverend Robert Hunt, Anglican chaplain to the earliest settlers in Virginia. Robertson and his wife Dede are charismatic Christians and possess the gift of tongues. Once he was a Stevenson Democrat, but he ran for the White House as a Reagan Republican. Contrary to many predictions, he made a poor showing. Even in the Southern primaries, he came in a weak third.

Despite the patrician manner, Robertson has much in common with Oral Roberts who, in a phase of pastoral pruning, amputated the law school from his university and presented it—lock, stock, barrel, and magnificent library—to Robertson's CBN University. The Virginian too confronts divers diseases by television. With his face contorted in prayer, he speaks of the miracles that are saving his viewers. Even Gloria (Hurricane Gloria, that is) exercised a lady's privilege and left his headquarters intact. Further south, Robertson's erstwhile assistant Jim Bakker followed the same theme but with variations. Heritage U.S.A. is a leisure park with the biggest water slide in the world and a dizzying array of holiday accommodations as well as the inevitable satellite uplink and TV studios. Following his disgrace and removal from the ranks of the Assemblies of God clergy in 1987, Bakker and his wife Tammy Faye enjoyed a comfortable exile in Palm Springs. As this goes to press, Jim Bakker is under indictment by the Federal Government, charged with 24 counts of fraud and conspiracy in connection with his management of the PTL television ministry. His trial is expected to begin sometime in 1989.

Jimmy Swaggart

Still further south, in Louisiana, evangelist Jimmy Swaggart transmitted programs to five continents. He is the cousin of country star Jerry Lee Lewis and is himself a noted gospel singer. He represents a tougher strand within the electronic church. Narrower, uncompromising, and straightforward, Swaggart exposed the sexual misdemeanors of Jim bakker. He also publicly poured contempt on the antics in the Tulsa Prayer Tower. He has little time for the traditional denominations and a clear idea of the worldwide significance of satellite broadcasting. His studios in Baton Rogue are famous throughout the industry for their technical standard and their expertise in language translation. But early in 1988 the sky fell in for evangelist Jimmy. His own sins were exposed and, after an excruciating public confession and a later defiance of his denomination, the Assemblies of God, he has decided to go it alone.

GIVING VIEWERS WHAT THEY WANT

Long before the major televangelist scandals, the questions were often asked: Is so-and-so genuine? Can a preaching star with so much fame and fortune possibly be anything but a clever showman? Dozens of liberal journalists have written knowingly about the sins of the televangelists or the hypocrisy endemic in the electronic church. Once it seemed to be the Charlotte Observer that stood out as a lone sentinel for sanity, pegging away, in season and out of season, pointing up the discrepancies of Bakker's PTL. Now there is a tide of condemnation. It has become the accepted wisdom that the electronic church is a thoroughly bad thing, bad for religion and bad for broadcasting. But when I hear the question, Is so-and-so genuine?, I have to turn it on myself. I am a preacher and I am a religious broadcaster. I do not have one millionth of the wealth or reputation or power of a Pat Robertson or an Oral Roberts, but I now know the problem. I have learned for myself that to be a preacher and to be a religious broadcaster are not the same. In my pulpit, I am "ten feet above contradiction," sustained there by a long suffering congregation if not by my own eloquence. Tomorrow (or rather next Sunday) is always another day. But, in the studio, I am as exposed as a matador. Tomorrow is not another day. Now is all that matters. Position, qualifications, learning, the ecclesiastical hierarchy—all mean nothing. All that matters is my ability to hold and multiply an audience. If I can do that, I will succeed. And I also have to consider the maxim which might hand over the studio door. It would sound better in Latin, in plain English, it is simply this: "the best way to satisfy the listener or the viewer is to give him what he wants for as much time as he wants."

For me, the important question is this: "Is religious broadcasting even possible? It is my belief that, if the televangelists risk corruption, the infection has come not from money or sex or power or even the size of their operations but from broadcasting itself. The televangelists have spent their lives trying to do the impossible, to square the circle. Rather than preach the word without fear or favor, to rich and poor, to large crowds or small groups, the televangelist has first of all to work at the illusion that he is a great success and then to recruit an invisible army of viewers/subscribers to turn that illusion into a financial reality. This is manifestly not the priority of the gospel but it is the starkest fact of broadcasting life and applies the world over.

Dr. David Clark, Pat Robertson's astute Vice President for Marketing, put the point to me without frills: "As far as I know, there are only three ways of paying for television. The government can pay, out of taxes. The advertiser can pay. Then again, the viewer can pay." The electronic church, the whole religious broadcasting industry of the televangelists, is entirely supported by its viewers. So audience size is crucially and immediately important. Relatively few fans send large sums to their chosen idol. Money comes in little by little, week by week, ten dollars here and there. This is a case of quantity over quality. The more viewers there are, the more tens of dollars there will be. If his audience diminishes or ages, then (in his financial manager's jargon) his donor base will have shrunk. He will have become a descending star and he will soon be forgotten.

THE EVOLUTION OF TV EVANGELISM

My church has stood since the thirteenth century. It is an Essex gem. Before this church, there was another on the same spot. Christopher Martin, Governor of the Mayflower, was married in the building. Long before him, the peasants of the area revolted against the king. No doubt they rest around us, buried irreverently in mass graves. Life has been quieter lately, although a German airship crashed in flames during the Great War and is still a talking point. Today, St. Mary's still overlooks the parish. She is so old now that most of her memories have gone. The collared doves fight for a perch on her tower and the grey squirrels run along her walls . . . "as it was in the beginning, is now and ever shall be, world without end. Amen."

Wrong! The collared doves are new arrivals. Ornithologists tell me that they are immigrants from Siberia. About ten years ago, they spotted an ecological niche. They have filled it with such spectacular success that the farmers now regard them as pests. As far as the gray squirrels, they too are interlopers with superpower connections. They are Americans. Years ago, they seized control of the habitat of the good old English red squirrel, who would have been so well known to crusader and peasant and to Christopher Martin. The weaker reds have succumbed. The more powerful grays have inherited the earth.

The television evangelists of North America have also come into a great inheritance. Some would say that God has smiled on the preachers and rewarded them mightily for their faithfulness to the Bible and for their evangelical zeal. I believe that their success story has a much simpler explanation. It is just the same as the squirrels' and the doves'. The TV preacher has filled a particular ecological niche. Unthinkingly, he has been sucked into a vacuum. He has filled a gap that is not of his own design. Charles Darwin (no hero of the evangelists!) would understand. When a window of opportunity blew open, the evolution of a species and the survival of the fittest became inevitable. If the television evangelist had not already existed, it would have been necessary to invent him.

Therefore, the real questions are, How did the window blow open? and "Why did the broadcaster's habitat change. Here, too, the answer is straightforward. Throughout most of its history, and until very recently, the shape of broadcasting on every continent has been determined by government regulation. The television evangelists exist and prosper where the government allows a broadcasting environment that is conducive to televangelism. Conversely, they cannot survive in countries where the government has set its face and its policies against them. In recent years, this simple rule of thumb may be changing. Broadcast satellites take little notice of national boundaries. Most of the television evangelists would claim to see the finger of God working for them in the space age. Indeed, are not the satellites the angels in the sky, foretold in the Bible? Many satellites even have wings and have the potential to preach the gospel to every creature . . . assuming, of course, that the every creature has a receiving dish. But the present power of the television evangelists was not forged anywhere but within the boundaries of the U.S.

Early in its history, radio in the United States was regulated. The concept of public service was held to be important. Stations were required to provide free airtime for religious and community affairs. The buying of airtime for religious causes was forbidden. It was expected that the mainline denominations should be heard on the airwaves. Indeed, from the broadcasters' point of view, mainline Christians were easier to deal with. The spokesmen for the established churches were temperamentally better suited to wide, generalist themes which sit more comfortably within broadcasts to anyone and everyone. Well-established national denominations can deal more conveniently with mighty networks and corporations. Evangelicals with their emphasis on change and personal conversation can be inconvenient and prickly colleagues underneath a transmitter that is beamed at as many people as possible.

Indeed, in the U.S. for four decades, evangelical Christians felt themselves excluded from the airwaves by a "sweetheart deal" between the major networks and the Catholic, liberal Protestant, and Jewish establishments. The "liberation" of evangelicals took place less than twenty years ago. American religious radio and television underwent a sea change. The pharaoh who began to let broadcasting go was Richard Nixon. Successive administrations have continued a process of deregulation which has (perhaps inadvertently) turned the religious tables in the studios. From the early days, federal regulations demanded that religious broadcasting be provided as a free service. Deregulation has led to a volte-face. Nowadays, religion still has to be given an airing—as a public service. But religious airtime can nowadays be sold to the highest bidder. Money is now the determining factor in American religious radio and television. Airtime has to be bought. As the costs are stupendous, the only way to find these huge sums is to solicit funds from the viewer.

THE ABSENCE FROM THE AIRWAYS
OF CATHOLICS AND MAINLINE PROTESTANTS

The television evangelists have multiplied and prospered simply because the U.S. government has, since the days of President Nixon, arranged (or permitted) a broadcasting environment which suits them perfectly. The Christian religion flourishes in North America. People attend Sunday worship in great numbers. The U.S. is probably the only country on earth where a new church building can be the cause of a bitter planning dispute. Suburban activists have been known to reach high levels of excitement over the increase of road traffic caused by churchgoers! Nowhere else in the Western world could their sheer numbers conceivably be regarded as an environmental hazard. The overwhelming majority of these Sunday (and indeed midweek) worshipers belong to the traditional churches. Millions belong to the mainline Protestant denominations that had their roots in Europe. More than one in three is a Roman Catholic.

But, when it comes to broadcasting, which in so many powerful ways influences the values and defines the culture of the modern state, the traditional American churches are almost silent and almost invisible. The televangelists' argument is that the old ecclesiastical-structured faiths are played out or that their members have nothing worthwhile to say. On the airwaves of America, they are now tongue-tied, and this is no doubt part of the justice of God. Liberal Protestantism has had its day and has been found wanting. As for Catholics, they are too numerous for a direct frontal assault, and, more importantly, they are too valuable and cohesive a fraction of the televangelists' donor base.

The interesting thing about Catholics is that a good number of them are temperamentally prepared for the certitudes of televised religion. Accordingly, there is an unspoken understanding between the new TV preacher and the Roman quarter of his congregation. Attacks on "liberals" are allowed. They are the common enemy. But the papacy and the doctrines of the Assumption and the Immaculate Conception are off limits. They are neither mocked nor condemned—nor mentioned. The Bible is presented as the common ground of Christendom. Biblical interpretation is fundamentalist. The teaching of the televangelists about Armageddon, the end of the world, and the State of Israel would hardly earn the imprimatur of any Vatican Biblical Commission. Religious broadcasting in the U.S. is now firmly in the hands of independent preachers. The only possible counterbalance could have been provided by North American Catholicism. But, in religious broadcasting, the country's fifty-three-million-strong Catholic population is either neutralized or collaborating with the occupying power. The traditional Protestant churches have different problems, but the result is the same. They too are in internal exile from their country's airwaves. Counted together, they are half as numerous as the mighty U.S. Catholic Church, and yet a visitor from outer space who dial-flips his television set could be forgiven for doubting their existence.

Their near-total banishment of the mainline Protestant and Catholic churches is a relatively recent phenomenon. It has nothing to do with an evangelical tide that is supposedly sweeping America and washing away all non-evangelical impurities. Pat Robertson's poor showing at the hustings was, if nothing else, an indication that his much-vaunted secret army of supporters may be little more than a regiment. Nowadays, born-again Christians may be on the crest of something like a wave, but their success in capturing the religious broadcasting marketplace is not an ideological or spiritual success. It is the straightforward, simple, and inevitable result of decisions by the federal government which turned religious broadcasting into a free-for-all. By handing over religious broadcasting to the highest bidder, the FCC guaranteed the preeminence of those capable of buying the airtime.

Of course, the sweetheart deal had two serious effects. For many years it cushioned most of the traditional American churches from the realities of broadcasting economics. They tended to regard their easy access to radio and television as a constitutional right. On the other hand, and with some justice, the evangelicals felt excluded. Evangelicals had seen the new broadcasting technology as an exciting new means to preach the good news to every creature. The radio antenna was simply an extension of the church pulpit—a means of reaching more and more people. Indeed, of all Christians, evangelicals are the ones who pride themselves on having something to say. Others would hold that "Christian broadcasting" is never achievable and is simply a contradiction in terms. Others will persist with the business of trying to do the impossible for the simple reason that it is only through TV sets and radio receivers that millions of human beings will ever hear anything remotely like the Christian gospel.

SATELLITES AND SALVATION

On the airwaves, the word certainly does not become flesh and dwell among us. The televangelists are themselves aware of too much reliance on the disembodied word. The search is on for "interactive broadcasting" and for audience response. Many different techniques have been tried. Oral Roberts and Pat Robertson feel moved to pronounce God's direct intervention in the health of some anonymous viewer in Albuquerque or Atlanta. Campus Crusade for Christ, using the new technology, has linked together one hundred different satellite downlinks in five continents. Whirring, million-dollar word processors, while not quite able to make the word into flesh, are at least able to present the televangelist as a personable and caring correspondent. Prodded by Billy Graham, the NRB has now adopted a new and stricter code of financial ethics and accountability.

Televangelists are better broadcasters than Catholics and liberal Protestants. They can present a straightforward, cut-and-dried message that is easily adapted to an information, entertainment, and advertising medium. But are there deeper reasons why televangelists prosper behind microphones and cameras and why Catholics and mainline Protestants have become the new outsiders? Many things changed on that day in 1957 when a man-made metal meteorite soared above Kazhakstan and then hurtled off round planet Earth. The art of warfare changed and became yet more terrible. Space travel began. Within a few years, Americans would journey to the moon. The most immediate and far-reaching effect of Sputnik, and the hundreds of artificial satellites that followed, was a revolution in electronic communication.

Wireless was discovered as the twentieth century began. Its development was speeded by two world wars. The main limitations were the result of nature's own trigonometry. Sputnik did nothing for the Flat-Earthers.

The world really is round! But radio, radar, and television prefer to travel in straight lines and, just like human eyesight, have problems seeing over the horizon. A television signal is rather like the beam from a hand-held torch. The beam expands but does not bend. Artificial satellites, launched by rockets and shuttles, and maneuvered into a stationary position 33,000 miles from the earth, can now act as electronic mirrors. Transmissions can be reflected. The beam from a broadcast satellite can now illuminate a continent. In the U.S., the effect on entertainment broadcasting has been spectacular. Twenty-one satellites are now available, parked over the equator. TV no longer has to be relayed, as a kind of electronic semaphore, from hilltop to high point. Nowadays television signals not only come over the horizon. They come downwards—out of the sky—and in profusion. Some satellites can transmit a dozen programs simultaneously.

One further step—much more down to earth—completes the revolution in North American broadcasting. As the descendants of Sputnik grow bigger and stronger, their transmitting beam will grow brighter. Increasing numbers of households will have their own (ever-more-compact) receiving dishes. Broadcasting will be a one-hop business. The broadcaster will send his product to the satellite waiting in the sky and, within one fifth of one second, it will be back on earth in the receiving dishes of the viewers. Sputnik 1 was put into orbit by self-declared atheists, but satellites have changed the nature of American religious broadcasting. TV preachers can now access every state in the Union. Anyone with a religious message can now buy half an hour on a "bird," hire half-hour spots on several cable systems and be in business as a genuine coast-to-cast gospel minister. What a transformation for an old tent crusader! He was a preacher who went from town to town as a kind of religious traveling salesman. Now he, or at least his children or grandchildren, can stay at home. He can look a camera straight in the eye and he can save souls, not just in western Kentucky, but . . . elsewhere. From the beginning, radio was an exciting medium for an evangelist. Surely this new power makes it possible to fulfill the New Testament commission to preach the gospel to every creature? And now it can be done without getting wet! Nowadays, the word of God can come from a studio pulpit. The only requirement is that every creature should have access to a TV set.

THE PROBLEM OF FINANCES

However, there remains just one serious and inescapable problem: dollars. Religious broadcasting has to be paid for. Evangelism has always cost money. From the days of St. Paul, there have always been subscribers and supporters. Even the crusade tent did not come cheap. Passing round the hat was a reasonable necessity. But the prices of American religious broadcasting—and in particular television—is now so sky high that religious fundraising has become an industry. The largest of the religious TV enterprises, Pat Robertson's CBN, buys time on more than five thousand cable systems. Each year, Robertson raises the bulk of the immense sums he needs from two mighty telethons. One way or the other, the hundreds of millions of dollars required to keep the televangelists on the airwaves of North America come from the viewers.

At one level, there is nothing in the least wicked about public support. If a campfire evangelist on the frontier could be supported by his audience, why can't a modern electronic evangelist enjoy similar backing? The problem is one of scale. The electronic church of the U.S. is very big business indeed. CBN has now surpassed American Airlines as the country's major user of toll-free telephone calls. In order to pull in such large sums of money, the preacher's overriding priority is in attracting an audience. This means that he has to be a competitive TV entertainer as well as an evangelist. He has to say what the audience wants him to say. He must reinforce the viewer's opinions and expectations. John the Baptist would not last thirty seconds in front of the camera. He would have to have his hair dyed, permed, and styled. His teeth would be capped and become pearly white. He would be allowed neither to alienate nor to challenge. Most probably, his producers would think more of him if he could sing just a little. The biggest problem for the televangelists is not their fire-and-brimstone message. Bible-believing Christianity has been a formative strand in the history of the U.S. The weakness of Robertson, Roberts, Schuller, and Bakker is not that they are prickly Protestants but that they have become thoroughly conformed to the world of commercialized entertainment broadcasting, a world in which ratings are all-important.

THE TV PREACHER AS ENTREPRENEUR

Televangelists speak much about the church, but they mostly stand outside ecclesiastical organization and discipline. This gives them a financial head start. They are able to raise the huge sums of money that are needed to buy time, not because of the clarity or excellence of their message, but because their lack of structure and constraints permits them to act as freewheeling business entrepreneurs. American revivalist preachers are (as they have always been) first and foremost individualists. They do not owe their pulpit to any bishop or board of deacons. In the beginning was the preacher. The congregation came on the second day. In the thirteen colonies and on the western frontier, ecclesiastical structures arrived very late on the eighth day—if at all.

The preacher is the leader and the decision-maker. In twentieth century media terms, he is the star. His is a highly-personalize ministry; hence the contortions of so many of the televangelists as they seek to hand over their earthly ministries to their natural, rather than to their spiritual, heirs. The campfire tub thumper of the Old West was financed by his audience. Only the fittest or the sincerest or the noisiest survived. In the same way but on an enormously enhanced scale, the televangelist is sustained by a scattered group of prayer partners which is simply and by any other name his fan club.

The independent preacher would pass round the hat at the end of the camp meeting in order to defray the necessary expenses. His great-grandson, the televangelist, has had to preserve the family's financial tradition but, in the process, has lost much of his forebears' message.

Meanwhile, the mainline churchperson finds it difficult to function as a fast-moving entrepreneur. To begin with, he is held in position in the ecclesiastical firmament by the role conferred on him by his church. Like the Israelites before them, Americans are pointed to God by both priests and prophets of a certain sort. Prophets mark themselves out by their own vision and charisma and drive. But priests are anointed by the collective will of their church. As a general rule, the priestly classes are unlikely to succeed as self-financing stars in the highly personalized and commercialized world of show biz religion.

SUGGESTIONS FOR FURTHER READING

Armstrong, Ben, *The Electric Church*. Nashville, TN: Thomas Nelson, 1979.
Fore, William F., *Television and Religion*. Minneapolis: Augsburg Publishing House, 1987.
Horsfield, Peter G., *Religious Television: The American Experience*. New York: Longman, 1984.
Lewis, Sinclair, *Elmer Gantry*. New York: Harcourt, Brace and Co., 1927.
Roberts, Patti, *Ashes to Gold*. Waco, TX: Word Books, 1983.
Robertson, Pat, *Shout it from the Housetops*. Plainfield, NJ: Logos International, 1972.

6

The History and Role of the Catholic Press

William J. Thorn

In the two hundred years since the first Catholic newspaper appeared in the U.S., the Catholic press has moved between two press models, public relations and public interest, responding both to the demands of American society and to the internal dynamics of American Catholicism. The unique American context has influenced editors, publishers, and readers of Catholic newspapers, and the church hierarchy as well. This reversal of a presumed order of things has caused successive generations of Catholic editors and bishops to reevaluate their roles, yet without resolving the pivotal question, Whose role is it to inform, educate, and persuade American Catholics?

Along with the forces of American society and American Catholicism, two other factors have come to bear on the history and role of the U.S. Catholic press: The American press in general has provided a professional standard by which Catholic journalists have measured themselves and been measured; and the economics of the Catholic press have been unusual, with publications functioning both as profitable commercial enterprises and as not-for-profit institutional organs. As a consequence, then, of its unique situation, the American Catholic press has periodically shifted from one model to the other. As public relations organization, it has been a partisan house organ, providing officially sanctioned views on controversies. Adopting the secular press's role as public interest organization, the Catholic press has aggressively pursued news about the church, even revealing its leaders' shortcomings and airing its dissidents' viewpoints.

THE SHAPE OF THE CATHOLIC PRESS

Reaching over 23 million Catholics, the Catholic press currently comprises 156 diocesan newspapers, 6 national newspapers, 11 Eastern rite newspapers, and 259 magazines. The newspapers have a combined audience of 5.5 million subscribers, and the magazines reach 17.7 million subscribers. Owned by dioceses, independent corporations, private individuals, and religious orders, these 400-plus publications do not share identical roles. Throughout its history, the Catholic press has identified numerous roles, internal and external, for its work:

External Roles:
Defend against anti-Catholic myths and stereotypes.
Provide a Catholic voice in debates on public issues.
Provide a Catholic interpretation of events.
Participate in the formation of public opinion.
Evangelize lapsed Catholics and those outside the faith.

Internal Roles:
Provide news of local, national, and international Church.
Unite the Catholic community.
Educate the faithful about church teaching and policies.
Provide inspiration and affirmation for Christian lifestyle.
Evangelize fallen away and lapsed Catholics.
Provide a Catholic perspective on major issues of the times.
Give the bishop an official platform.
Provide reliable, official texts, statements, and opinions.
Provide a forum for debate on Catholic issues and teaching.
Create a dialogue within the Catholic community between leaders and members.

Most of the roles are part of the public relations model, with the debate, forum, and dialogue roles uniquely public interest. News, however, can be defined to fit either model, which has made it the focal point for the struggle over public interest and public relations models. Many magazines are public relations organs which limit their roles accordingly; a few emphasize analysis of current events and issues in the public interest model. Primarily the work of religious communities and lay owners over whom bishops have no direct authority, these magazines reflect the diverse interests of their publishers. Newspapers, because of their frequent publication and immersion in news and controversy, have been the primary focus of the hierarchy from its first efforts to build a voice for American Catholicism. It is among newspaper editors and bishops that the tension over the public interest and public relations models continues to produce the sharpest and most prolonged struggles.

American society has not always tolerated or welcomed Catholics, but American values have inspired and influenced Catholics who responded to the same societal forces, whether immigration, urbanization, feminism, or education. The Catholic press serves the Catholic subculture as an interpreter of the American experience; it also speaks to American society about the Catholic vision of life. The core values of democracy and citizenship shape each Catholic's view of church and their role within it; other values conflict sharply with those of Christianity. Integrating American cultural values with Catholicism remains a major, long-term effort of theologians, hierarchy, and laity. The expectations Catholics have of their religious leaders, religious practices, and religious press bear the stamp of American culture.

STAGES IN AMERICAN CATHOLICISM
AND THE CATHOLIC PRESS

Catholicism in America has passed through several stages, from immigration to assimilation, each imposing different demands on the press. The institutional church evolved as the product of Vatican policies and the vision of the American hierarchy. Bishops have, from the first years, looked to the Catholic press as the teacher of the Faith, a means of instruction and a platform for personal expression. And bishops, who take their role as official teacher very seriously, relied on the Catholic press to assist them. The Second Vatican Council produced a different, less hierarchical structure with a freer press, altering the expectations of bishops.

Catholics themselves changed, rising from illiterate immigrants through Catholic enclaves to captains of industry and members of the intellectual elite. The press that once served immigrants became ill suited for physicians and physicists. Vatican II transformed America's Catholics by demolishing their isolationist ghetto and propelling them into full encounter with American life. It also replaced an absolute monarchy with a more democratic one, and urged a dialogic model of communication within the church rather than "top down" monologue. Each change reverberated through the press, altering the relationship between individual Catholics and their leaders, forcing a new balance between public interest and public relations models.

American Catholics, as Jay Dolan wrote, have always posted a special problem for the Church:

> The United States prided itself on freedom and democracy, and new immigrants as well as longtime citizens cherished these qualities. Time and again, European priests bemoaned this "spirit of independence" prevalent among Americans, since such a spirit weakened the respect for authority deemed so necessary in the church. American culture encouraged such freedom and independence, especially in things religious;

church authorities recognized this not only as a weakness of the culture, but as a threat to Catholicism as well.[1]

Diversity, even fractious debate have marked the internal dynamics of Catholicism in the U.S., and the Catholic press has been intimately involved in the battles. A stereotype of Irish Catholic dominance in the 1800s disguised the hostility among various ethnic Catholics who brought their nationalistic animosities to the Catholic press. At other times, the press has been the instrument of the bishops, urging on the faithful a common vision and common action, trying to mend the rift by force of authority. In more recent times the press has sought to be a forum for working out the debates and bridging the divisions by force of argument—while remaining a source of reliable, authentic teaching.

At the core, the Catholic press has always been a religious press operating within a free press system; in this it has more in common with the *Illinois Baptist* and *Jewish Exponent* than with the *Boston Globe* or *Portland Oregonian*. The Catholic press exists, as John Deedy, Jr. wrote, "to serve definite apostolic purposes, some of them selfish, some of them humanitarian, and all of them bound up with or complementary to the Church's evangelical and social missions."[2] The public relations and public interest models provide a complement to the apostolic drive.

American journalism developed its core values out of the right of individual citizens in a democracy to be informed, to know what their leaders are doing and thinking. Because power lies with the people, the press serves the people's right to know and be heard. The free press system imbues its reporters and editors with norms and values which conflict with the instincts of institutional leaders. By constitutional design, the American press is set against malfeasance and inept governance so that citizens can remove their elected leaders. Democracy requires airing conflicts and challenging views, and rejecting cover-ups and dissembling.

As an authoritarian institution or government operates from a different premise, namely that power resides in the leadership, which decides what the people need to know. Because it moderates the right of people to know, an authoritarian institution sharply curtails reports of dissent and conflicts. As an authoritarian institution within a democratic society, the Catholic church can not allow its press to operate only under the norms of the secular press. But Catholic editors are journalists who share the values of their professional peers in the secular press.[3] These values lead them,

---

1. Dolan, *American Catholic Experience*, 222.
2. Deedy, "Catholic Press: Why and Wherefore," 67.
3. See Scotton and Thorn, "Journalists in the Catholic Press Today," 67.

for example, to demand the freedom to produce a credible source of news and opinion. The tension between bishops and editors is least where the bishop shares the public interest norms or absolutely rejects them; it is most pronounced where the public interest model is the pronounced ideal but undercut in practice by the demands of the institution.

Economics, in the form of ownership and economic cycles, are inescapable for publications, even those of non-profit groups. The Catholic press has always included profit-making ventures of independent lay owners or religious organizations. Because ownership is closely linked to status as the "official" Catholic voice, it has shaped the debate over public relations and public interest models. Questions of "official" status recur under private ownership, particularly when the editor proclaims the Catholic view. After bishops became intent on Church ownership or control of an official newspaper, they mandated a subscription for each Catholic household, and the parishes paid the costs. As a result, diocesan newspapers had guaranteed access to virtually every Catholic home from 1930 to the end of Vatican II. Mandated circulation relieved editors of economic pressure to attract readers and conspired with official status as a license to bore readers with unrelenting attacks on anti-Catholicism, insipid chancery information, and lackluster features. More importantly, it reinforced the need to avoid scandalizing the faithful and abetting the enemies of the church, the reasons for avoiding stories about dissent and internal problems. Ultimately, ownership decides how much theory or philosophy will be put into practice. Institutional ownership of publications committed to the theory of a free press creates constant, inevitable friction, even when the institution is committed to the information rights of individuals members.

The Catholic press has moved through five major stages: immigrant expansion, consolidation and institutionalization, professionalization, Vatican II exploration, and reinstitutionalization.[4] As they moved through each stage, editors struggled to articulate Catholicism for Catholics, resolve their relationship to the official structure, achieve a higher standard of professionalism, and speak to the larger society. The resulting newspapers and magazines represent an ongoing dialogue between freedom of expression, American journalism, and the Catholic experience in America.

4. Others have used different criteria. Baumgartner identified three periods based on complexity, Deedy used a similar number based on editorial focus and professionalization, and Real used six stages based on focus and hierarchical authority over content. See Baumgartner, *Catholic Journalism*; Deedy, "Catholic Press: Why and Wherefore"; and Real, "Trends in Structure and Policy," 265–71.

Immigrant expansion stage: 1789–1884

As Old World Catholics moved into the New World, they created a Catholic press which would help them overcome their homesickness and the strangeness of the new land. This press had two overriding roles: to unify the ethnic Catholics and to defend against the vicious attacks of nativists and other virulent anti-Catholics. Because immigrant Catholics were minimally American, their newspapers were printed in German, Italian, Polish, French, and other European tongues. As Deedy has observed, "the hyphenated Catholic had his hyphenated Catholic press, absorbed in Old World causes and attitudes that spilled over into competitions, jealousies and frictions in the New."[5] Private entrepreneurs served up hundreds of Catholic newspapers, many proclaiming the church's position inaccurately or inadvisedly. Bishops contended with the problems of private ownership, publicly denouncing those which tried to draw the Church into Old World problems and correcting misstated church teaching. They also cherished the defense against anti-Catholicism.

Sadly, anti-Catholicism ran unchecked through many secular newspapers of the time. The extent of anti-Catholicism can best be illustrated by the Charlestown Riots of 1834 in Boston. Boston had at least nine ethno-religious riots between 1823 and 1838, several aimed at Catholics and Irish immigrants. Such riots were hardly unique to Boston.[6] Fear of popery and anti-Catholic nativism reigned powerfully among staunch members of the Church of England, New England Congregationalists, and Presbyterians.[7] Catholics were denounced as infidels from numerous pulpits and characterized as conspirators in the press.[8]

Stirred by inflammatory newspaper accounts of a young woman being kept in an Ursuline convent against her will, a mob attacked, ransacked, and burned the convent at Charlestown, driving the nuns and young girls into the night. Even graves were opened and desecrated. Anti-Catholicism and disregard for accuracy were clearly evident among three of the five daily Boston newspapers before, during, and after the riots.[9] Against such problems, the bishops demanded Catholic newspapers which explained

5. Deedy, "Catholic Press: Why and Wherefore," 71.
6. Between 1830 and 1850 Boston, Baltimore, New York, and Philadelphpia had thirty-five major riots. In 1834, *Niles Weekly Register* clipped five hundred references to civil disturbances from U.S. newspapers. See Brown, *Strain of Violence*; Beals, *Brass Knuckle Crusade*.
7. Billington, *Origins of Nativism*.
8. Samuel F. B. Morse launched a campaign against Catholics as foreign conspirators with articles in the *New York Observer* entitled, "Foreign Conspiracies Against The Liberties of the United States"; see *Protestant Clergy and Public Issues*, 69.
9. Finnegan, "The Press and the Charlestown Riots."

Catholic teaching and exploded the anti-Catholic myths perpetrated by nativist fanatics.

Huge waves of immigrants continued to wash into America until 1922, bringing large numbers of Catholics from Ireland, Germany, Italy, Poland, France, Canada, and Mexico. By 1916, these six groups represented 75 percent of the Catholic population of nearly sixteen million.[10] For the balance of the nineteenth century, reaching these new Catholics and defending the church would be the dominant roles of the Catholic press.

Lack of a Catholic middle class and costs of publishing made a Catholic newspaper a financial gamble, for even the secular press survived by serving either political partisans (usually at a loss made up by the party) or the merchant class. The first Catholic-oriented newspaper, *Courier de Boston* came off the press in 1789, nearly a century after the first American newspaper. Edited by a Harvard University professor of French, the *Courier* began 23 April 1789 and lasted for six months.[11] Twenty years later, Detroit pastor Father Gabriel Richard brought a printing press back from Baltimore and established the *Michigan Essay* or *Impartial Observor*. Written in English with some columns in French, this newspaper died soon after it began. A long string of Irish national newspapers began to appear in 1809, sympathetic to Catholic values and ideas.[12] The *Shamrock* or *Hibernian Chronicle* suspended publication four times in its brief life. Philadelphia spawned two short-lived Spanish publications, the newspaper *El Habanero* (1824) and the magazine *El Mesagero Semanal* (1829).

United States Catholic Miscellany was the first successful newspaper and the first official newspaper. Begun on 5 June 1822 as the newspaper of Bishop John England, the *Miscellany* continues today as the *Catholic Banner*. The bishop and his sister, Joanna England, edited the *Miscellany* and sold it through distributors in thirty-one cities. Supported by church funds after financial difficulties, the *Miscellany* continued until the Civil War, when it suspended publication until peace reigned.

Countering anti-Catholicism was a major role:

> [*Miscellany*] revealed as if by drawing aside a curtain the number and the influence of a score of anti-Catholic journals, now happily forgotten, but then in the heydey of their power. The secular press of the time was by no means the suave and impersonal kind of journalism we possess today.

10. Dolan, *American Catholic Experience*, 135.
11. Paul Guerard de Nancrede was its editor, according to Baumgartner, *Catholic Journalism*, 2.
12. Foik, "Pioneer Efforts in Catholic Journalism," 258.

Anti-Catholic sermons were welcomed in its columns, and thus on all sides Catholics found themselves at the mercy of this hostile group.[13]

In 1829 the *Jesuit* appeared in Boston, soon renamed *The Catholic Intelligencer*, and renamed once again as the *Literary and Catholic Sentinel*. At first supported by Bishop Fenwick, the newspaper became a source of discord within the church, so the bishop threw his support to the newly founded *Boston Pilot*. Thus sanctioned, the *Pilot* survived, and it continues today as the diocesan newspaper of Boston.

The third successful newspaper among the pioneers, *The Catholic Telegraph*, was founded in Cincinnati in 1831 with the gift of a European press. Like the *Miscellany* and the *Pilot*, the *Telegraph* was created to "meet the constant attacks upon the doctrine of the Church, her clergy and her people."[14] The era of cheap mass newspapers brought dozens of other Catholic newspapers into existence, dedicated to countering anti-Catholicism.[15] The first Catholic magazine, *Metropolitan*, began in Baltimore in 1830 and became the authoritative publication of American Catholicism.

The foreign language press in the U.S. could boast daily Catholic newspapers and great financial health. Neither was a notable condition among English language Catholic newspapers, whose daily newspapers failed soon after opening. Even English language weekly diocesan newspapers struggled to stay afloat despite hierarchical exhortations. Of more than 1,300 publications begun before 1900, only four hundred survived.

Continuing internal controversies among bishops, clergy, laity, and ethnic groups rocked the church and brought the immigrant expansion press to an end. Scarcely limited to European problems, these battles found willing partisans among American Catholic editors, who earned a reputation for rough exchanges and nasty dissent. Pope Leo XIII expressed his dismay at the contentions within the American Church.[16] Whenever the bishops gathered formally, their decrees and discussions always involved the Catholic press.

In the Plenary Councils of 1854 and 1866, the bishops warned that not every newspaper which called itself Catholic was authorized to speak for the church. The bishops stated that the only content which could be considered absolutely reliable was the bishop's signed column containing his teaching.

The immigrant phase of the Catholic press reached its conclusion with

13. Guilday, *Life and Times of John England*, 451.
14. Shea, quoted by Baumgartner, *Catholic Journalism*, 9.
15. Foik, "Pioneer Efforts in Catholic Journalism," 267–268.
16. See *Testem Benevolentiae*, an apostolic letter of 22 January 1899 written to James Cardinal Gibbons.

the Third Plenary Council of Baltimore in 1884, where the bishops devoted a chapter of the *Acta et Decreta* (Acts and Decrees) to the press. After affirming the importance of the press for defending the church and explaining doctrines to Catholics and the outside world, the bishops called for a Catholic newspaper in every province of the church. They urged consolidation of struggling newspapers into one subsidized publication for an official Catholic newspaper.[17]

Consolidation and institutionalization: 1884–1945

The Baltimore Council of 1884 reflected the growing authoritarianism of Rome which Vatican I had asserted in 1870. As Martin Marty has observed, nineteenth-century society was moving religion to the periphery.[18] The Vatican response was to insist more forcefully on its own authority. From Vatican I to Vatican II, Catholicism stressed the authority of the pope.[19] American bishops, exceptionally loyal to Rome and leading a church constantly assaulted by American anti-Catholics, built a powerful authoritarian culture and defensive enclave. The Catholic press became a voice from the ghetto, a press primarily concerned with the authority of the hierarchy and protection against enemies. Consolidation took on overtones of official newspapers owned by dioceses, and the Great Depression of 1929 virtually completed the process. Professionally, the Catholic press became a cooperative system with its own professional association, news service, newspaper chains, and university journalism programs. The press reflected the Catholic world between the Councils: pope, bishops, clergy, and nuns as ranking authorities; laity as obedient followers.

At first, the Baltimore Council's plan triggered expansion of private ownership, but by the turn of the century, "official" newspapers meant the demise of any whose editor did not submit completely to the authority of the bishop. The press had given bishops ample cause for insisting on submission to authority through irresponsible, vitriolic attacks on hierarchy and fellow editors alike. Editors proclaimed their own views as church doctrine. Thus bishops asserted their authority over any publication which wanted to be defined as "Catholic." The tests for a truly Catholic publication became: explain and defend the church, describe the progress of the church at home and abroad, and be subject to the authority of the church in all things. To underscore their meaning, the bishops warned

17. *Acta et Decreta*, Third Plenary Council of Baltimore, Chapter IV (translation from Latin).
18. See Marty, *Modern Schism*, 18–58.
19. Dolan, *American Catholic Experience*, 222.

editors that canonical procedures would be brought against editors whose Catholic newspapers scandalized the faithful by misrepresenting church doctrine or policies or by ridiculing the hierarchy.

A distinct chill settled in with the circulation of *Testem Benevolentiae*, Pope Leo XIII's apostolic letter to Cardinal Gibbon in 1899. Citing the many controversies which plagued the church in the U.S., the pope urged greater internal harmony. The press was clearly on the pope's mind, for he ordered journalists to treat bishops with reverence befitting their "lofty position of authority." The pontiff defined any criticism of bishops as injurious and disastrous to the Catholic cause. Defending Catholicism was to be the journalist's primary goal.[20]

The Pope's letter had its desired effect: editors became suddenly respectful, even docile. Bishops brusquely challenged the use of "Catholic" by unreliable publishers; when lay publishers proved recalcitrant, bishops bought an existing paper or started their own. If a bishop could not afford to start his own newspaper, he could contract for a local edition of the national Catholic chains. Taking their cue from secular media, Catholic publishers built newspaper chains. *The Register* was the largest with thirty-five papers; *Our Sunday Visitor* had twenty; and others had fewer than ten. A major contribution of the chains, particularly *Our Sunday Visitor*, was "effective apologetics," particularly against the more virulent anti-Catholic publications of the twenties and thirties.[21]

The economics of publishing also worked against the weaker Catholic publications. By 1892 New York City contained, in addition to seventeen English language dailies and at least seven foreign language dailies, eight Catholic weeklies, one Catholic semi-weekly and a German Catholic weekly.[22] Baumgartner cites over eighty Catholic newspapers begun between 1884 and 1900. Like the secular press of the time, the Catholic press

20. [Journalists] who desire to be of real service to the Church, and with their pens heartily defend the Catholic cause, should carry on the conflict with perfect unanimity. . . . In like manner, their work instead of being profitable and fruitful becomes injurious and disastrous whenever they presume to call before their tribunal the decisions and acts of Bishops, and, casting off due reverence, cavil and find fault, not perceiving how great a disturbance of order and how many evils are thereby produced.

The Bishops placed in the lofty position of authority are to be obeyed and suitable honor befitting the magnitude and sanctity of their office should be paid them. Now this reverence, which is lawful to no one to neglect, should of necessity be eminently conspicuous and exemplary in Catholic journalists. From *Testem BeneVolentine*.

21. Deedy, "Catholic Press: Why and Wherefore," 73.

22. *Ibid.*, American Newspaper Directory, cited in Deedy, "Catholic Press: Why and Wherefore," 72.

had become seriously overdeveloped. Periodic depressions thinned the ranks, but the Great Depression fundamentally altered the ownership pattern. Foreign langauge Catholic papers, the healthiest of the 1800s, faltered as Americanization drew the young away from the culture of their elders. By 1930, fewer than fifty remained.[23] Just over seventy English newspapers remained in publication by 1931, so bishops began buying the strongest local newspaper simply to ensure its survival. By 1936, dioceses owned over seventy-five percent of Catholic newspapers.[24] They had become official publications of the hierarchy.

But if the immigrants' children spoke English, they remained ghetto Catholics, isolated in cultural enclaves within the Protestant culture: "Ethnicity and religion were the major elements in this culture, and they shaped Catholicism into a very ethnocentric and religiously exclusive community."[25] The local parish became a cultural and social center whose multiple groups offered a full range of activities and attachments sufficient to fill the needs of all parishioners. Above the parish enclave existed a whole complex of Catholic institutions and businesses which encouraged Catholics to move in a world of mutually shared values.

The ghetto mentality drew Catholic publications into a supporting role. Catholic social groups like the Knights of Columbus, produced their own magazines; diocesan newspapers focussed almost exclusively on the Catholic community. A Catholic book publishing system flourished, serving both the general audience and the far flung network of Catholic schools, colleges, and universities. Mass circulation publications provided inspiration, information, defense of the faith, and devotional materials. *St. Anthony Messenger* provided a Franciscan approach from its founding in 1893. *Ligourian*, begun in 1913 by the Redemptorists, specialized in short, readable articles. *Catholic Digest*, the counterpart to *Reader's Digest*, began condensing articles from other Catholic magazines in 1936.

Not all publishers or editors acquiesced without question to the authority of the bishops. Humphrey Desmond, head of the *Herald* chain based in Milwaukee, openly challenged hierarchical priorities, particularly the construction of parallel Catholic institutions within the society. Debates over church policies also echoed through the pages of intellectually oriented magazines written for a more educated audience. *America*, founded in 1909 by the Jesuits, analyzed current issues and culture from a Catholic perspective, and it quickly became a bellweather of American Catholic intellectual life. *America*'s Jesuit editors held open the window

23. Baumgartner, *Catholic Journalism*, 93–99.
24. Ridder, "U.S. Catholic Exhibit at Vatican City," 38.
25. Dolan, *American Catholic Experience*, 203.

between the Catholic ghetto and American public life. *Commonweal*, established in 1924, offered a distinctly urbane lay view, unconvinced by pleas for unquestioning loyalty. These and a few other kindred publications reviewed the arts with strong emphasis on the products of the Catholic culture, particularly literature. Still, "the vast majority of Catholics remained relatively impervious to the intellectual movements of their time."[26]

The most unique and independent publication was the *Catholic Worker*, which from its first issue in 1933 expounded a radical Christian social activism and pacifism which was neither understood nor accepted by mainstream Catholics. Dorothy Day, its founder and premier journalist, confounded the church of her day with total dedication to care for the poor and to oppose war. The hierarchy kept Day at arm's length, defending her right to live a radical Christian lifestyle but refusing to endorse her. The Catholic Press Association, reflecting the suspicions of bishops, rejected the *Catholic Worker*'s membership application.[27] Nonetheless, Day and the *Catholic Worker* inspired at least two generations of young Catholics.

In 1890 Catholic editors met to form an association of Catholic publications, following the lead of secular press associations.[28] In 1893 editors met in the Congress of Laity as the "Apostolate of the Press."[29] The first CPA convention of 1911 demonstrated how completely the editors and their association would support the goals of the bishops: "The Catholic viewpoint, not the editor's personal opinion, should be the only one given on topics of the hour."[30]

Perhaps the most significant professional development was the National Catholic Welfare Conference News Service, begun after World War I. NCWC News demonstrated that the Catholic press was serious about news, and that bishops supported a major, long-term commitment to Catholic newspapers. Funded primarily by its clients, NCWC News also received a subsidy from the U.S. bishops. NCWC News quickly became the pacesetter for reporting within the church, covering Europe

26. Ellis, *American Catholics and the Intellectual Life*, 24.
27. See Miller, *Harsh and Dreadful Love* and *Dorothy Day*; Roberts, *Dorothy Day and The Catholic Worker*.
28. In the period 1880–1900, publishers, editors, circulation managers, and advertising managers formed professional associations, first as counterbalances to trade unions, then as professional groups for advancing their skills, knowledge, and legislative agenda.
29. Reilly, *History of the Catholic Press Association*, 22.
30. Reilly, *History of the Catholic Press Association*, 36.

and North America. Though sometimes less than autonomous from powerful bishops who demanded a public relations service, National Catholic News Service (as it was renamed) earned a reputation as a credible source.

Catholic colleges and universities, heeding the urging of the pope and American bishops, began journalism education at two Jesuit institutions years before Columbia University established journalism education in the East. Santa Clara University offered the first courses in 1907; Marquette University began the program in 1910 for its College of Journalism. Trained professionals, critical services for existing publications, and research grew out of these and other Catholic journalism schools. Catholic journalism educators, while supporting the existing system, brought professional values and norms into the Catholic enclave. Oriented primarily to students seeking careers in the secular press, the schools also graduated priests, nuns, and an occasional lay student who carried American press norms into Catholic publications.

Apart from the pacifist *Catholic Worker*, the Catholic press threw its full support to World War II efforts, in part to prove that Catholics were patriotic Americans. The war fundamentally altered American society, breaching regional, ethnic, and religious isolation. The GI Bill had far greater impact on the Catholic ghetto, for it paid the children of working class immigrants to go to college. Catholic veterans marched into state and Catholic institutions, where they imbibed the knowledge and worldview which laid the foundation for a new integration of Catholicism and Americanism.

Professionalized institutional stage: 1945–65

Vatican II (1962–65) almost perfectly fit the middle age of those Catholics who took advantage of the GI Bill to launch a successful assault on upper-middle-class status. Widespread college education shifted the ground under the Catholic press, even as it brought a number of top flight editors like Bernard Casserly, Donald McDonald, Gerald Sherry, Richard Guilderson, Robert Burns, John Deedy, Robert Hoyt, and a dozen more into its editorial offices. These editors joined a rapidly expanding press whose circulation of twenty-six million in 1960 was the fruit of mandated circulation and a growing Catholic population.

The best young editors began articulating the need for a Catholic press which functioned less as a house organ and more as an independent voice operating on behalf of the people. Prof. David Host of Marquette University aided professionalization with the establishment of the Institute for the Catholic Press in 1948. The role of the Catholic press was a recurring topic at conferences and CPA conventions, reflecting the impact of professionalization.

The first effect of lay editors from the best journalism schools was physical: Catholic publications looked sharper, read better, and handled advertising like professionals. Magazines like *The Sign*, *Ave Maria*, and *St. Jude* blossomed; diocesan newspapers like *St. Louis Review*, New Orleans's *Clarion-Herald*, and the *Long Island Catholic* were widely respected as pacesetters.

The larger debate was joined when Donald McDonald, editor of the *The Catholic Messenger*, declared that 50 percent of the news content of the best Catholic newspapers was useless information: "It is about time that we begin to reward the loyalty of our readers by giving them something to read besides the monotonous and often useless diet of anti-Communism, anti-Protestantism and anti-sin."[31] McDonald triggered a torrent of abuse for his criticism, though he was simply applying the standards of the Hutchins Commission Report in American Journalism, the Catholic humanism of French philosopher Jacques Maritain and the profession: the press should fill the informational and spiritual needs of the readers.

Pope Pius XII added support one month later when, in *Humani Generis*, he sought to stimulate the intellectual life of the Church by urging a balance in the press between "mute servility" and "uncontrolled criticism."[32] The Pope challenged the press to contribute to formation of Catholic opinion. *Commonweal,* under the guidance of John Cogley, John O'Gara, and John O'Connor, became a leading voice forming Catholic opinion. Other intellectuals joined the reform, but the Catholic press remained frozen in its defensive mindset and came under increasing assault. From 1957–1959, the press was criticized for not reflecting the pluralism of opinion in the Church on the social and political issues of the day.[33]

Through the late 50s, the debate over roles of the press raged ever stronger. John Finnegan identified and ranked several themes for the roles of the press which emerged during the debates in this transitional period:

1. Blend professional and Christian principles into a workable journalistic model.
2. Form public opinion within the Church.

31. McDonald, "State of the Local Catholic Press," 460.
32. Pope Pius XII, *Humani Generis,* 15 March 1950.
33. Finnegan, "Trends in Criticism," 16.

3. Report news in a context of meaning.
4. Provide accurate and useful information.
5. Promote Christian values.
6. Present undistorted truth.[34]

Other themes cited by Finnegan which reflect the deeper trends moving through the debates include:

1. Roles of editors and journalists.
2. Dull, colorless, predictable content.
3. Coverage of pluralism within the Church and the world beyond the walls of the Catholic ghetto.
4. Growing rift between editors and bishops over autonomy, particularly as it related to accurate portrayal of bad news, emphasis on news-worthy content, and house organ status.[35]

The new Pope, John XXIII, brought the issue to a head when he opened the Church windows for some fresh air by calling the Second Vatican Council. "Aggiornamento" was about to become a household word which abruptly demolished the carefully cloistered world of American Catholics. Vatican II broke ground as a powerful lesson in modern press relations within the Church. For three years (1962–1965), American Catholics faced a process of change for which they were totally unprepared. Between displays of pageantry and grandeur, journalists and the public saw plural-ism of opinion within the ranks of the bishops and cardinals—battles between liberals and conservatives. "By midpoint of the first session, the American bishops had set up a regular press panel in which bishops, *periti* [theological experts], and professors from Roman universities partici-pated."[36] The Council itself was shaped by press coverage which gave greater detail and play to the liberals than to the conservatives, who gener-ally avoided reporters.[37] By 1965, "the Council had given certain bishops a new tolerance for freedom of the press."[38] It also created a need for reliable news and emphasized aggressive reporting.

Catholic press coverage of Vatican II was often insipid. The very best reports of a Catholic priest, Xavier Rynne's work, appeared in the *New Yorker,* and the Protestant press and secular press seemed better tuned to controversies and more balanced. The Catholic press seemed unsure about how to cover the disagreements, factions, maneuvers, and personal-

34. Finnegan, "Trends in Criticism," 52.
35. Deedy, "The Catholic Press: The Why and the Wherefore," 77.
36. Hennesey, *American Catholics,* 310.
37. Whalen, "The Press Opens up Vatican II," 53–61.
38. Real, "Trends in the American Press," 267.

ities. Like American Catholics, editors seemed completely unprepared for
the fact that the Church could countenance fierce disagreements, much
less abandon centuries of accumulated practices. The official press of the
ghetto led its readers into Vatican II with few hints about the issues which
had been blowing through the Church, and its editors had neither experience nor skill at aggressive journalism amidst hierarchical confrontations. The public relations model had failed, and the public interest model
was on the rise.

Vatican II Exploration: 1965–1970

When American bishops returned from the final Council meeting in
1965, the renovation of Catholicism had just begun. Vatican II smashed
the ghetto walls to let American attitudes rush in. Avery Dulles' *Models of
the Church,* a seminal book which became a commonly accepted basis for
rethinking every aspect of the Church, reflected the newly unleashed intellectual energy. The resulting revolution revamped the way readers, editors, and hierarchy perceived the roles for the Catholic press. In dividing
the Church, the turmoil also divided the press which both covered the
turmoil and urged its own vision, whether traditional or liberal.

Vatican II documents defined the Church, among other images, as the
People of God and the Pilgrim People. The stunning implication for
Americans was that the laity in the Church have a role nearly identical to
that of citizens in the American political society. The Catholic press, then,
would have the same role within its sphere as the secular press has in
American society. Responsible to the Church as People of God and to the
Church as hierarchy, the press becomes an official one which covers the
institution in open, even adversarial fashion: the public relations and
public interest models collided head on. Wrestling with changing roles
proved to be an exhilarating, then painful experience, but ultimately
fruitful.

Editors, supported by bishops, pushed back the boundaries of hierarchical control. Virtually overnight the turmoil within the Church was
reflected in its press: traditional pieties took a back seat to "critical,
controversial news coverage, even muckraking. . ."[39] Month after month,
previously unheard dissent appeared in issue after issue: birth control,
racism, religious garb, role of clergy and nuns, rituals for Mass and prayer,
parochial schools, even limits on the authority of pope and bishops. Turning their investigations inward, editors also reported on diocesan finances,
priests and nuns who left and sought laicization (or married without it),
even alcoholism among clergy.

39. Real, "Trends in the American Catholic Press," 267.

The *National Catholic Reporter*, which began as a diocesan newspaper and became wholly independent, was a leading voice of the fresh, new wave of journalism: feisty, investigative, intensely suspicious of anything "pre-Vatican" or "old church." When, in 1965, it ran an article questioning celibacy for clergy, it was accused of showing bad taste and being un-Catholic. However, its circulation rose to nearly one hundred thousand within the decade. Progressive Catholics found the *Reporter* a refreshing delight; traditional Catholics urged the hierarchy to have "Catholic" removed from its nameplate. To traditionalists, such openness began to look like scandal mongering, even thinly disguised disloyalty to the church.

On the right, a new newspaper, *Twin Circle*, joined an existing conservative voice, *The Wanderer*. Patrick Frawley, conservation publisher of *Twin Circle*, gave voice to the fears and hopes of traditional Catholics by calling for an end to experimentation and liberalization. When he later took control of the national edition of the Register chain, the *National Catholic Register*, it joined the ranks of the conservative papers. The battle joined, conservative and liberal Catholic editors fought in ink the very battles each parish and diocese was fighting face-to-face.

Responses among the hierarchy to the sudden shift were mixed. Cardinal Ritter of Saint Louis openly encouraged the *St. Louis Review* in its pursuit of the public interest model. Of bishops surveyed, however, half were dissatisfied with Catholic newspapers for failure to balance their approach with church doctrine, and for their fascination with those who deviate from church teaching.[40] Nonetheless, three-quarters of the bishops were satisfied with their own diocesan newspapers; most of their dissatisfaction focussed on two national newspapers, *National Catholic Reporter* and *The Wanderer*.

In 1967 National Catholic News Service found itself caught between editors and bishops when it refused to run any material on a report leaked from the birth control study commission appointed by the pope. According to the report, a majority of members supported eliminating the ban on artificial contraceptives. Enraged editors, supported by Bishop James Shannon of Saint Paul, demanded a formal policy rejecting such censorship. The distance between bishops and editors increased in the wake of *Humanae Vitae*, as did the distance between many Catholics and their church. According to priest-sociologist Andrew Greeley, *Humanae Vitae*, not Vatican II, caused the disaffection of huge numbers of Catholics.[41]

---

40. Hannan, "What Bishops Think of the Catholic Press," 42.
41. Greeley, *American Catholic*, 149. *Humanae Vitae* (*Of Human Life*) is Pope Paul VI's 1968 encyclical letter which reaffirmed Catholic opposition to all forms of artificial contraception.

The Catholic press found itself drawn deeply into the resulting fire-storm which pitted pope and bishops against articulate theologians and laity. Clearly, Paul VI had drawn the line on changes in doctrine. *Humanae Vitae* signalled that Rome still retained final authority, but its signal met with outright, vocal opposition. Dissenting theologians mod-elled their use of media after that of the bishops in Vatican II. Constantly accessible and skilled at press conferences, the dissidents found the press anxious to report the latest and biggest controversy following Vatican II. Bishops blamed the Catholic press for the laity's widespread opposition to *Humanae Vitae's* birth control teaching, arguing they best served the Catholic community by defending the pope and curtailing coverage of the dissidents. Editors argued that reporting dissent was precisely the role of the Catholic press, a role essential to the new style of Catholicism which emphasized openness and full accountability to the laity.

But conservatives had already reversed the pendulum. Cardinal Ritter of Saint Louis was replaced in March 1968 by Archbishop John Carberry, who oversaw the *St. Louis Review.* Donald Quinn, its highly respected editor, resigned in 1969, charging that Carberry was suppressing the *Review* as part of a broader effort to dampen liberal Catholics. Quinn pre-dicted a wave of repression which he called the "purple backlash." Later that year, *National Catholic Reporter* was "condemned" as a destructive force by the same bishop who had helped found it.

Financial problems began to mount in 1967 as bishops, some under pressure from clergy and parish councils, began abandoning the mandated circulation plan. James Doyle, executive secretary of the Catholic Press Association, rushed letters to bishops urging them not to destroy their newspapers. Prominent liberal newspapers were particularly hard hit. As circulations plummeted, CPA income shrivelled, because membership fees were based on newspaper circulation. In desperation, Doyle cut his staff and worked without pay to keep the association solvent.[42] The ripple spread to NC News, whose subscriber fees were also based on circulation.

A 1969 meeting of bishops and leading editors, sponsored by the Catholic Press Association, sought to dampen the growing rift between bishops and editors and simultaneously clarify the roles for the Catholic press and its journalists. The agreed-upon statement: "The basic purpose of the diocesan press is to enlighten the Catholic about his world and his role in it."[43]

The document then listed nine ways in which diocesan newspapers fulfill this purpose. A deft blend of public relations and public interest

---

42. Interview with James Doyle, May 29 1988.
43. *Resource Papers and Consensus Paper of the Bishops-Editor Conference at Bergamo Center,* 5.

models, the consensus stressed the relation of the Catholic press to its readership. The first seven roles elaborated direct service to the faithful; the eighth role placed the press under the authority of the local bishop; the ninth embraced direct service to the entire community:

1. Interpreting fully, fairly, and accurately the events of the day as they relate to the Christian in his community.
2. Helping to create that community.
3. Informing and instructing its readers.
4. Reflecting the prophetic mission of the church, through exhortation and inspiration.
5. Helping readers to see God speaking to man in the events of the times.
6. Continuing education leading to an enlightened public opinion.
7. Providing a forum for dialogue within the body of the church.
8. Helping to fulfill the bishop's obligation to teach and instruct the people of God . . . and to hear them in return.
9. Striving to convey the Christian meaning of human events to all segments of the general community.[44]

These statements bring together the basic elements of the Hutchins Commission, Maritain, and Vatican II: "The editor must recognize the bishop's pastoral responsibility, and the bishop must recognize the editor's necessary freedom. Both should recognize the right to information is a right of the reader which should not be abridged."[45] Whatever the agreed-upon roles, the conference was unable to resolve the core problems: can an institution tolerate and support editors of its own press who are committed to serving the members with public interest news, even if that means the embarrassing exposure of institutional weaknesses?

Experimentation with the heady wine of renewal left the press and the bishops a bit remorseful, more sober, but actively working out a different relationship befitting the new approach to Catholicism. Seeking a balance in diocesan papers involved four entities, each with their rights: the church hierarchy, the journalists, the faithful, and the larger community. By the end of this period, there could be no return to the absolute authority of the consolidation era.

Reinstitutionalization: 1970–present

As the hierarchy applied the brakes to the freewheeling explorations, editors and bishops began searching for a new balance between the public interest and public relations models. Editors drew the practical balance in

44. *Resource Papers and Consensus Paper of the Bishops-Editor Conference at Bergamo Center,* 5.
45. *Resource Papers and Consensus Paper of the Bishops-Editor Conference at Bergamo Center,* 5.

their publications in response to more complex pressures: declining circulations; new-style Catholics; important news about open disagreement among bishops and between bishops, clergy, and nuns; aggressively secular coverage of the church; and professional journalism norms. The result was a distinct split between the diocesan and national press. Diocesan newspapers took a middle course between public relations and public interest, the precise stance influenced by the bishop's expectations. National newspapers split along political lines from ultraconservative to moderately progressive, but committed more to public interest than public relations.

The debate over press roles was ongoing, open, and national. *Communio et Progresso*, a 1971 document on media requested by Vatican II, contributed key arguments for both public models. Cognizant of the media age, the Vatican also urged bishops to expand their communication activities into electronic media, creating a new communication framework within which the press would have to find its unique place. Serious audience research contributed additional material to the debates. The U.S. Catholic Conference, through its new Department of Communication, sponsored "A Vision All Can Share," a series of national discussions among media professionals designed to build cooperation on communication priorities. And the bishops provided their reflections with a document on communications, *In The Sight of All*. Through it all, no retreat was sounded from commitment to serve the needs of individual Catholics. Rather, a new and more complex task began to emerge as the crucial role: to mediate between church leaders and laity by carrying on a dialogue, which Pope John Paul II identified as the heart of a community. Vatican II's principles had taken root, and the resulting challenges were to avoid the pressures from all sides to bias the dialogue and keep the debate civil.

The debate over roles often took second place to the more critical issue of survival. Declining readership and reduced advertising forced some publications out of business and put others on the largesse of sponsors until workable solutions began to emerge. When a major conference, "The Future of the Catholic Press," was held in 1979, many wondered if the press had any future. Revisions based on readership studies and skilled marketing brought success to some newspapers. A profound change in Catholic life sent readership tumbling, for the Catholic press suddenly faced a more heterogeneous and independent audience.

A new form of Catholicism had begun to take shape by 1970 as Vatican II principles sank their roots deeply into Catholic life, displacing the accumulated practices and mentality. Pluralism in rituals, prayer, even theology characterized the new Catholicism. As Jay Dolan observed,

"There are various ways of being Catholic, and people are choosing the style that best suits them".[46] Greeley found a rise in "communal Catholics," people who identify themselves as Catholic but selectively accept beliefs and practices.[47] "Dialogue" became a standard call for Catholics who wanted a voice in policy decisions affecting them. The Catholic press was pulled in both directions: toward an open forum where the church could dialogue on crucial issues and toward a source of authentic teaching and officially sanctioned theologians. On the one hand, Vatican II provided a new tolerance for the professional judgments of editors and for diverse views of readers and the faithful. On the other, the chaos of the times increased the pressure for reliable, orthodox, even approved content. "Problem" articles triggered confrontations over the freedom of the editor, the authority of the bishop, the rights of faithful, and the role of the paper.

Communio et Progressio broke new ground in the debate by explicitly basing its discussion of church and media on the right of all individuals to information and communication media, and the right of all religions to have access to their members through the media.[48] The formulation seemed to support those editors who urged the public interest as an important part of any role formulation. With "common good" and "human dignity," understood in the light of Christian teaching, as central elements in the discussion of the value of media, *Communio et Progresso* seemed to mesh almost perfectly with American journalistic norms. It also encouraged the public relations model by stressing the responsibility to teach and form public opinion on moral issues.

Crafted with the assistance of media professionals, the encyclical condemned national censorship of media, particularly religious media. This liberal stance became the ammunition of American editors who applied it to the Catholic press. It continues to create a powerful block against those within the institution who prefer a more censorious posture toward the Catholic press. While not resolving the debate, *Communio et Progresso* supported responsible editorial freedom and demolished the notion that biased or suppressed news was appropriate.

Low readership closed major magazines like *Ave Maria* and led to the creation of *Catholic New York* and *Chicago Catholic*. *National Catholic Reporter* entered the period with about seventy-thousand subscribers and watched the figure fall below fifty-thousand. The circulation of *Our Sunday Visitor* fell by one-third over a four-year period. The hierarchy had

---

46. Dolan, *American Catholic Experience*, 453.
47. Greely, *American Catholic*, 270–74.
48. *Communio et Progressio*, 293–349.

provided subscribers; now editors had to find their own. As parish councils and bishops abandoned the mandated circulation plan, newspapers did not adapt to the new reality of direct sales to Catholics. The magazine problem, on the other hand, was caused largely by the breakup of the ghetto: publications could no longer survive solely by being Catholic, and the traditional pious content and images were simply outmoded. Understanding the audience and developing publications to serve readers' needs suddenly emerged as the key to survival.

Magazines worked hard to identify and serve the new audience. *U S Catholic*, aided by fine writing and outstanding graphics, showed how to reach the younger, progressive Catholic. *Ligourian* developed a major readership research project which provided article-by-article analyses of its appeal to nearly five hundred thousand subscribers. *St. Anthony Messenger*, another circulation giant, adjusted its blend of news, features, and reviews to keep pace with middle-of-the-road Catholic families and lead them through the changes. *Maryknoll* shifted to critical analyses of the political and economic conditions of its mission countries.

NC News brought major innovations to the aid of its subscribers. In 1967, Director A. E. P. "Ed" Wall initiated full wire service. In 1985 Director Richard Daw established satellite delivery. During this period *NC News* strengthened its reporting from Rome and established an international link by satellite to Asia and Australia through UCA News, a Catholic news agency in Hong Kong. Resisting hierarchical pressure to slant or suppress unfavorable news, *NC News* became the pacesetter in credible, responsible, independent news coverage. In order to save its client, *NC* began a special financial service to aid failing newspapers. A team of specialists provided marketing and financial advice to newspapers judged salvageable. A key element in the flying squad's approach became the working board, a group of lay experts in media who helped with readership studies, marketing, and product improvement.

READERSHIP STUDIES

A CPA-funded readership study produced a depressing portrait: readers averaged fifty-plus years old, and were largely female and highly religious. Readers under forty were few and far between. Magazines fared somewhat better, but the point was made: editors were reaching an older audience and had to take steps to improve their product or be content with preaching to the choir.

Later, more sophisticated research pointed to the same conclusions:

Catholics were interested in publications that serve very specific needs, ranked as follows:

1. Information and news about the church, and the problems and issues facing it which lets them "know what's going on."
2. Information which helps readers cope with the changes in the church and with the world.
3. Material which allows participation in the life of the church through a clear portrait of the community and individual members.
4. Information which may be useful for solving problems or used in conversations.

When asked, more than three in four readers will cite the following as their motivation:

1. To find out what's going on in the church.
2. Be aware of the teachings of the church.
3. Keep up to date.

Nearly half cite these:

4. To get information that can't be found elsewhere.
5. To remind myself of my values.
6. To feel like I'm participating in the events of the church.

And, only one in three reads for these reasons:

1. To get spiritual guidance.
2. To get details about stories reported elsewhere.
3. To be informed in discussions with others.
4. To help cope with the challenges of life.[49]

Almost none of the readers cited relaxation or entertainment, which are significant motives for reading secular newspapers. The results of such research, which provides important audience input for the debate on roles, has only just begun to enter the discussion. Three motives bring it forward: circulation problems, changed norms in the secular media, and the ideals expressed in Vatican II and *Communio et Progressio*.

A new generation of bishops accustomed to media attention seemed more comfortable with an open and responsible discussion of problems, even if friction seemed inherent in the new relationships with their editors, who were now respected as professionals. Archbishop Rembert

---

49. Griffin, "Information Seeking and Usage," 23–31; Sly, *Three Catholic Readerships*; Gallup, *U.S. Catholics and the Catholic Press, Five Diocesan Newspapers, Four Catholic Magazines*.

Weakland argued for five specific tasks for Catholic editors: report events of the church and those which affect it; reflect on and interpret events; create growth of a forum for legitimate dissenting views; teach and evangelize through events; and create a cultural environment which reflects gospel values.[50]

The average bishop publisher and his journalist editor agreed on the three dominant roles—news, intra-diocesan communication, and religious education—but they strongly disagreed on the order of priority. Bishops ranked intra-diocesan communication first, religious education second, and news a distant third.[51] Editors, as a group, give strong primacy to news with intra-diocesan communication and religious education far below. The other, lower-ranked roles include: provide forum for dialogue, bishop's communication instrument, develop awareness on moral issues, interpret news from Catholic perspective, link Catholics to the church. One of the lessons editors and their bishops learned slowly is that participation, or linking Catholics to their church, ranked high among Catholic readers. The dialogue on press roles has only begun to work out the triangular relationship between laity, hierarchy, and journalists.

Editors jealously guarded their role as official voice while new diocesan communication offices sprang up across the country. The internal strife became public over the creation in 1977 of a special national collection or financial offering at masses for communication activities. Editors and the Catholic Press Association challenged the need for work in broadcasting and cable television. UNDA-U.S.A. (*unda* is Latin for wave), the professional association of diocesan communication directors, began as part of the CPA then split from it. The 1984 conference, "A Vision All Can Share," brought representatives of all church media people together to develop priorities and means for collaboration across media. The conferees recommended that each diocese develop and support its own newspaper and affiliate with NC News Service.[52] But clearly, newspapers were no longer the only voice of the diocese, and this became another factor in the search for their role.

THE FUTURE

Immensely talented, charismatic, and consummately skilled with media, John Paul II became both an international media figure and an

---

50. Weakland, "Need for a Catholic Press," 4–11.
51. Thorn and Garrison, "Institutional Stress," 51.
52. *Vision All Can Share*, 37–39.

influence on the role of media within the church. With every means at his disposal, the pope has reasserted the gravity of the center, labelled the "Catholic Restoration."[53] At the same time, he has urged upon the press a special role within the church, that of carrying on the dialogue between the leadership and the membership. Without dissent, the pope wrote in *The Acting Person*, there is no authentic community life because community solidarity often triggers dissent, as do new ideas. Thus was framed the central dilemma for the reinstitutionalized press: how to provide a forum for dissent and accurate news while remaining officially sponsored by the diocese. As the Catholic Restoration proceeded through the appointment of conservative bishops and cardinals, John Paul II sent a clear signal that dissent has limits and the hierarchy is responsible for maintaining them.

Facing the 1990s, the Catholic press continues to debate its public interest and public relations roles. *National Catholic Reporter* demonstrated the vital role of public interest in its coverage of the pedophilia problem among clergy. *National Catholic Register* and *Our Sunday Visitor* contribute important perspectives from the center and right. Diocesan newspapers, reflecting the view of the bishop, range from near-autonomy to the instrument of the bishop. Magazines range from public relations organs of their sponsoring religious communities to those oriented to special groups such as *New Covenant* (charismatic Catholics), *Catholic Health World* (health care and hospitals), *Modern Liturgy*, or *Today's Catholic Teacher.*

This diversity demonstrates how much Vatican II revolutionized the role of the press. The Catholic press expresses the balance of roles adopted by the publisher and bishop and supported by the readers. Still, the fact remains that the publisher of most Catholic newspapers is a bishop. That triangular relationship, bishop-editor-readers, provides the dynamic for ongoing adaptation of the press to the needs of the community. It places editors squarely in the center of the community as mediators between bishop and faithful and between the various factions and groups.

53. Johnson, *Pope John Paul II and the Catholic Restoration.*

BIBLIOGRAPHY

Acta et Decreta. Third Plenary Council of Baltimore, chapter 4.

Baumgartner, Appollinaris, *Catholic Journalism: A Study of Its Development in the United States, 1789–1930.* New York: Columbia University Press, 1931.

Beals, Carleton, *Brass Knuckle Crusade: The Great Know-Nothing Conspiracy, 1820–1860.* New York: Hastings House, 1960.

Billington, Raymond Allen, *The Origins of Nativism in the United States, 1800–1844*. New York: Arno Press, 1933, 1974.

Bodo, John R., *The Protestant Clergy and Public Issues, 1812–1848*. Princeton, NJ: Princeton University Press, 1954.

Brown, Richard M., *Strain of Violence: Historical Studies of American Violence and Vigilantism*. New York: Oxford University Press, 1975.

Deedy, John G., "The Catholic Press: The Why and the Wherefore." Pp. 65–122 in Martin Marty, ed., *The Religious Press in America*. Westport, CT: Greenwood Press, 1968.

Dolan, Jay P., *The American Catholic Experience*. Garden City, NY: Doubleday & Co., 1985.

Dulles, Avery, *Models of the Church*. Garden City, NY: Doubleday, 1974.

Ellis, Msgr. John Tracy, *American Catholics and the Intellectual Life*. Chicago: Heritage Foundation, 1956.

Finnegan, John, Jr., "The Press and the Charlestown Riots of 1834." Unpublished manuscript.

———, "Trends in Criticism: The American Catholic Press 1957–1977." Unpublished Plan B MA Project. University of Minnesota, 1978.

Foik, Paul J., "Pioneer Efforts in Catholic Journalism in the United States." *Catholic Historical Review* Oct. (1915): 221–29.

Gallup, George, *U. S. Catholics and the Catholic Press*. New York: Catholic Press Association, 1978.

———, *An In-depth Study of Five Diocesan Newspapers*. New York: Catholic Press Association, 1980.

———, *In-depth Study of Views on Four Catholic Magazines*. New York: Catholic Press Association, 1981.

Greeley, Andrew, *The American Catholic: A Social Portrait*. New York: Basic Books, 1977.

Griffin, Robert, "Information Seeking and Usage by Milwaukee Area Catholics." Pp. 23–31 in *The Future of the Catholic Press*. Milwaukee, WI: Institute for Catholic Media, 1979.

Guilday, Peter, *The Life and Times of John England*. Vol. 1. New York: The American Press, 1927.

Hannan, Bishop Phillip, "What Bishops Think of the Catholic Press." Pp. 41–49 in Resource Papers and Consensus Paper of the Bishops-Editor Conference at Bergame Center, NY. Catholic Press Association, 1970.

Hennesey, James, SJ, *American Catholics*. New York: Oxford, 1981.

Johnson, Paul, *Pope John Paul II and the Catholic Restoration*. Ann Arbor, MI: Servant Books, 1981.

Marty, Martin E., *The Modern Schism*. New York: Harper & Row, 1969.

McDonald, Donald, "The State of the Local Catholic Press." *Commonweal* Feb. 3. (1950): 459–61.

Miller, William D., *A Harsh and Dreadful Love: Dorothy Day and the Catholic Worker Movement*. New York: Liveright, 1973.

———, *Dorothy Day: A Biography*. New York: Harper & Row, 1982.

Papal Commission for Social Communication, *Communio of Progressio.* Available in *Documents of Vatican II*, ed. Austin Flannery. Grand Rapids, MI: Wm. B. Eerdmans, 1984.

Real, Michael, "Trends in Structure and Policy in the American Catholic Press." *Journalism Quarterly* 52 (Summer 1975): 265–71.

Reilly, Sr. Mary Lonan, OSF, *A History of the Catholic Press Association.* Metuchen, NJ: Scarecrow Press, 1971.

Ridder, Charles H., "The United States Catholic Exhibit at Vatican City, 1936." *Historical Records and Studies* 27 (1937): 28–51.

Roberts, Nancy, *Dorothy Day and the Catholic Worker.* Albany: State University of New York Press, 1984.

Sly, Julie A., "A Uses and Gratifications Study of Three Catholic Readerships: The National Catholic Reporter, The Tidings, and The Times Review." Unpublished master's thesis. Marquette University, 1984.

Testem Benevolentiae. An apostolic letter of 22 January 1899 written by Pope Leo XIII to James Cardinal Gibbons.

Thorn, William J. and Bruce Garrison, "Institutional Stress: Journalistic Norms in the Catholic Press." *Review of Religious Research* 25, 1 (1981): 49–62.

A Vision All Can Share: The 1984 Conference. Milwaukee, WI: Institute for Catholic Media, 1985.

Weakland, Rembert J., "The Need for a Catholic Press." Pp. 4–11 in *The Future of the Catholic Press.* Milwaukee, WI: Institute for Catholic Media, 1979.

Whalen, James, "The Press Opens up Vatican II." *Journalism Quarterly* 44 (Spring 1967): 53–61.

The History and Role
of the Protestant Press

Charles Austin

When a theological, social, or political movement begins within American Christendom, it inevitably spawns a magazine or newspaper. When church members are angry at their denominations, they are likely to (a) cancel their subscription to the church's magazine, (b) write an angry letter to the editor, or (c) blame the magazine or newspaper for whatever is troubling them.

American Christians, especially American Protestants, have been aficionados of the printed word since pre-colonial days. This orientation is a trait they inherited from Reformation printers. And it seems that, subliminally, the power the Reformers gave to the Word of God was partially transferred to other words put on paper to read as faithfully as one read the scriptures.

While Catholics found their unity in the language and ritual of the Mass and the unchanging verities of parish life, Protestants connected with one another through preaching and publishing.

The Protestant press, therefore, has had a distinguished history, paralleling the steady influence of Protestantism on the development of American society. But this parallel means that as the church itself has become less important to Americans and their society, the influence of the Protestant press has declined. It therefore needs to seek a new role and identity, win its credibility anew, and adapt to the more pluralistic nature of modern times.

Unfortunately, it also faces the onslaught of the "non-literary" age, when the printed word is devalued, cogent expression is corrupted by political jargon and trendy newspeak, literary illiteracy runs rampant, and attention spans are compressed into twenty-second television-commercial simplicity.

When Protestants came to these shores, they brought with them their love of publications and their desire to publish. The publications sometimes served "ethnic" purposes, since they were written in the language of the immigrant's homeland. But those generations of immigrants were quick to seek assimilation into American life. In pre-colonial days, for example, newspapers such as the *Geschicht-Schreiber*, published for German Lutherans, took a political turn with editorials critical of British rule.[1]

The words of sermons thundering across the pews from the pulpit of a Cotton Mather or Lyman Beecher burst through the church doors and into the streets through newspapers and magazines, carrying the weight in their day that contemporary newspaper editorials or op-ed columns bear today. The writings of the early abolitionists and prohibitionists appeared in church-related publications. And, though American Christians have always been wary of writings considered "too literary," the works of such authors as James Russell Lowell and Richard Henry Dana found a publisher in the church press.

Perhaps the earliest religious magazine in the country was *Christian History*, first issued in 1743 and edited by Thomas Price, son of the pastor of Boston's Old South Church. *Christian History*, which lasted only a few years, was an outgrowth of the Great Evangelistic Awakening.[2]

Publications that weren't ethnic served denominational purposes or became the standard-bearers for theological movements, a characteristic of Protestant publishing that continues to the present time.

In the first quarter of the nineteenth century, according to a study done for the Associated Church Press, there were sixty-seven denominational weekly papers, and at least eighteen monthlies or quarterlies.[3]

Within the denominations were dozens of other publications.

As American theology cut its ties to the European homelands and began developing its own style, magazines and newspapers and theological journals reflecting the American continent flourished. *Dial*, edited by the mystic Margaret Fuller, became the major publication of transcendentalism. The *Mercersburg Review*, edited by John Williamson Nevin, spread the intellectual revival of the Mercersburg theology.

1. Ashlstrom, *Religious History of The American People*, 377.
2. Lipphard, "The Associated Church Press," 3.
3. Lipphard, "The Associated Church Press," 5.

Modern readers with any interest in contemporary theology will have felt the influence of Charles Clayton Morrison's *Christian Century*, founded in 1908 and still the chief vehicle for liberal ecumenical Protestantism, or C.F.H. Henry's *Christianity Today*, the news and opinion journal for a major segment of conservative evangelicalism.

Until well into the twentieth century the Protestant press was the source of ethnic identity and unity, inspiration, and polemics, as well as general news. As American society became more pluralistic and "less Christian," the church press took on the role of being more genteel. In the late nineteenth century, "Christian" literature self-consciously and piously stood apart from the lurid, worldly, impious headlines of the secular press.

At the same time, movement-centered periodicals coaxed, rallied, and harangued readers from the pulpits of crusading editors.

ROLE OF THE PROTESTANT PRESS TODAY

There are probably more than five hundred nationally circulated church publications today. The membership of the Associated Church Press, an organization for major Protestant publications, stands at 173. The Evangelical Press Association, composed of evangelical and conservative magazines, has more than three hundred members.

And there are hundreds of unaffiliated newspapers and magazines, many of them regional or serving the needs of smaller special interest groups. So it is safe to assume that the Protestant press has millions of readers and access to large numbers of people who may not read much else or mistrust what they read in the secular press.

Many of these serve the relatively narrow interests of denominations or special groups, acting as conduits of information from national or regional offices to local churches and members. Depending upon tradition or the tenacity of the editors, these publications may or may not consider themselves free of denominational or bureaucratic strictures. They have their purpose and readership.

But by far the more interesting segments of the Protestant press today are those publications that have inherited a sense of journalistic freedom or those that have championed movements within various sections of the church. Often beset by their sponsors, publications like these attempt to take the American tradition of a free press and make it work within the church.

Some such publications and news services receive their support from church or church-related units willing to let the press have free rein.

Religious News Service, begun in the 1930s under the auspices of the National Conference of Christians and Jews, and purchased in 1983 by *United Methodist Reporter*, is a truly independent news service, carrying news of the churches that is free from any actual or unconscious denominational influence.

The clients of RNS, which publishes four times a week, are religious and secular publications interested in news about religion. Like a wire service, its success depends upon the confidence its clients have in its coverage and the use they make of RNS news stories and features. (The U.S. Conference of Catholic Bishops sponsors National Catholic News Service to provide news to diocesan papers. Though sponsored by the bishops' conference, it too is known for its high journalistic standards and is generally free from interference by the sponsors.) RNS, in addition to being a model for responsible religion journalism, has helped religious groups know more about each other by disseminating news to both the religious and secular press, crossing all denominational lines.

Some denominational news services, providing stories to church and secular publications, also try to operate with high journalistic standards and shun the role of denominational mouthpieces. With conservatives and fundamentalists fighting for control of the fourteen-million-member Southern Baptist Convention, *Baptist Press*, the denomination's news service, has attempted to report openly and in a balanced fashion on the sometimes bitter struggle. Their stories have drawn hostility, and the organization has been subjected to close administrative scrutiny, primarily from the fundamentalists who champion a rigid conformity and strict biblical literalism.

When the Lutheran Church-Missouri Synod battle over doctrine began affecting inter-Lutheran and ecumenical relations, the News Bureau of the Lutheran Council in the U.S.A., sponsored by the LCMS and three other Lutheran denominations, began carrying stories on the turmoil. Unable to dictate how those stories would be written and angry that the strife was aired so publicly, the LCMS eventually withdrew its financial support from the Lutheran Council News Bureau.[4]

More recently, the Presbyterian Church (U.S.A.) has engaged in long discussions on how "open" denominational meetings should be, whether its news service is free to quote people speaking at certain meetings and whether the practices of secular journalism are acceptable within church circles.

4. The writer was assistant director of the Lutheran Council News Bureau from 1971-75.

These battles—and they are widespread and occur in nearly every denomination and organization at one time or another—generally pit those with an understanding of journalistic freedom against those who feel that information put out by an organization should more narrowly "serve the needs" of the organization. Stories on controversial subjects, "bad" news, embarrassing mistakes, or failed programs, though "newsworthy," might not serve these needs and therefore should be squelched, say the organizationally-minded.

They are opposed by those who argue with equal fervor that "news is news." It should be reported honestly and fairly, letting the chips fall where they may. Freedom of information, they contend, is a higher value than denominational peace.

In recent years, with churches facing controversy at every turn— mergers, declining membership, difficult subjects such as sexual ethics, and scandalous discourses in the secular press—the discussion has heated up and taken some unusual turns. Told that *The Lutheran*, the magazine of the new Evangelical Lutheran Church in America, was going to publish articles by former bishops discussing the issue of ordination for homosexuals, bishops of the ELCA went around the editor of the magazine and cajoled the authors of the articles into withdrawing the pieces, even after they had been set in type. Thus the ELCA bishops avoided directly interfering in the magazine's editorial decision-making but nonetheless suppressed something they did not want to have printed.

That decision took on more significance since *The Lutheran*, with a circulation of about one million, has a strong history of editorial freedom, a freedom clearly stipulated in its organizational mandate from the ELCA.

Struggles like these lie at the heart of the Protestant press as it seeks a new identity. It is hard for editors to be bold when their churches are in turmoil or when the rapid changes bring other difficulties. There are so many troubles already, why add the uproar of news stories on AIDS, errant ministers, declining finances, and denominational squabbling?

Richard Ostling, religion editor of *Time* magazine, told the 1988 conventions of the Associated Church Press and the Evangelical Press Association that editors had to constantly battle the "tendency to timidity" and strive for current, lively copy. "All too many church periodicals are slow or sluggish in responding to the issues of the day," said Ostling, a former news editor for *Christianity Today* magazine.

The situation puts the editor on a tightrope. If the publication is too bland, readers fall away. Furthermore, good editors will suffer within themselves, knowing they are making editorial decisions about what should be printed based on their fear of angry responses. On the other hand, an editor who turns over too many rocks may find funding decreased or discover that the publication is cut off from the institution it is supposed to report on and serve.

Despite the conflicts, most editors of general-interest church magazines claim that editorial freedom is a reality in their worlds and is important to their mission. Some exercise the freedom more boldly than others, but nearly all carry the banner.

THE "MOVEMENT" PRESS

Another segment of the Protestant press makes carrying the banner its reason for existence. Ranging from theological journals to shabbily-printed tracts, the "movement presses" have always been active in American Protestantism. The fact that abolitionist and prohibitionist publications were often church-related has already been mentioned.

No movement can exist without a regular way to inform, inspire, and stir up its followers. And when crusaders or revolutionaries or just people with unpopular views are excluded from the "official press," they will always start their own. When ideas don't seem quite ripe for the multitudes, the initiated share them through small publications, newsletters, and journals.

The Presbyterian Lay Committee, a group of conservatives within the more moderate Presbyterian Church (U.S.A.), publishes *The Layman*, a regular tabloid pointing out what the Lay Committee thinks is wrong with the denomination. Persistently critical, the publication has become a force within Presbyterianism, though the numerical and ideological influence of the Lay Committee is hard to pin down.

The schism that divided the Lutheran Church-Missouri Synod in the 1970s may have been inevitable; but it was certainly brought about more quickly by the constant, intemperate, often vicious carping of Herman Otten, whose independent publication, *Lutheran News*, later renamed *Christian News*, chewed away at alleged heresy in the denomination and then supported the presidency of J.A.O. Preus, under whose administration the 2.6 million member denomination split. A feisty, ideologically conservative editor to whom fairness was doctrinal compromise, Otten's independent publication reached a circulation of twenty thousand and kept conservatives stirred up and moderates on the defensive until the schism.[5]

Motive, a magazine published for Methodist youth, became the focal

5. Adams, *Preus of Missouri*, 130–31.

point for social activism within the denomination. Other church-related and independent publications oriented toward religion took up such causes as racial justice, world peace, American Indian rights, ecology, and inter-church cooperation. Most remained small, and most folded after their special concern or a charismatic editor passed from the scene.

In addition to representing the special concerns of a movement, these publications often served as an "alternative media," reporting and editorializing on matters ignored by the official media or secular journalists.

THE NEED FOR "ALTERNATIVE MEDIA"

American media, especially the broadcast media, simply ignore religion and are often inept when it comes to reporting on religion-related concerns. There are many good religion writers for daily newspapers, but too many daily newspapers do not have religion writers and therefore ignore the segment of their readership interested in religion and current affairs.

Futhermore, broadcast news has become slick-packaged and homogenized due to the power and influence and competition of the networks. Concerned with quick-study politics, power, high finance, sensationalism, celebrities, and entertainment, broadcast news is not likely to pay much attention to the religious faith that influences the life of the average believer. Nor are the major national media as "on top of the news" as they often claim.

In the early 1970s, Americans were jolted into concern for famine in Ethiopia, largely because of some British television footage and the ensuing major stories about the famine in American newspapers. Editors and regular readers of the church press may have smiled at the furor, for the church press had been reporting on the ongoing famine in Ethiopia for several years.

In a like manner, the church press was reporting on South Africa's brutal occupation of Namibia in violation of a U.N. mandate long before much of the secular press noticed the struggle at all, or discovered that churches in Namibia were in the forefront of the independence movement.

As clergy and others began providing sanctuary for refugees from Central America who were denied refugee status and faced deportation by the U.S. government, the church press developed the story before the secular press took much notice. It took a truly major event—a federal trial in Phoenix in 1986—for the general press to report extensively on the sanctuary movement.

THREE ROLES FOR THE PROTESTANT PRESS

The Protestant press, therefore, can lay a historical claim to three critical roles in American society. First, it shares with the secular press the role of the responsible journalist who questions, probes, and reports with the objective truth and the readers' interest, not the publisher's pocketbook, at the forefront. (It must be said, of course, that this is a role often abrogated by the secular press, an admission which does not reduce the importance of the task.)

Second, the journals of church-related movements, both theological and social, can keep new ideas before the public, stimulate participation, rally supporters and test viewpoints. If the journals last long enough, as the *Christian Century* has, they can later begin a "how my mind has changed" series giving even more reflections on recent history by participants in the events.

Finally, the church press can serve as an "alternative media" that looks at current events from the perspective of faith. Lutherans and Anglicans, for instance, became interested in Namibia quite early not because the country had international geo-political significance, but because of the large numbers of Lutheran and Anglicans in Namibia asking for prayers and support. The secular press is often blind to or simply ignores the role that religion plays in newsworthy events; and it is incumbent upon the church-related press to fill in this gap.

THE NEED FOR PROFESSIONALS

Journalists like to quote the biblical phrase, "You shall know the truth and the truth shall make you free" (John 8:32). But journalists know that truth is not a simple thing; and despite the much vaunted claim of "objectivity,' that, too, is elusive.

Like any ministry, then, those who aspire to church journalism need to have or develop the proper charisms. Church periodicals need editors and writers whose journalistic skills have been well-honed. The words they write compete with every other written word that comes before potential readers. There may be only one preacher or congregation in the life of the average believer; but that believer is exposed to dozens of journalists daily.

This means that the church journalist must develop the skills of discernment. "And that's the way it is!" was the sign-off line of Walter Cronkite, one of the century's most trusted journalists. But suppose that *isn't* the way it is from another perspective? Discernment is the mysterious ability to know what's important, what counts, to weight the goofball and ephemeral against the signs of the coming age. Public awareness of events, however small, can catapult those events onto the world stage. Public ignorance of events, however large, can rob them of all meaning. And it is often the journalist who determines what the public will know. (Exasperated by long discussions with non-journalists about what constitutes news, most editors will end up admitting "news is what I say it is.")

It is a heady task.

The protection against the ill-effects of misuse, of course, is the existence of many media. The economics of publishing today have robbed most cities of more than one newspaper and reduced the number of national general interest publications. But church publications—smaller, more flexible, with a more loyal readership—have been less affected by the changing fortunes of mass media economics. Futhermore, modern technology such as computer typesetting and desktop publishing should cause the kind of alternative, "movement" publications mentioned above to flourish. What formerly took a printshop, heavy equipment, and years of apprenticeship can now be accomplished with a few thousand dollars used to purchase a computer and a laser printer.

CONCLUSION

The Protestant press may be languishing, buffeted by the ill winds that have diminished denominations and made the church less important to society than in former days. But church newspapers and magazines nonetheless bear a noble heritage that cannot be denied and waits to be revitalized.

BIBLIOGRAPHY

Adams, James E., *Preus of Missouri and the Great Lutheran Civil War*. New York: Harper & Row, 1977.

Ahlstrom, Sydney E., *A Religious History of the American People*. New Haven and London: Yale University Press, 1972.

Lipphard, William B., "The Associated Church Press: A Brief History (1916–1961). Unpublished paper.

SUGGESTIONS FOR FURTHER READING

Bachman, John W., *Media-Wasteland or Wonderland: Opportunities and Dangers for Christians in the Electronic Age*. Minneapolis: Augsburg, 1984.

A scholarly look at the church's use of the print and broadcast media.

Beck, Roy H., *On Thin Ice: A Religion Reporter's Memoirs*. Wilmore, KY: Forum Script, 1988.

A veteran journalist talks about covering religion for the church press and the secular press.

Gentz, William and Lee Roddy, *Writing to Inspire: A Guide to Writing and Publishing for the Expanding Religious Market*. Cincinnati, OH: Writers Digest, 1988.

While not journalism in the strictest sense, the publication of devotional literature is a major part of the Protestant publishing enterprise. This how-to book explains what that segment of the media is like.

Haselden, Kyle, *Morality and the Mass Media*. Nashville, TN: Broadman, 1968.

Some moral and ethical issues raised in the print and broadcast media.

Hensley, Dennis E. and Rose A. Adkins, *Writing for Religious & Other Specialty Markets*. Nashville, TN: Broadman, 1987.

Another look at the devotional press in America.

Olasky, Marvin, *Prodigal Press: The Anti-Christian Bias of the American News Media*. Westchester, IL: Crossway Books, 1988.

A very idiosyncratic book which begins with the premise that all journalism in America began as religious journalism designed to spread the gospel, and that, having lost this objective, the media has become a tool of the devil.

Osmer, Harold H., *U. S. Religious Journalism and the Korean War*. Washington, D.C.: University Press of America, 1980.

How church publications, newly awakened to journalistic responsibility, handled the Korean war.

Ross, Robert W., *So It Was True: The American Protestant Press and the Nazi Persecution of the Jews*. Minneapolis: University of Minnesota Press, 1980.

A somewhat harsh indictment of the Protestant press; it does indicate that had Protestants been more ecumenically and internationally involved in the days prior to World War II, the public might have known more about the pending Holocaust.

8

The History and Role of the Jewish Press

Herb Brin

Unlike with the press of other faiths, coverage of religious news constitutes only a portion of what the Jewish press is all about.

Only in the Armenian press in America is there a parallel.

Jewish editors are concerned not only with faith but with survivability of a people. To be sure, the Jewish people have their disparate movements: Orthodox, Conservative, Reform, Reconstructionist, and something called Humanist where one rabbi has proclaimed the thesis that God is dead.

And Jews are concerned with ancient rules of *kashrut* which require Jewish families not to mix meat and dairy foods—rules talked about for the most part but generally observed in the breach, unless the family is Orthodox.

Intermarriage is of utmost importance, having directly to do with survivability of the people. And so the Jewish press must be a social calendar to enable Jewish boys and girls to meet. Alas, it is largely a losing cause with huge percentages of young Jewish people marrying outside the faith.

With all the pressures of ritual and social awareness and because of the traumatic history of the Jewish people, the Jewish press in essence is a super conscience for humanity itself. Perhaps it is because of the Good Book, given to the world by the Jews, that this small people of less than 13 million worldwide is forever in the news.

THE TASK OF THE JEWISH EDITOR

The task of the Jewish editor is formidable. Such an editor receives no doctorate in conscience from universities of the world. Courses in Jewish editorial standards are not taught in the rabbinic schools.

There is no formula for selectivity of items covered in such a press, but if there is a human factor involved, if freedom is involved, if survival of the species is involved, or justice, the Jewish editor is concerned. Or ought to be.

It may be a presumption to suggest that the Jewish press is the oldest in history. But our reporters were covering events from the days of Eden. They sailed the sea with Noah and covered the Exodus to the Promised Land. Our op-ed writers were called prophets and we covered the arts passionately in the Song of Songs. And even way back then our Jewish press was reporting on the culinary arts of the people. It's all there, in the Good Book.

When the Roman dispersion came, Jewish publications were found in all cities of the known world—from Damascus to Toledo, Spain and along the northern crescent of Africa. A People of the Book, indeed. If the publications weren't exactly in the form of newspapers, tabloid size, offset, the street singer reporters called out the warning news of impending attacks from behind their city walls.

Who else was there to tell the story of the destruction of a Golden Age in Spain? Jewish songs are still heard in Espana where Spaniards don't seem to understand why the six-pointed Star of David—Estrella de David—can be seen everywhere in Iberia and Majorca.

It is no wonder that issues of church and state—and quotas—are among the foremost topics on a Jewish editor's menu of events to cover.

Ours is a press of many languages. Events of the Jewish people are chronicled in Hebrew, Aramaic, Greek, Yiddish, Ladino, Chinese along with almost all the languages of the western world.

Following the expulsion of Jews from Spain in 1492, a Jewish press flourished in Salonika and Amsterdam. Poland had an exciting Jewish press in both the Polish and Yiddish languages. The Warsaw publication, *Heint*, in Yiddish, was one of the most sophisticated in the history of journalism. It, along with Jewish life in Poland, was destroyed in the Holocaust, that inhuman watershed of tragedy. But even as the Holocaust raged, an active underground press existed in Warsaw and Lodz to alert victims to world events.

THE YIDDISH PRESS

In America, the Yiddish press served as a major education force for the integration of nearly three million immigrants who came to these shores at the turn of the century.

Daily newspapers in Yiddish were to be found in New York, Chicago, Montreal and Toronto. Hundreds of magazines were established to describe the transplantation of a people. Yiddish writers included the novelist Sholem Asch and Nobel Laureate Isaac Bashevis Singer.

The ten daily Yiddish newspapers had a combined circulation of nearly eight hundred thousand. As Yiddish readership began to disappear, the Yiddish press all but vanished in the United States and Canada. Into that void came a vibrant English-Jewish press.

The English language Jewish newspapers emerged wherever a sizable Jewish community existed. Editors of these journals were treated by the communities which they served with benign neglect. Status came painfully and slowly for the new breed of Jewish editors.

There are today nearly 250 Jewish newspapers and magazines in the English language in the United States and Canada. There are 12 Jewish publications in Mexico City. Most are subvented by Jewish federations or similar communal groups, while about 30 or 40 newspapers in the U.S. and Canada are independently owned. Only a handful of the independents are really making ends meet. Hardly an arena for making it, American style.

To survive, most independent Jewish publications must augment their income by putting out "happiness editions"—greetings to the community on the various holidays. But then, that's what is also done to help sustain other religious publications.

Despite life for these independents which has them on the razor's edge of survivability, the publications are in the forefront of the ongoing human struggles. And if an editor can stick it out with his integrity intact for thirty-five years, he is among the honored in Israel.

During the 1920s a great transformation in Jewish life occurred. Jewish students were no longer engulfed in the ways of their fathers, devoted to studies of the tradition. They began climbing out of the ghettoes, transplanted onto magic ladders to suburbia. They entered countless professions, the arts, the sciences. Few chose to become Jewish editors.

THE GROWTH OF THE ANGLO-JEWISH PRESS

It was during the Hitler years that much of the viable Jewish press in English came to life in America, Canada and Britain. Jewish editors covered nazi marches in the parks of America's great cities. While shudders swept through Jewish life in America, Jewish editors infiltrated the nazi German-American Bund and told of plans by the bundists for a Hitlerian takeover of the nation.

A multitude of quality publications was born ranging the political spectrum from left to right. Journals such as *Midstream* and *Commentary* made strong impacts on the Jewish community and on American readers in general. Each branch of the Jewish faith had its own high quality magazine. The Jewish Telegraphic Agency was born and fed an expanding number of English language weeklies that began to sprout everywhere in the land.

In time, an American Jewish Press Association came into being as standards for coverage of Jewish life in America started to improve. Jewish editors were invited to White House conferences and some were honored by their own communities.

FAILURES DURING THE HOLOCAUST

Jewish publications found it possible, and of course necessary, to carry reports on the developing Holocaust in Germany and Poland long before the *New York Times* got the stories.

But Jewish publications had their failures also.

The Jewish press—both in Yiddish and in English—failed to demand of President Franklin Roosevelt that he permit victims of the terror abroad to enter the United States as refugees. The Roosevelt name, once honored in Jewish communities across the nation, tarnished in the process. The highly cultured and creative Jewish communities of Central Europe were savagely destroyed, their creative works plundered.

Accepting the advice of national Jewish leaders, the Jewish press agreed not to rock the boat during wartime. Innocent people, among them a million and a half children, died of that tragic fearfulness. The burden of the English-Jewish press is heavy.

The basic charge assumed by any Jewish editor is to be sure that he will never write an obituary on the continuity of his people. Jewish editors came close to that in the days of the Final Solution.

PROTECTING JEWISH VALUES

With the rebirth of Israel out of the ashes of Holocaust, the Jewish press came into its own on the world scene. The battles of Israel for survival affect Jewish life in Timbuktu. The Kansas City milkman, if he is Jewish, must read of the battlefield sorrows or euphoria as reflected in his Jewish newspaper. There are understandably levels of special Jewish values which the Jewish press must explore and which the metropolitan media cannot. These are values, of course, which place no burdens upon the vast other religious presses in America.

While Jewish newspapers tell of the bat mitzvah of Debbie Goldfarb or of the bar mitzvah of Kelly Doyle (ah, the names of the Jewish people range the gamut of civilization) or the plans of a canter's upcoming concert at the Christchurch Synagogue (there is one, indeed, in New Zealand), the joys or sorrows of Israel are as close to the editor's desk as the bakery where he obtains his Sabbath bread . . . the bakery that refuses to advertise because the Jewish owner can't abide, he says, Jewish customers. He bakes his bread, the Sabbath *challah*, for *Auld Lang Syne*, one would suppose. And God forbid Debbie's mother doesn't come around to buy that *challah* he baked for her.

Everybody wants a free ride.

While most Jewish editors do not follow traditional kosher strictures in their personal lives, all treat the subject of kosher foods with respect. One would hardly insult the spiritual image of his grandparents for whom the ritual of a kosher home meant having a spiritual altar in the kitchen.

Religious holidays are always reported with reverence by most editors of the Jewish media. Great care and innovation underscores the search for special holiday features. The history of Jewish life on the planet is vast enough to suggest a magnitude of perceptive articles to fit all such occasions.

Fundamental to coverage by all Jewish publications are reports affecting the survival of Jewish spiritual values here in the United States and throughout the world. The survival of Israel is a *sine qua non* to Jewish coverage of the news. Forget that there is often rancor among the Israelis. As David Ben-Gurion said: "Show me two Jews and I'll give you three opinions."

The vibrancy of this people, its essential vitality, must be somewhat frightening, perhaps staggering, to those who cannot comprehend Jews and turn to consuming hatred.

Jewish editors are unable to find Jewish genes which impel our students to excellence and achievement. But Jewish editors cannot pontificate, they cannot write down to readers who know more about every subject that must be tackled than do the editors.

But the editors quickly discover that this is a community that is incredibly devoted to educational excellence, perhaps because in that pursuit the Jewish people have found some measure of communal safety.

There. That's the basic Jewish secret. In telling the secret, many editors (if male) may now have to submit to a second circumcision.

By aiding in the process of Jewish young people to get to meet one another, an editor perceives his role to be one to halt the losses that are inevitable via assimilation in a free society. Unless the publication is sponsored by a specific branch of the faith, no Jewish publication will make a litmus test of the qualities of faith required of any Jewish family. Most Jewish publications have refused to support the demands by the religious parties in Israel for a change in the Israeli Law of Return. Under that law, any Jew can come to Israel and receive immediate citizenship. The extreme Orthodox groups in Israel and the United States have demanded exclusion of Jews who were converted to Judaism by other than Orthodox standards, thus bringing into question the religious values of Conservative and Reform Jews.

The question became moot in the fall of 1988 when a new unity government was formed in Israel and the issue was ignored.

Jewish publications avoid taking sides in Israeli political events. In one Jewish publication, half its staff of five editors supported one major Israeli party and half supported the other. How does an editor divide himself in half? It's not easy.

Fundamental to the role of the Jewish press is a firebrand support of the cause of Soviet Jewry. With an estimated 2.5 million Jews living in the Soviet Union, the problems of the refuseniks—those refused exit visas by the government—become an important issue for editorial concern in the Jewish press.[1]

CHALLENGING THE SECULAR PRESS

Jewish publications have come a long way from being newspapers of merely social events. Editorial interests range from the thoroughly religious aspects of communal life to the widest possible news arenas on the state, national and international levels. Often these publications have the audacity to hold up mirrors to the metropolitan press, challenging them when it is perceived that certain attitudes are clearly harmful to the Jewish community and to the spirit of freedom generally.

Editors are beginning to enter the Jewish press after years of service on metropolitan publications. These journalists cover all sorts of news of direct Jewish interest, such as the rise of white supremacists on the West Coast and the threats posed by youth groups called the skinheads.

The Jewish press covered the civil rights movements in America and

---

1. *Editor's Note*: Author Brin and his associate editor at Heritage Publications, Tom Tugend, were the first journalists to contact the Jewish Community of Moscow, in January, 1960, and to learn of the calculated attempt by Soviet authorities to destroy Jewish life in the U.S.S.R. They subsequently brought their findings to Israeli Prime Minister David Ben-Gurion.

played an important role in exposing the hate antics of activists such as Louis Farrakhan and Lyndon LaRouche.

While the Jewish Telegraph Agency is happily improving the quality of its news coverage, many independent publications maintain their own news bureaus in Washington and Israel. There is hardly a Jewish newspaper without a respected feature writer offering material from overseas.

This chapter is being written aboard an Israeli container ship, the Zim-Tokyo, crossing the Pacific with a cargo of nearly 1,000 large containers of products destined for ports from Japan to Korea, Hong Kong and Taiwan.

The Zim company invited this writer to tell how a small country the size of Israel can develop one of the ten most important shipping lines in the world. For Jewish readers it is a story dramatic enough to cover, describing how the flag of Israel is flying in peace in major ports of the Far East where Pacific nations are pulling away from Atlantic countries in the competition for world trade.

A major story? We think so.

Several Jewish publications covered both the Republican and Democratic conventions of 1988. A number of them reported from the scenes of the presidential debates. These reports were of extreme interest to Jewish readers.

The visits of the chief rabbis of Britain and Israel have special interest for Jewish readers. And so does the visit of the pope to America.

ADVOCACY JOURNALISM

Finally, a comment on issues raised by advocates of objective versus advocative journalism. This is a debate which should have no standing in the case of a religious or ethnic journal confronting a life issue.

An Armenian newspaper clearly ought to be mindful of its readers' basic concerns: to win recognition from Turkey of that nation's unfortunate and tragic role in the Genocide of 1.5 million Armenians during World War I; to report on the tragedies that struck Armenians in the recent killer earthquake in Soviet Armenia that killed nearly forty thousand of their coreligionists.

The great Jewish sage, Hillel, once said: "If I am not for myself, who will be?. . .If not now, when?"

Jewish editors in America must be mindful of the Hillel injunctions. They are hardly platitudes for a people of history. Jewish editors are charged by that history to refract the truth in utmost honesty. But then, that is the essential calling of all journalism.

SUGGESTIONS FOR FURTHER READING

Silverman, David Wolf. "The Jewish Press: A Quadrilingual Phenomenon," in Martin E. Marty (ed.), *The Religious Press in America*. New York: Holt, Rinehart and Winston, 1964.

An historical survey of the four languages in which the Jewish press operated in America—German, Yiddish, Hebrew and English—with special attention to the transition from Yiddish to English as the medium of culture and of communication for American Jews.

9

Religious Organizations and Public Relations

William J. Thorn

Public relations has been part of every religion and every church that ever existed. More than publicity and press relations, public relations embraces every aspect of how an institution communicates with people— the public(s)—around it. As such, it is dynamic: speaking and listening, sending and receiving. From architecture and art to worshipping and zeal, churches and other religious organizations relate to the public constantly, sometimes clearly, sometimes powerfully, sometimes visually, sometimes verbally, sometimes by what is said or done, and sometimes by not saying or doing anything. Because communication—whether of sacred texts or values or ideas of God—is central to religion, public relations forms a crucial link between a church and its faithful as well as the larger public. Public relations begins with the leadership and core of the denomination or local church and extends outward, forming images of the church and its belief system.

Variations in ecclesiology alter the strategies for implementing public relations, but they neither reduce nor expand the fundamental need for it. A highly democratic congregational denomination has different problems and resources then the National Conference of Catholic Bishops or the National Council of Churches, and those differences shape the implementation but not the fundamentals of public relations. As Edward Greif has written, "An objective for Jews may not be suitable for Catholics. Among Protestants, the objectives of Methodists may vary from those of Seventh Day Adventists."[1] Comparable differences exist at the local level: a rural Mississippi Baptist congregation, a Jewish congregation on the north side of Chicago, and a Catholic parish in the heart of San Antonio have substantially different communication problems. But whatever the differences, public relations is part of their work, and the local minister or

1. Greif, *Silent Pulpit*, 21.

rabbi or priest is the public voice, the "public relations man" for both the congregation and the community.[2]

THE IMPORTANCE OF PUBLIC RELATIONS
TO RELIGIOUS GROUPS

The importance of public relations work at the local level can be judged by the number of handbooks written specifically for parish and congregation. The Religious Public Relations Council has produced four editions of its *Handbook for Local Congregations* since 1969. Like others produced for denominations, this handbook contains specific, practical advice for producing a newsletter, writing a press release, and handling media relations, photography, direct mail, cable, radio, television, and special events. An older, Lutheran handbook, *Telling the Good News,*[3] extends public relations to "What Does Your Building Say?" and "Exhibits, Displays, and Floats." Every form of media pressed into the service of communication at the local level falls within the ambit of public relations. The amateurism of some efforts is both a charm and a problem, for media effectiveness requires skill.

As Paul Tillich observed, the gospel cannot be hurled at people like a stone; it must be integrated with the human condition. In the media age, media are part of the human condition. Moreover, in a mass society, public dialogue through the media immerses a church and its leaders in the human condition. The research required for effective public relations lays a foundation for that dialogue as well.

Modern media, because of their influence on American life and information, form an inescapable part of public relations strategics. David Moberg argues that increased public relations activities are one of the major factors in the recent revival of life in churches.[4] Yet, many religious leaders have been suspicious and frightened of media, preferring to shun journalism, press conferences, and advertising. The scandals of the electronic church have done little to reduce those fears. Public relations has all too often seemed to some clergy like glitzy sensationalism, half truths, and devious manipulation. Perhaps they have had in mind Rabbi Bernard Cohen of California, who added art, drama, mime, music, and magicians to his services in order to overcome the boredom they created. But publicity stunts are not public relations.

Public relations in its complete sense, communication with the public,

2. See Moberg, *Church as Social Institution.*
3. Johnson, Temme, and Hushaw, *Telling the Good News.*
4. Moberg, *Church as Social Institution,* 41.

has been part of major church documents. In 1968 the Fourth General Assembly of the World Council of Churches adopted "The Church and the Media of Mass Communication," a clear-eyed statement of the reality of mass media for religion. The document encourages effective public relations as part of the use of these media to communicate the church to the people. The Vatican issued its major document on communication, *Communio et Progressio* in 1971. It, too, emphasized effective use of mass media to communicate with the faithful and the world. The Lutheran World Federation reached similar conclusions in the "Joint Report of the Task Force on Mass Communication and the Task Force on Publication Strategy" in 1972. But if these documents, and more local statements of rabbis and ministers, concur on the need to use media, their public relations efforts have not been identical.

As institutions, churches create a corporate culture which defines not only "how things are done around here," but the basic relationship between the church, its members, and the larger community. Ranging from denominations with loose affiliation among certified pastors to highly structured denominations with strong central authority, each church addresses issues and communicates itself as part of a religious culture. The culture goes beyond structural issues to the core concepts about the role and mission of the denomination and each local church. Evangelization drives some as the prime priority, while active work on peace and justice issues or spiritual growth among members ranks first with others. As a communicator, each religious group provides an insight into itself.

The church and its values must remain the center of religious public relations lest the relationship become distorted. The media carries messages; the church leaders decide the content. Marjorie Hyer, former head of the Office of Communication of the United Church of Christ, said that the power to ready-make ideas for mass media, like consumer goods, poses an ethical problem:

> It is easy for religious groups to follow the tested pattern of success and rely on the repetitive slogan and soothing formula of positive thinking, instead of the hard task of expounding the absolute demands of the Gospel. . . . We must not compromise our principles in the thought that we must adapt to accepted practices. Our obligation is greater than that of anyone else.[5]

Hyer touches a central point in church public relations: the act of communication conveys values, images, and other messages of considerable significance to the audience. The risk of deception, in fact, led Malcolm

5. Hyer, "Communication for the United Church of Christ," 82–85. Hyer is now a religion writer for the *Washington Post*.

Muggeridge to declare that Christ, were he alive today, would not use television.

Another distortion of public relations is the use of public opinion polls to adjust church posture and activity to avoid the unpopular. Moberg has argued that overconcern for how the public will react hinders the church's task as media and social critic.[6] To be sure, the mass media culture has reshaped the social context for reading, discussing, and thinking. Criticizing the values of soap operas, for example, is bound to raise the ire of faithful viewers in the congregation. To avoid the challenge because of popular opinion, however, undercuts the basis of public relations, which is a dialogue between church and public.

The marketing aspect of public relations, that is, the response to the needs and interests of the public, has troubled some clergy because it seems to turn church into another form of hamburgers or aspirin . . . a slick image and catchy jingle. But religion operates with its own symbols—a menorah or a cross—in a world of media symbols carefully engineered to amuse or sell. Media symbols and images are inescapable, even during a media fast, for the jingles and phrases and images pop out as though our consciousness were programmed: "the night belongs to Michelob"; "you deserve a break today." Each of those images was conceived through a process which began with the communication goals and continued through the content. The public relations task is to apply the same creative skill to the goals of church communication. Ultimately, public relations is the talented servant, the messenger who moves between church and public, conveying words and images.

Public relations among churches remains a lesser activity. A flurry of activity between 1957 and 1960 produced a handful of conference reports and handbooks, apparently in response to television's impact and potential. A decade later, major church documents appeared. Cable television and the media success of televangelists, coupled with more aggressive religion reporting, have once again stirred interest. But the Religious Public Relations Council's efforts echo the research on those involved in public relations at the local church level: the ideas have been accepted, but hiring competent professionals and keeping them is a second-level priority. A study of diocesan communication directors in the Catholic church disclosed that the average length of time in office is less than two years, and that the burnout rate is caused by too many communication demands and too little time for effective public relations work.[7]

---

6. Moberg, *Church as Social Institution*, 176.
7. Unpublished study by Rev. John Geaney for UNDA-USA, the Catholic association of communication directors, 1983.

MASS MEDIA SOCIETY

Americans live in a country which leads the world in communications technology, and, like people elsewhere, find themselves unified, divided, and shaped by their mass media habits. So highly dependent are Americans on mass communication for their social and personal lives that a day without media has become unthinkable. Moreover, the media which serve America have become a complex mixture of printed and electronic systems which read into the personal, social, and business lives of virtually every American. The pervasiveness of mass media as measured in numbers of radio sets per household (seven), average television viewing time (seven-plus hours per day), numbers of newspapers sold (almost one per household), and similar statistics tends to minimize the profound effects of a mass-mediated life on the communication patterns, expectations, and worldview of Americans. Media inform, lecture, entertain, and deliver audiences to the advertisers. By satellite, Americans have watched wars, the shooting of Pope John II, and the failings of Jim Bakker and Jimmy Swaggert. The system can bring a majority of Americans to their television sets for the same program, offer detailed news analysis through 1,700 daily newspapers, and yet offer something uniquely appealing for different groups within the population.

The media's role in the life of each American—pagan or theist, Christian or Jew or Muslim—places special demands on church communications by offering a competing vision of life and values and raising images which must be publicly addressed. Television's emphasis on the tangible and the present make it more difficult to frame the transcendent and the afterlife so they can be understood. The church, which must preach to all people and communicate with the faithful in the media society, is called to voice the moral implications of mass media content and labor for their improvement as part of its public relations. Each media portrayal of religion and religious leaders offers images to the faithful and unchurched alike. Images of faithless ministers, hysterical religious fanatics, and church corruption become part of the fixed image in the minds of some in the audience unless challenged through the same media—by public relations.

Through prime time heroes and heroines, media teach our children values and tell the stories by which the culture is formed. In order to attract the audience which brings profits, the media all too often seek to tickle the eye and ear of Americans, presenting an affluent world of violence, sex, narcissism, and manipulation. Media also have some glaring shortcomings in dealing with religion. News about religion, sparse to begin with, too often concentrates on conflicts, scandals, and events as seen through the insensitive eye of the ill-prepared. They also avoid mention of God, Christ, and religious ideas except in early morning "ghetto hours." The portrait of religion in the everyday life of "Family Ties" or "The Cosby Show" suggests an America where no one prays, few attend church apart from weddings and funerals, sacrifice has no meaning, penance has no purpose, and religious figures are innocuously weak or naive. These images create part of the real world for television viewers, the "pictures in their heads" by which people make decision about life.

Churches are called to be a sign of contradiction to the dehumanizing aspects of mass media as both shepherd and corporate citizen. As shepherd, a church takes care of its flock and protects them, nourishes their religious hunger, and supports their worship of God. As citizen, the church actively participates in public life, debating salient issues, giving voice to the voiceless, explaining itself, urging its moral vision, and prophetically calling the society to recognize God's presence in everyday life, even of the least of the citizens. Thus the media society poses three formidable challenges to churches, each involving a form of dialogue:

1. Assess the impact of media on people and address the public about the results through words and actions.
2. Correct and counter falsehoods and distortions which appear in news and entertainment content.
3. Use media to communicate religious ideas and values to faithful and to the public.

Just as religious leaders eventually mastered manuscripts and then printing, they are called to master communication through modern media. The sophistication of both media and audiences requires professional skill. Americans are a tough audience. Not only do they have multiple choices constantly before them, they expect technically skilled presentation, whatever the message. Religious public relations provides strategies for both challenging media content and using the forms of media to convey ideas.

The mass media society creates several other realities:

1. If something seems important or interesting in religion, media will cover it, either in news and documentary or entertainment programs.
2. Every worthwhile idea or concept should be explicable in language and images intelligible to a mass audience.
3. The average citizen will judge a church on images presented through mass media (which is a form of personal experience).
4. The media presentation of a church's response to an issue, problem,

crisis, tragedy, or scandal will become part of the public image of the church.

5. Public discussion of a church's issues and problems, including internal ones, is the expected pattern among American audiences, activists, and journalists.

6. Misquotation and misrepresentation are inevitable, and should be corrected through the media with a press statement or news conference.

7. If an individual or institution wants the public to know something, it will use the mass media, most often through a press conference or release.

The media are the means for the society to speak to itself about everything from labor negotiations and court cases to fashion and lifestyle. They are also the means by which segments of the society speak to themselves and others. So pervasive are the media that the old philosophical question might be rephrased; If the forest burned and it wasn't covered on the media, did it happen? The media society requires significant church public relations efforts in order to participate in the life of society. This context means the church must communicate with the faithful and society through each available medium and through several forms of media content, and it forces leaders to think and react in categories and images which can move through the media with minimal distortion. Public relations is the professional key to church communication with its internal and external audiences.

CHURCH AS COMMUNICATOR

Both as shepherd and as corporate citizen, a church or other religious body speaks to diverse audiences on several levels. Public relations is part of the communication effort, and a product of the structural and theological differences.

Some implications of differences in structure are instantly obvious: the scale and complexity of relating to a particular public or the general public varies dramatically by level of church. National offices and regional headquarters offer the preferred location for addressing some issues; local responses are more suited at other times. A centralized, hierarchical denomination will speak with a more unified and therefore more powerful voice than one local congregation on regional and national issues; the local congregation will speak more powerfully to local issues. Urban media demand different approaches than small town or rural media.

But deeper differences have a more profound effect on public relations, because they flow from the very communicative goals of each church. No denomination has a single communication goal. The Vatican identified three for Catholic communication efforts: create dialogue within the church; create dialogue between the church and the world, and give the Good News.[8] While most church people might agree with those very broad goals, each might stress a particular priority or add a special emphasis.

For some, including William Leidt, evangelization is the primary communication effort, and public relations becomes part of that goal: "Publicity is a way of life. Said differently, it may be a call to witness, an evangel."[9] Leidt's call to ministers instructs them on leading the public relations effort of a single congregation. For others, maintaining a coherent identity in a pluralistic and swiftly changing society becomes primary. American Jews have stressed it, first in the Jewish ghettoes, then in the suburbs.[10] One of the media goals stated by the Jewish Theological Seminary of America is, "To introduce and elucidate and interpret Jewish ritual, ceremony and society." A closely related goal is, "To define the place of the Land of Israel in Jewish religious aspiration."[11] The National Council of Churches of Christ cited, "To build a stronger Christian family" and "To make known the Christian Gospel to every person everywhere."[12]

Avery Dulles analyzed church communication from the perspective of the church's self-perceived and defined model. While Catholic in inspiration, Dulles's models seem catholic in application to public relations:

> The theology of communication does not deal with the entire range of God's saving work but studies in particular how God brings about attitudes, convictions, and commitments connected with religious faith. Since God normally does this by means of the church, the theology of communication is closely connected with ecclesiology. Under one aspect, the church may be seen as a "vast communication network designed to bring men out of their isolation and estrangement and to bring them individually and corporately into communion with God in Christ."[13]

8. See Papal Commission, *Communio et Progressio.*
9. Leidt, *Publicity Goes to Church,* 5.
10. Nathan Glazer's, *American Judaism,* cited by McKinney, and Carroll, *Varieties of Religious Presence,* 12.
11. Greif, *Silent Pulpit,* 19. The list of goals also includes, "To extol all who sanctify God's name; to emphasize the sanctity of the human personality; to demonstrate the fundamental character of the democratic in a good society."
12. Greif, *Silent Pulpit,* 20. Other goals included, "To win listeners and viewers to the Christian faith; to help the different religious groups to understand each other; and to work with the radio, television, and film industry toward the presentation of the best in religious programming."
13. Dulles, *Reshaping of Catholicism,* 110, quoting his article, "Church Is Communications," 7.

Dulles developed the communication implication in five models of church: institutional or hierarchical, community or communion, sacramental, herald, servant, and secular-dialogic.

In the *institutional* model, the church is a large society, and the communicator works in a strong hierarchical system to proclaim official church teaching to the members, to convert, and to project a strong corporate identity. This assumes authoritative speakers and faithful listeners.

The *communion* model, which stresses the bondedness of small communities and spiritual unity amidst pluralism, creates a far different role for the communicator, one of leading people to communion with the divine and of linking together a network of open, loving communities. The communicator also helps communities grow together. Fellowship is an important characteristic.

The *sacrament* model recognizes communication through people and events as well as words. Worship incorporates powerful communicative elements, including signs and symbols. As Christ communicated the Father by his life, each community is called to do the same. Public relations here would stress the living example of religious calling, the witness of individuals and communities.

In the *herald* model, a theology of the word, the communicator will have a central role as proclaimer of the Word and developer of the language of faith. The congregational style of this model forces the communicator to emphasize response to the gospel. The communications of this model would extend preaching and perhaps be full of the power of God to save those who hear and believe.

The *secular-dialogic* model involves dialogue with non-Christians and with secular ideologies, not for conversion but "as a realm in which the creative and redemptive will of God is mysteriously at work."[14] The goal of public relations in such a model is to learn as well as teach, and perhaps to jointly witness for authentic human and religious values.

As communicators, churches have other tasks involving public relations: producing newspapers, magazines, radio and television programs, films, audio-visual displays, and the like. These aspects of public relations, whether corporate communication or press relations, profoundly reflect the character of the institution.

Churches and other religious bodies are also complex social organizations, with semi-autonomous agencies and offices who work in alliance with the church in reaching desired goals. The public relations efforts of

---

14. Dulles, *Reshaping of Catholicism*, 118.

the Anti-defamation League of B'nai B'rith have inspired leaders in several denominations. Like other Jewish groups, the League monitors media and public debate for anti-Semitism, then relies on public relations to correct the image.

The church organization may also include hospitals, universities, schools, homes for the elderly, religious communities and lay associations, museums, and other operations which all have a public relations dimension to communicate their values and ideas. The problem facing reporters and the public, and one which public relations must address, is how to understand these co-religionists in their religious context. If, for example, a hospital takes a stand on euthanasia which differs from that of denominational leaders, how is this interpreted.

PUBLIC RELATIONS

Public relations is a deliberate, planned, and sustained effort to establish and maintain understanding between the church and its publics.[15] The definition implies that public relations is far more than publicity or mere public information. In a Christian context, competent public relations is a managerial function which faithfully communicates the church and the gospel through planned, widespread information efforts. In maintaining understanding, public relations is a dialogic form of communication which tries to identify desires and misconceptions, in order to develop and maintain a healthy relationship. Public relations experts favor an approach which is research-based and "proactive," or favoring action.

Research and evaluation run through the public relations effort, primarily in the form of public opinion and attitude surveys. But evaluation can be done through clipping services (which monitor the stories), records of telephone calls to an advertised number, critique by a panel of experts, and reflection on the process itself. Public opinion has always been an important element in public relations, less as the determinant of response than as an indicator of communication effectiveness. Attitude surveys disclose problem areas which may be addressed through public relations.

Among the environments influencing the effectiveness of church public relations, several identified by George de Lodzia bear close examination by research: the culture of the religious organizations, the larger religious culture of the U.S., and the general culture.[16] Because each of

---

15. Cutlip and Center, *Effective Public Relations,* 16.
16. De Lodzia, "Managing Survival," 46–49.

these affects the members of the faith, they comprise an important part of public relations strategies.

Reliable studies provide knowledge about the audience, about the perceptions of the church about contemporary issues, and about the effectiveness of communication activities. Standard surveys provide profiles about church members which can be compared to those of other churches in the same denomination or across denominations, as Gallup studies of religion regularly do. Attitude surveys provide more precise information about how the congregation or denomination is perceived locally. Research also evaluates the impact of each public relations activity to identify not only success or failure, but to locate specific strengths or weaknesses with particular parts of the audience. Given the complexity of modern American communities, public relations' emphasis on attitude and demographic studies provides a scientifically reliable line of communication from the public.

During the 1965 New York World's Fair, the Church of Jesus Christ of Latter Day Saints surveyed fairgoers' attitudes toward the Mormons. To their chagrin, they discovered two strongly negative attitudes: Mormons are anti-family and Mormons do not collaborate with people of other denominations. The discovery became the springboard for a long-term public relations effort to demonstrate the pro-family aspects of the faith and to collaborate more, particularly on public issues of mutual concern. The campaign involved television and radio spots, among other efforts. The result, twenty years later, was a complete reversal in public perception of the denomination's attitude toward family.

The Mormons demonstrated a proactive public relations stance. That is, they identified a problem and set communication goals to correct false perceptions. By contrast, reactive public relations is limited to a response to public criticism or challenge. The proactive attitude enables the congregation or denomination to control the issue rather than be controlled by it. More importantly, a proactive approach ensures that the church is always abreast of the views and changes in the community.

The constant goal of public relations is control of the image of church, its teachings, and its public views presented through the media, particularly through news accounts. Image here does not mean something false, but rather a portrayal which accurately depicts the gospel message, the nature and teaching of the church, church members, the religious life, or the role of religion itself. Whether working closely with the media or by creating its own content, religious public relations activities fall into four broad categories: corporate communication, counseling, press relations, and public advocacy.

Corporate communication

The first task involves use of external and internal communication to help the church understand itself and to communicate the church to those outside. In the ideal, public relations is a management function, one which allows the communications expert to participate in decision-making. One of the common frustrations of religious public relations people is that they are excluded from key decision-making but called into control the damage that could have been avoided.

Internally, this may take the form of a newsletter or part of the newspaper and broadcast content, and in essence it explains the church to its members and employees. The focus may be narrowly aimed at employees or clergy, or it may be aimed at a broader group of co-religionists. Externally, this involves planning, developing, and implementing media campaigns which present the church and the scripture to everyone within reach of the media. The content may range from programs to explain a pastoral letter, through seasonal projects to bring lapsed members back to church, to efforts to evangelize. Whatever the specific goal, the public relations campaign seeks to explain some aspect of the teachings of the church and to project an accurate image.

Disaster strategies prepare the church leadership for the inevitable disaster: major fire, clergy with AIDS, choirmaster who absconds with the Easter collection. Such preparation enables the leaders to think the problem through outside the heat of the moment and prepare a statement which reflects the theology and serves the needs of the audience. Disaster plans also allow the leadership to identify the spokesperson well in advance to avoid the confusion of too many voices.

Long-term strategy also builds or refines or corrects an image or message. To invite people to its churches, the Wisconsin Evangelical Lutheran Synod built a major event around the theme "Come to the WELS." A well-executed campaign, this involved every media aspect from bumper stickers to ads and billboards. The media blitz supported an extended effort by each congregation to invite and welcome fallen-away members and everyone else.

Counseling

This task involves advising the pastor, rabbi, or denominational leadership about public issues, church positions and image, and possible responses. Most often, counseling helps church or synagogue formulate immediate responses to current events as part of a crisis plan. Counseling also includes strategic planning for church responses to developing public issues and enduring problems. Public opinion research about the church is the research base for developing programs to correct distortions in the image and enlarge limited perceptions. A skilled public relations unit can prepare officials for press conferences, help focus attention on the desired message, and generally improve presentations for all media.

Press relations

Broadly defined, press relations is "the planned effort to influence public opinion through good character and responsible performance, based on mutually satisfactory two-way communication."[17] In this work with the public, church communication faces five major problems:

1. The intangible nature of many religious activities.
2. The sacred nature of many activities, which requires a dignified approach.[18]
3. The problem of showing the practical worth of religious values.
4. The problem of interpreting a program that follows a more-or-less traditional pattern.
5. The difficulty of knowing at which level to project ideas so that they will appeal to people of all ages.[19]

Another organizational concern is access to the pastor or religious leader who can speak to an issue. Here, structure becomes exceptionally important. Research indicates that the Catholic Church gets a disproportionately large amount of coverage in newsmagazines and major newspapers.[20] Andrew Greeley has argued that this is because Catholics are actually great theater with quaint titles, garb, rituals, and fierce internal battles. Another reason is that Catholics have clearly identified leaders in each diocese, and those leaders have public relations offices. Moreover, the structure creates official spokesmen from pope to local bishop, who are authorized to speak for the church. Congregational faiths like the Southern Baptists or Assemblies of God have no such counterparts.

Press offices, nonetheless, have become a common part of each denomination's headquarters. The National Council of Churches established its public relations office in 1950, because its primary communication was through the media. Lutherans produce their own world news

17. Cutlip and Center, *Effective Public Relations*, 17.
18. Appropriate dignity is a critical concern, because every aspect of a public act communicates. The Dean of St. Paul's Cathedral in London sent a very odd message, for example, when he parachuted from the cathedral steeple to make a point and attract the young. See Kotler, *Marketing for Nonprofit Organizations*, 392.
19. Cutlip and Center, *Effective Public Relations*, 484.
20. Hart and Turner, "Religion and the Rhetoric of the Mass Media," 256–75.

service from Switzerland and make it available to the press as part of their work. In many denominations, the church press is produced by a press office or office of communication. Many religious newspapers and magazines, however, are privately owned and operated, and they take considerable professional pride in their journalistic autonomy. National Catholic News Service has taken great pains to avoid any public relations work in order to establish itself as an autonomous news service focussing on Catholic news. The U.S. Catholic Conference has a separate press office for public relations.[21]

The press office provides a stream of information about potentially newsworthy events and a point of access for journalists. Access increases the likelihood of news coverage and the probability of accurate reporting. Most importantly, it demonstrates that the church is concerned about its role in community life, about being open. For the news media, the public relations unit is both a constant source for reliable information and a simple means of reaching the proper official or agency. During the pope's 1987 visit, the U.S. Catholic Conference supported a computerized press center at Marquette University which provided instant on-line access for the press to official texts, "backgrounders," press releases, press advisories. Wire services and newspapers used the press center to feed their computers. In major metropolitan areas, commercial public relations services provide similar on-line services to media for churches and other institutions.

A press officer who establishes a working relationship with reporters is also a source for articles on aspects of the church other than the purely institutional or potentially embarrassing. Press offices also evaluate the work of individual reporters and correct errors or distortions.

Public advocacy

The fourth task involves activities—from pastoral letters and church commissions to political lobbying and demonstrations—which seek to affect laws and policies on behalf of the public good. In advocacy, the church stays abreast of legal and political actions in communications, as in other issues, and clearly states its case, publicly and privately. Whether ensuring public access channels to cable franchise, testifying against pornography, or lobbying for specific language in bills, public relations helps to fulfill its responsibility as a major institution and a "corporate citizen."

21. During the 1987 papal visit, NCNS refused to allow the USCC press office to use downtime on the wire service to distribute "backgrounders," press releases, and press advisories on the visit, even though editors wanted the material. (The writer was a participant in the discussions.)

The church is one of the few remaining voices for the public good amidst the special interest voices, and it needs high quality public relations to make its voice heard and its message understood. Public advocacy is particularly important in the area of communication law; few others have a moral view rooted in the right of individuals to communicate and recognize the potential for social sin in communication.

Lobbying on behalf of children's television began for the United Church of Christ within its communication office. Peggy Charon has spearheaded the effort for over a decade, challenging misleading food advertising during cartoon hours on Saturdays, violence in children's programming, and a host of related issues. The U.S. Catholic Conference commissioned a handbook for citizens reviewing local cable franchises. Interdenominational groups have taken up the problems of broadcast regulation and dial-a-porn services.

Yet, in its public witness, the church is called to argue on behalf of the common good in the following issues:

1. Defend the freedom of the press, particularly the religious press, against any governmental intrusions.
2. Defend the right of people to accurate information.
3. Defend the right of religious groups to comment on public issues.
4. Guarantee public access to cable systems and representative community control.
5. Point out the moral issues of media-promulgated consumerism and oppression by control.
6. Protect the public from pornography, particularly when it is accessible to the young, degrading to women, and blatantly promulgated.
7. Protect the weak and powerless in telecommunications legislation, such as telephone costs or Third World access to satellite orbital parking places.

Advocacy on such issues completes the circle. Public relations provides the expertise to use media for church communication goals—evangelization, public opinion, dialogue with the faithful and the community. Media's crucial role in modern society, which requires church public relations, also requires church advocacy in order to prevent it from being used against the best interests of the audience.

BIBLIOGRAPHY

Cutlip, Scott M. and Allen H. Center, *Effective Public Relations*. 5th ed. Englewood Cliffs, NJ: Prentice-Hall, 1982.
De Lodzia, George, "Managing Survival Is a Public Relations Paradox."

Pp. 46–49 in *The Challenge of Modern Church-Public Relations.* Syracuse, NY: Syracuse University Continuing Education, 1972.

Dulles, Avery, "The Church Is Communications." *Catholic Mind* 69 (Oct. 1971): 7.

――――, *The Reshaping of Catholicism: Current Challenges in the Theology of Church.* San Francisco: Harper & Row, 1988.

Greif, Edward L., *The Silent Pulpit: A Guide to Church Public Relations.* New York: Holt, Rinehart and Winston, 1964.

Hart, Roderick and Kathleen Turner, "Religion and the Rhetoric of the Mass Media." *Review of Religious Research* (Summer 1980): 256–75.

Hyer, Marjorie, "The Office of Communication for the United Church of Christ." Pp. 82–85 in *The Church and Communication Arts.* Washington, D.C.: U.S. Catholic Conference, 1960.

Johnson, Phillip, Norman Temme, and Charles Hushaw, *Telling the Good News.* Saint Louis: Concordia Publishing House, 1962.

Leidt, William E., *Publicity Goes to Church.* Greenwich, CT: Seabury Press, 1959.

Moberg, David, *The Church as a Social Institution.* 2d ed. Grand Rapids: Baker Book House, 1984.

Papal Commission on the Means of Social Communication, *Communio et Progressio.* Available in *Documents of Vatican II.* Ed. Austin Flannery. Grand Rapids: Wm. B. Eerdmans, 1984.

SUGGESTIONS FOR FURTHER READING

Craig, Floyd, *A Christian Communicators Handbook.* Nashville: Broadman Press, 1977.

Kotler, Philip, *Marketing for Nonprofit Organizations.* Englewood Cliffs, NJ: Prentice-Hall, 1982.

National Catholic Welfare Office, *The Church and Communications Arts.* Washington, D.C.: The United States Catholic Conference, 1960.

Reagan, Michael, ed., *The Challenge of Modern Church-Public Relations.* Syracuse, NY: Syracuse University Continuing Education, 1972.

Religious Public Relations Council, *Religious Public Relations Handbook for Local Congregations.* 4th ed. Gladwyne, PA: The Religious Public Relations Council, Inc., 1988.

Swann, Charles E., *The Communicating Church.* Atlanta: Office of Media Communications of The Presbyterian Church in the U.S., 1981.

Part III

Ethical Issues

10

Religion's Role in the Media Reform Movement

Elizabeth Thoman, CHM, with Ira Rifkin

Institutional religion has sought to develop professional approaches to media almost since the dawn of the modern communications age, creating denominational news services, newspapers, audio visual departments, and radio and television programming in an effort to compete with the mainstream media for the public's attention.

Nor have the latest advances in communications been ignored. With the advent of modems that allow personal computer owners to electronically talk with each other, denominations have established computer networks such as Presbynet, UNCOMM Teletalk, the United Church Christnet and Lutheran RELIGION-ONLINE so members could exchange news and information.

There is another side of institutional religion's involvement in communications, however, one that has been less obvious to the average media consumer. This is the values-based reform movement that has challenged the very structure and intent of mass media as an institution in society.

As far back as the advent of the Communications Act of 1934, religious leaders expressed concern over whether broadcasters would serve the public good or merely their own commercial interests. Not until the 1960s, however, did this reform movement begin to take hold as media joined the list of institutions called to explain themselves during that era of increased public scrutiny and reflection.

The print media has also been criticized for tending toward superficiality, excluding minority and alternative viewpoints and pandering to its readers with excessive sensationalism. But film and particularly television have been the primary focal points of the movement because of their pervasiveness and powerful ability to subtly manipulate the emotions of their audiences.

In 1964 the Office of Communication of the United Church of Christ joined in the landmark and ultimately successful effort to challenge the license of a Jackson, Mississippi, television station on the grounds that its programming was blatantly racist and discriminatory.

Another strategy adopted by religious activists involved stockholder resolutions. Citing the need for corporate responsibility, activists tried to dissuade companies from supporting television programs that stereotyped people and to convince them to implement affirmative action policies in TV advertising.

And in the early 1970s, the Media Action Research Center was created by a number of mainline church leaders to develop media education materials and promote their use in youth and religious education programs. Its most successful projects were "Television Awareness Training," an adult workshop process, and "Growing with Television," a Sunday school curriculum program.

Of course, the media reform movement also gained important impetus outside the sphere of institutional religion. Parents in a Boston suburb—fired by the growing realization that violence and hard-sell commercials on television were teaching their children more than they wished for them to learn—banded together in 1968 to form Action for Children's Television (ACT). ACT's petition to the Federal Communications Commission to limit commercial advertising during children's programming drew an unprecedented one hundred thousand letters of support, mostly from parents, and forced broadcast executives to take note of the growing dissatisfaction with policies that unabashedly exploited audiences of all ages.[1]

Meanwhile, attorney John F. Banzhaf III asked a New York television station for free equal time under the Fairness Doctrine to respond to the claims of cigarette advertisers. In 1969 Congress passed the Public Health Cigarette Smoking Act that banned cigarette advertising from television on the grounds that media licensed in the public interest should not be promoting products that the Surgeon General had determined to be unhealthy.[2]

Others, including the National Parent-Teacher Association and the National Black Media Coalition, the National Organization for Women, and the Grey Panthers, also joined the effort, each seeking to force broadcasting executives to pay more attention to the needs of their individual constituencies and to stop acting as if society was composed of willing blocs of consumers waiting to be served up to advertisers.

1. Brown, *Keeping Your Eye on Television*, 57.
2. Brown, *Keeping Your Eye on Television*, 57.

WHY REFORM?

To regard TV-watching as the new American ritual has become so widely accepted a premise that to repeat it is to state a cliché. Yet like most clichés, it is based in solid fact.

According to Nielsen Media Research, adult American men watch an average of three hours and fifty-nine minutes of television each day. Adult women stay glued to the tube even longer. They watch for an average of four hours and fifty-three minutes. Teenagers watch for three hours and twenty minutes and young children ages three to eleven, the most impressionable age grouping, watch for three hours and forty-three minutes.[3]

And what is it they watch? In a word, entertainment. And too often to keep viewers entertained (and watching) that means action and violence of the physical, emotional, and spiritual varieties. Dr. George Gerbner, dean of the Annenberg School of Communications at the University of Pennsylvania, summarizes the problem this way:

> For the past 17 years, at least, our children grew up and we have all lived with a steady diet of about 16 entertaining acts of violence (two of them lethal) in prime time every night, and probably dozens if not hundreds more for our children every weekend. We have been immersed in a tide of violent representations that is historically unprecedented and shows no real sign of receding. Humans threaten to hurt or kill, and actually do so, mostly to scare, terrorize, and impose their will upon others. Symbolic violence carries the same message. . . Violence as a scenario of social relationships reflects the structure of power in society and tends to cultivate acceptance of that structure. . . It is clear that women, young and old people, and some minorities rank as the most vulnerable to victimization on television.[4]

That all this has an impact on the people that watch it has also been so widely accepted that it, too, is a cliché. Ever since the 1950s, Congressional hearings and presidential commissions have compiled and released evidence of the negative effects on society of gratuitous TV violence.

However, television programming has other subtle impacts that, in the long run, may be even more influential on human attitudes and behavior. William F. Fore, Assistant General Secretary for Communications of the NCC, calls them TV's "central myths."

They include:

(1) "The fittest survive," and in the world of TV, "the fittest are not lower-class, non-white Americans."

3. Cf. Fore, *Television and Religion*, 16–17.
4. Gerbner, *Gratuitous Violence and Exploitative Sex*, quoted in Fore, *Television and Religion*, 140.

(2) "Power and decision making start at the center and move out," a notion that is contradicted by, among other sources, the Declaration of Independence, which states that government derives its power from the people.

(3) "Happiness consists of limitless material acquisition," giving property rights the nod over human rights.

(4) "Progress is an inherent good," making it hard to say enough is enough or to consider the price society pays for these "advances."

(5) "There is a free flow of information," a myth that leads to "the illusion of media independence [obscuring] the existence of propaganda and censorship. . . Radical, even non-establishment, points of view have almost no opportunity to find expression in mass media, especially television."[5]

In short, the mass media, led by television, create an image of the world and of society that is, from the standpoint of the media reform movement, fragmentary at best, destructive of the values that nourish and sustain society at worst. At the very least, the media reform movement argues, consumers should be aware of the messages conveyed by the media.

WHAT SORT OF REFORM?

The values-based media reform movement is grounded in an ethic that is at once Judeo-Christian, self-actualizing, and liberating. Its intent is to bring fresh, critical insight to bear on such questions as:

How are media decisions made?
Are there any limits to artistic or commercial expression?
How do we deal with material we find objectionable?
How can media enhance the human condition?
How does media impact or influence the kind of society we want our children to grow up in?

The objective is to help people separate what they consider positive about the mass media from what they consider negative and to give them the tools to initiate the sort of change they want to occur within both the mass media system and their own participation in it.

Movement values include:

Concern for family and justice.
Equal access to the media for all as an aspect of justice.

5. Fore, *Television and Religion*, 64–66.

The dignity of the individual.
The value of diversity, ethnic and otherwise.
The right of children to be children, that is allowing them to explore and learn, protected from crass commercialism.

In a very real sense, the movement for values-oriented media is part of the consistent ethical approach championed by those in the liberal wings of the Roman Catholic and Protestant worlds who see the social order as a single, complex fabric of interconnected threads, each of which contributes to the overall texture.

Before we can properly use the tools of media, we need to be aware of what they are and what we want from them. And we need to know how to express—and create—the desired result. This is the value of media awareness education, which helps consumers to identify the techniques and languages used by the media to convey information and construct an image of reality, to understand the influence of media and to enable people to produce their own media products.[6]

But the values-based media reform movement is concerned with far more than merely altering the content of mainstream media, as significant an achievement as that might be. Its focus is not what the Rev. John Pungente, Director of Programs at the Jesuit Communications Project in Toronto, Ontario, has labeled the "innoculation theory."[7] This theory holds that media is essentially bad, and such people, especially the young, must be taught to resist its evil influence. Instead, what the values-based media reform movement is most concerned with is empowering people to be "proactive" participants in creating the media environment that permeates the culture.

The problem is not only that the popular media's content is vapid, but that audiences have been socialized to passively consume media. Viewers have been taught to consume TV by the clock, rather than by the program. Most people do not turn on their sets because they want to watch a specific program. They turn them on just to pass the time.

The media awareness movement, however, seeks a society that is educated to make choices, to browse, if you will, through the media library, to be aware of individual needs and how media can—or cannot—satisfy them. "When you flip the channel, where and why do YOU stop?" asks media theologian George Conklin.[8]

If audiences begin to think of media consumption as less an automatic

6. Pungente, *Getting Started on Media Education*, 17.
7. Quoted by Greer, "Putting the Mass Media into Our Classrooms," *Toronto Star*, 17 Oct. 1987.
8. Conklin, "Find Your Video Values," 16.

function and more an act of intention, then the very nature of the media environment itself will change.

This is not to ignore the accountability of those who create the images and the stories of popular media, or not to ignore the capitalistic economy that drives the entire media industry. But the issue of media's influence in our lives is not resolvable by placing blame or pointing fingers. Viewers make choices, too. And those choices send a message to media owners and producers.

In the vicious cycle that is commercial mass media, the only entry point for effective, long-range change without censorship is the consumer. The signs are growing that mass media is the next arena for a values-based consumer movement.

MEDIA & VALUES MAGAZINE: THE PAST

Seeing the potential for the positive in media and putting communications in its proper context are hallmarks of *Media & Values* magazine, a staunch exponent of the growing values-based media reform movement. Since 1977 it has struggled along on a shoestring budget, operating out of an overcrowded apartment-cum-office situated in a lower-middle-class minority neighborhood of Los Angeles. The magazine is very much a cause, and its offices reflect that attitude. Walls—that is, what little have not been blocked by file cabinets and piles of books and magazines—are covered with inspirational notes, posters, and cartoons intended to keep the magazine's largely volunteer and part-time staff from caving in to the magnitude of the task *Media & Values* has set out for itself.

If one were to trace *Media & Values's* religious roots to their tap, the Second Vatican Council of 1962–65 convened by Pope John XXIII to renew the life and structure of the Catholic church in the context of the latter half of the twentieth century would soon emerge. Vatican II opened the church to ecumenical contacts, new forms of worship, and increased lay participation. It also loosened the reins that previously had kept priests and sisters under tight control.

This newfound freedom in the church, coupled with events in the larger society, produced a generation of socially involved church people who marched for civil rights, worked in voter registration projects, publicly agitated for the ordination of women, and spoke out against corporate greed. It also led to a new emphasis on church involvement in media, one more aspect of the church's commitment to the modern world.

All this had a profound effect on me as I watched the church changing, becoming more open and progressive. As a young nun, I taught English and journalism and worked with TeleKETICS Films at the Franciscan Communications Center in Los Angeles. Then, in 1976, while attending the University of Southern California's Annenberg School of Communications, I received a small grant from the Lilly Endowment to start the National Sisters Communications Service. The purpose was to help usher Catholic women's orders into the media age by teaching them how to write press releases, prepare radio spots, create print ads, and the like.

At USC, one of my courses was communications and social values, where we discussed at length the impending breakthrough in media technology—the advent of the personal computer, cable TV, portable video—and their eventual impact on family life, education, leisure, and the workplace.

Excited by the challenging ideas presented in these discussions, I decided to share these concepts with other sisters, with priests, and with lay leaders. Through religious education programs, youth ministries, and family renewal events in thousands of churches and schools, they were struggling to help individuals and families find meaning and purpose in a contemporary society heavily influenced by media. The result was *Media & Values*. The first issue was, in reality, a class project for that seminar.

From the beginning, *Media & Values* has sought to be a visual magazine, designed for easy reading. The people it was intended for—religious professionals in education, youth work, and pastoral ministry—lead incredibly busy lives and are inundated with things to read. The magazine also needed to stand out from the usual run of cause-related newsletters, which generally lack a graphics approach in favor of "wall-to-wall" typography. Boring people does not move them to action, and *Media & Values*'s audience, given the excess of causes in the world that cry out for immediate attention, had to be convinced that media activism was an issue worthy of consideration.

The first issue of *Media & Values*, all twelve pages of it, reflected the emphasis on display as well as a "convince me" line-up of articles. The front cover pictured a TV antenna atop a church steeple, and carried a quote from Pope Paul VI: "If religious . . . wish to be a part of modern life and also be effective in their apostolate, they should know how the media work upon the fabric of society and also the technique of their use . . . Indeed, without this knowledge, an effective apostolate is impossible in a society which is increasingly conditioned by the media."[9]

The back cover offered definitions of common media terms, including such basics as "mass media," "cable television," and "network feed." The

9. Appeared on the front cover of *Media & Values* 1 (1978).

need for such basic definitions was indicative of the little information on media that had previously been available to most members of religious organizations.

In between were short items about using audio cassettes in visiting the sick and building community in a public housing project through a low-watt radio station. The feature article was excerpted from a speech I had given that spring to the National Catholic Education Association. Entitled "I Hate It, But I Love It; Television and Listerine," the article explored the challenge of media education for those in religious ministry and noted:

> We complain that advertising is turning us into a consumer society, but are we doing anything to educate young people to understand how media seduces them into believing that happiness comes from brushing with Ultrabrite, keeping spots from their glasses and joining the Pepsi generation? Is anybody doing anything about this?
>
> Take note of two facts: 1) Catholic schools proclaim, every year, they are "different where it counts." 2) A majority of American Catholic sisters and their congregations are still committed to education.
>
> That's a lot of teacher-power and a lot of opportunity to mobilize effective media education, not just for elementary and secondary students; but through the parish school, adult programs and religious education, a chance to reach parents and adults. They, like anyone over 35 who can remember when there wasn't television, are still reeling from the information and communications explosion that has shattered forever the smaller, quieter world into which they were born.[10]

Although significantly modified today to be more inclusive of other faiths, this graphic approach and philosophical ideal of media awareness remain the quarterly publication's trademark.

Those first few years were one long, protracted struggle as *Media & Values* sought to find its voice and pay its bills. (The magazine still accepts no advertising and depends entirely on subscriptions, donations, and grants). By late 1981 the masthead no longer carried the subhead "A Resource Newsletter of the National Sisters Communications Service." In its place was "A Quarterly Review of Media Issues and Trends." That change occurred when NSCS evolved into the Center for Communications Ministry, a move intended to broaden its training base beyond Catholic women. After just two years, however, it became clear that CCM was unable to financially sustain itself. In the fall of 1983, the Center announced it would close at the end of the year. *Media & Values* would cease to exist along with all other Center training and resource projects.

10. Thoman, "I Hate It But I Love It: Television and Listerine," 6.

But like the proverbial phoenix, the publication miraculously survived its near-demise. Attending the annual December gathering of the North American Broadcast Section of the World Association for Christian Communications (NABS-WACC), I encountered a number of primarily Protestant communication executives who expressed concern that the magazine was ending. They formed a "Friends of *Media & Values*" committee, explored a number of options, and within a week created a funding pool to purchase the publication under the aegis of the Media Action Research Center, the same organizational umbrella that had developed the highly acclaimed "Television Awareness Training."

With MARC's involvement, Methodist, Episcopal, Lutheran, Church of the Brethren, Mennonite, United Church of Canada, Unitarian Universalist, and other faith groups came into the picture. Catholic sponsorship continued along with participation by the American Jewish Committee.

Practically overnight, *Media & Values* went from being a nearly moribund publication to one with an international, interfaith perspective and reputation. Over the years nearly one hundred additional groups, ranging from the YWCA to the National Black Media Coalition, came aboard, too, as co-sponsors to help finance and distribute particular thematic issues on such topics as racism or militarism in the media, media handling of ethnicity, advertising and consumerism, and violence and sexual violence in the media.

MEDIA AND SOCIAL ANALYSIS

The magazine's current success, however, has come only after a slow evolution in philosophy and methodology since the activist heyday of the sixties and seventies.

In the early 1980s media education fell into disfavor as the mood of the nation changed. In Washington, Department of Education funding dried up with the Reagan Administration's budget cuts. Around the nation, secular reform groups lost income and moved on to other issues.

At *Media & Values*, a mood of self-reflection set in. With the emergence of home video, personal computers, MTV and ever-more-sophisticated media marketing, it was clear that some form of media awareness education would be useful for families, especially those with children. But what approach would be most effective?

Much writing, thinking, and discussing of various approaches took place as we looked at the methodology behind social causes, such as the peace movement, and consciousness movements, such as those around nutrition and physical fitness. A breakthrough came with the connection to social analysis, a systemic approach to problem-solving developed by Brazilian educator Paulo Freire and liberation theologian Juan Luis Segundo.[11] Popularized in the United States by various peace and justice efforts, it seemed to offer a powerful framework for empowering individuals and families to both take charge of their own media usage and to promote change in the larger media culture.

In the fall of 1985, *Media & Values* made a major editorial shift to incorporate a social analysis approach, giving the publication a strong framework for effecting media awareness education through churches, schools, youth programs, and family agencies. Social analysis identifies four "moments" in problem-solving an issue: awareness, analysis, reflection, and action. What that means in terms of magazine format is that each issue of *Media & Values* focuses on a specific media concern. As one issue stated:

> The way we see a problem determines how we respond to it. Looking at an issue through social analysis allows us to broaden our vision and transcend our internal blinders. Depending on the problems at hand, working through an issue using social analysis may take hours—or months. In some ways analysis never stops because even when we organize for action, that experience will lead us to new awareness which in turn requires another level of analysis, reflection and action.[12]

Each issue features a lead article followed by supporting pieces that focus the reader's awareness on the particular topic in question, analyzing it from various perspectives—economic, political, historical, legal, and cultural.

Recent issues titles include:

"Violence and Sexual Violence in the Media"
"Rock and Its Roll"
"Wide World of Media Sports"
"Advertising and the Consumer Economy"
"Racism in the Media"
"Militarism: The Media Connection"
"Tuning in to Television: How the Magic Bow Shapes Our Views, Vision
   and Culture"
"Home Video: The Revolution in Choice"
"Ethnic Diversity: Challenging the Media"

The twenty-four-page issue on militarism in the media, for example, led off with an article about a resurgence of pro-military sentiment in the

11. Freire, *Pedagogy of the Oppressed*; Segundo, *Liberation of Theology*.
12. Thoman, "Blueprint for Respons-ability," 13.

United States in the years since the end of the Vietnam era. That was followed by essays on how stereotyping the enemy masks feelings of fear, how American media covers the Soviet Union, and a review of the hype that surrounded the TV mini-series "Amerika." Additional articles dealt with war toys, an assessment of the impact of war movies, and how the military markets itself to young people, particularly minorities and the poor.[13] The contributors to this issue were researchers and media practitioners, most of them out of the academic and religious/social justice worlds, people in influential positions writing for people who have "formative influence" as leaders and program planners in schools, churches, and other institutions involved in conveying values. Their language bends over backward to avoid being "churchy" in an effort to be even more inclusive and to avoid being associated with religious institutions who in past have often been oppressive stumbling blocks in the way of change.

In keeping with the social analysis model, the magazine followed those articles with short pieces written by a regular stable of columnists who reflect and prescribe action that might be taken to deal with media issues. One columnist addressed his remarks to youth workers. Another placed the subject in the context of racial minorities. A third gave pastors tips on how to incorporate the subject into sermons, and a fourth spoke of militarism in the media in relation to women. Throughout the issue were sidebar "Re:Action" articles providing questions and group activities to help teachers and leaders build effective classroom or discussion processes. "Getting Involved," a back cover feature was devoted to the efforts of Canadians Concerned About Violence in Entertainment to counter the violence inherent in militaristic toys. The point was to show an example of grassroots action, the fourth "moment" in the social analysis model. A list of some two-dozen resources—films, videos, books, and organizations—to help readers deal with media militarism rounded out the issue.

MEDIA & VALUES: THE FUTURE

When MARC took *Media & Values* under its wing in January 1984, the magazine had a circulation of one thousand, no bank balance, two full-time employees (myself as Executive Editor and Associate Editor Rosalind Silver), and a handful of dedicated volunteers and student interns. In early 1988 *Media & Values* had a circulation of about three thousand, with bulk sales of single issues for use in college courses or professional semi-

13. *Media & Values* 39 (Spring 1987).

nars often totalling several thousand more. The issue on violence and sexual violence in the media, produced in conjunction with the NCC, has sold more than twelve thousand copies.

Money, while still extremely limited, had begun to trickle in somewhat more steadily and in larger amounts. (In 1983 the magazine's operating budget was about $75,000; in 1988 the budget was set at $246,000, about 40 percent of it coming from subscriptions and sales, the remainder from grants and fund-raising). And plans are being formulated for *Media & Values*'s second decade.

What is being proposed is a national, not-for-profit media organization—the Center for Media and Values—that would assume a philosophy leadership role in the reform movement for media awareness. As envisioned, the Center would serve as a coordinating agent for individuals and organizations nationwide wanting to explore and exchange common concerns about media. An important aspect would be to serve as a bridge between the religious and secular communities; between media consumers and media producers; and between media researchers and professional practitioners in education, youth work, family social services, and family counseling to promote technology and programming that enhance human growth and development.

Partnership—the need to work together to achieve desired results— would be one of the Center's foremost concerns as it works to develop a network of media education and reform movement individuals and groups. Functioning as a "voice of values," the Center would develop conferences and training programs, provide print and electronic resources for media education in homes, schools, communities, and religious organizations, and seek to build a constituency that cares deeply about the socialization that takes place in the media environment.

The long-range goal of *Media & Values* is not to put out a magazine, but to create a media literate society by the year 2000. When the Center is fully operational the magazine will take its place as the Center's ongoing periodical, but it will be only one benefit of membership in the Center.

A step toward realization of the Center concept was the formation in early 1988 of a *Media & Values* Speakers Team—seven men and women from around the U.S. and Canada—who are available as keynoters, panelists, or seminar presenters to help spread the movement's message. Development of the center is crucial if the reform movement for a values-oriented media is truly to become a recognized public policy question addressed by the grassroots as well as the media elite.

How do you get people to act? Where's the link between what is put in the pages of *Media & Values* and what can happen in a church basement or a classroom in Lawrence, Kansas, or Nashville, Tennessee? The answer is in a network of people around the nation with resources that motivate others to act. That's why the Center is so important.

CAN IT WORK?

Putting forth plans by no means insures success, and after a decade in the trenches it is clear that the movement for values-oriented media still has a long way to go. A readiness on the part of growing numbers of people to take up the issue can be discerned. At best, though, the movement is still in its infancy, and at times it seems premature to say even that much.

Perhaps it's because media issues do not mobilize people like hunger or disease, or because media touches the intimate part of people's lives (self-identity, self-esteem, family and societal relationships) where change is slow.

Perhaps the movement, and *Media & Values* in particular, has been reticent to toot its own horn and reluctant to use its insider knowledge of how media works to exploit opportunities and gain a wider public voice. Part of that comes from being sensitive to the indulgent exploitation evident in much of the mainstream media and a strong desire to avoid falling into the same trap. Part of it also stems from the heritage that hampers most movements in the religious sector: the willingness to put up with shoestring budgets and the lack of organizational "savvy" that drives profit-making enterprises. Laura J. Lederer, Social Concerns Program Director of the L.J. and Mary C. Skaggs Foundation in Oakland, California, a philanthropic leader in the media reform movement, says fear over just whose values are being spotlighted also keeps the movement from going forward.

Private and corporate foundations are willing to give monies to media producers who work outside the mainstream media and to non-profit organizations developing hands-on programs for children and adults to give them practical knowledge of media. But they are hesitant about getting involved with the question of values because of the ambiguities and potential for conflict that the word conveys to many, Lederer says. "People don't want to face the issue of values because they're afraid it will not be their values that will be pushed."[14]

Still, there is a budding involvement of philanthropic organizations, such as the Skaggs Foundation in media reform, and that is a hopeful sign that the movement is on the verge of stepping onto the public stage in an

14. Telephone interview with Ira Rifkin, 20 May 1988.

effective manner. Still, Lederer believes it will be some time before a great many foundations make money available to any significant degree.

It takes a long time to get a movement going. One criticism of the media reform movement over the years is that it has had too short a vision. Media reform was expected to happen almost overnight, as if a letter-writing campaign would change everything, as if boycotting a product would turn the industry around. The strength of *Media & Values*, it seems to me, is that we recognize we're in there for the long haul. The mistakes that characterize the birth of any movement have been made, and *Media & Values* now has a consciousness-raising methodology that can work over the next decade.

In some ways, though, we will never have a completely enlightened media society. All we can do is keep raising the questions, just as it's done within the political and economic processes that continually need retooling. We must remember, that as Howard Beale in the movie "Network" implored, what is important is not to confuse real life with the illusion of real life.

BIBLIOGRAPHY

Brown, Les, *Keeping Your Eye on Television*. New York: The Pilgrim Press, 1979.
Conklin, George, "Find Your Video Values." *Media & Values* 40–41 (1987): 16–18.
Fore, William F., *Television and Religion: The Shaping of Faith, Values, and Culture*. Minneapolis, MN: Augsburg Publishing House, 1987.
Freire, Paulo, *The Pedagogy of the Oppressed*. New York: Herder and Herder, 1970.
Gerbner, George, *Gratuitous Violence and Exploitative Sex: What Are the Lessons?* New York: Study Committee of the Communications Committee of the National Council of the Churches of Christ in the U.S.A., 1984.
Greer, Sandi, "Putting the Mass Media into Our Classrooms." *Toronto Star,* 17 Oct. 1987.
Pungente, The Rev. John J., *Getting Started on Media Education*. London: Centre for the Study of Communication and Culture, 1985.
Segundo, Juan Luis, *The Liberation of Theology*. Maryknoll, NY: Orbis Books, 1976.
Thoman, Elizabeth, CHM, "Blueprint for Respons-ability." *Media & Values* 35 (1986): 12–14.
———, "I Hate It But I Love It: Television and Listerine." *Media & Values* 1 (1978): 5–7.

11

Journalistic Ethics: Can Fairness and Objectivity Be Achieved?

George E. Reedy

In the United States of the twentieth century, we have launched a quest to reach one of the most unattainable goals in the whole history of human thought. It is the establishment of an institution which will present the public with the facts and opinions they need to make prudent judgments on the management of our society but which will not bring to bear any value judgments on those facts and opinions. The theory behind this goal goes by the name of "objectivity"—a word which has taken on an aura of sanctity in our society.

So deeply embedded is the word in our consciousness that most Americans are startled over the discovery that objectivity in journalism is a relatively new concept. Its root can be traced back to the philosophers of the Enlightenment—Hobbes, Locke, Hume, Voltaire, and Diderot, among others—who postulated that nobody really knew "truth" and that society was the product of compromises among varying groups of people with different points of view. Before that era, human beings were generally convinced that they knew the truth with such certainty that it would be foolish to permit the publication of error. The new way of thinking led inevitably to a demand for the publication of "pure" facts to serve as a base for social judgment.[1]

These philosophers did not have an immediate impact upon the American press which was founded (chiefly in conjunction with job printing establishments) to advance partisan causes and which continued to do so, in varying degrees, right up to the middle of this century. But the philosophy of the Enlightenment did foster a popular belief that it was possible to give an account of an event that was so faithful to "what really happened" that it could not be disputed by any honest person. As this was

1. For an excellent intellectual analysis of the Enlightenment, see Gay, *The Enlightenment*.

assumed to be feasible–and as it was obviously a desirable practice in a pluralistic society—it became the socially approved standard for judging journalistic performance. This was muddled thinking and a far cry from the intentions of the philosophers. But this bothered neither journalists nor their readers. What they believed they were doing was substituting "real" truth for "official" truth. They were not troubled by the thought that "truth" and "objectivity" were two different things.

PARTISANSHIP AND SENSATIONALISM

The early American press was unabashed in its partisanship. Generally speaking, the so-called newspapers of the post-colonial era were little more than political tracts. The only verifiable facts they presented consistently were in the ads for rum and tobacco (below the Mason-Dixon line, add slaves)—the commodities which seem to have loomed largest in the minds of the early settlers. It was not until the period of the Civil War that newspapers in the U.S., as a whole, began to put any stress on accuracy. This was probably due to the market that the huge battles created for valid information. People wanted to know whether they had lost friends or relatives and whether their homes were threatened by the retreating and advancing armies of the North and the South.[2]

Since that period, the history of the American press has been a constant advance toward higher degrees of factual verification. Sheer fiction (such as the famous case in which Edgar Allan Poe sold a phony story to a Baltimore newspaper about a balloon crossing of the Atlantic[3]) gave way to accounts that at least spelled names and places correctly. The process has continued, so that the journalistic standards of the 1920s (my father's time) had become totally unacceptable when I entered the profession. The twenties were known as "the era of wonderful nonsense," and the sole criterion for the time and space granted to a story was its salability to the public at large. Newspapers were hawked on the streets, and a household had to be far removed from civilization not to hear the nightly cry: "Extry! Extry! Extry! Read all about it! Sex maniac loose in city!" Usually the sex maniac turned out to be a somewhat dubiously reported Peeping Tom. But that was not the fault of the police reporters who were the kingpins of

2. The history of the early American press is well documented in Kobre, *Development of the Colonial Newspaper;* Bleyer, *Main Currents in American Journalism*; and Mott, *American Journalism.*

3. For an account of this incident see Mankowitz, *Extraordinary Mr. Poe;* and Sinclair, *Edgar Allan Poe.*

journalism at that time. They were in a constant search for salacity and violence, and it was not too difficult to find either or both.

The urban reporters of that time were generally uneducated, with the exception of one or two "rewrite men" who took verbal accounts over the telephone and translated them into readable English. The newsmen who roved the streets were usually familiar with the territory from birth, as the major stories involved low-grade hoodlums with such sobriquets as Scarface Al, Greasy Thumb, Little Diony, and Golf Bag (whose bag held machine guns, not golf clubs), who had emerged from the same streets. These thugs had been hoisted incredibly into the ranks of millionaires by the passage of an act making the sale of alcoholic beverages illegal. No city journalist could last for any length of time without knowing a few thugs on a first-name basis.

There were, of course, journalists who did spend full time on the booze wars. They were known as "Sob Sisters," and their task was to cover sex scandals and high jinks among members of the upper class. Like their police counterparts, they were not above manufacturing some evidence, but they were paid chiefly for their ability to "needle" a relatively dull event into headline shockers. The outstanding example of the genre centered around the "Peaches" Browning case. Because the case leads to some basic understanding of the role of journalism in society, it is worth taking a look at the facts.

Peaches Browning was a teenage girl who had managed to marry a wealthy, middle-aged gentleman.[4] In 1927 she sued him for divorce, and for weeks it was almost impossible to find anything else in the American press. The public was fed a constant diet of the pet names which they called each other (Peaches and Daddy) and the games they played in the boudoir (punctuated by such phrases as "Woof! Woof! You're a goof!"). One New York newspaper known as the *Graphic* succeeded in obtaining one picture of Peaches in her negligee and another of Daddy in pajamas and pasted them together in what was labelled a "composograph"—supposedly alerting the reader to the fact that it was *not* an action shot. The whole episode is not one present day journalists boast about, and it is generally presented in journalism colleges as the prime example of "yellow" newspapering.

In justice to the Fourth Estate, it should be said that in the same year newspapers gave equal, if not greater, coverage to Lindberg's epoch-making solo flight across the Atlantic. But a more important point emerges

---

4. See Allen, *Only Yesterday*, 215–16.

from exploring why so much attention was paid to a sordid divorce case that would merit only tertiary play in the modern world. It is not enough to dismiss it as "sensational," as this merely means that many people were interested in it. The more interesting thought emerges from asking what there was about the Brownings that led to such press concentration.

There is a very obvious clue that appears when one puts the 1920s into historical context. It was a decade in which Americans were obviously reacting to two major developments. One was the impact of veterans returning from World War I, and the other was the influence of belt-line production. New methods of assembly spawned, among other things, cheap automobiles and easily available radios, which could be used by ordinary citizens without training or skills in electrostatics or complex machinery. Almost overnight, or so it seemed, a new world of wide mobility and communication opened to the American people, and it was bewildering indeed. A new social structure arose and with it new concepts of morals and manners.

One must be my age to have a feeling of the violent wrench all this meant. As a child, I heard the older men and women in my family devoting most of their conversation to the fallen moral standards of the era. The flapper, with her thigh-high skirt and her "boyish" bobbed hair, was under constant condemnation from my aunts, who had been reared to believe that the display of an instep was immoral and that womanly virtue required hair that hung down at least to the waist (but was seen in public only in the shape of a bun). My uncles hastened to agree, even though I had the impression that they were enjoying the new visibility of feminine charms. But there was nothing mild about their feelings on divorce. They had plenty of opportunity to express those feelings because the subject was on everyone's mind. I gathered from the conversations that before World War I a divorced woman was about one step above a hooker, and a divorced man was a little more comfortable socially but definitely not to be invited into one's home or introduced to one's daughter or sister.

The returning soldiers and the young women whom they "dated" had other ideas. They had been in contact with an alien culture in France, and the experience was more intoxicating than the rotgut booze dispensed by the bootleggers. There was even a song about the situation entitled "How 'Ya Gonna Keep 'Em Down on the Farm (After They've Seen Paree?)." Perhaps even more important was that they had lived in an atmosphere of "Eat, drink, and be merry for tomorrow you die!". That was not true for most of them. But it had engendered a spirit of snatching whatever enjoyment was available and departing when it was over. The public dialogue centered around divorce more than any other single subject that I heard discussed.

"Public dialogue" has become one of those phrases which is pronounced solemnly (pompously might be a better word) in contemporary conversation. It is generally assumed to be the equivalent of a debate under the Oxford rules. The reality is quite different. Public dialogue is what takes place in bars and at lunch stands, in homes over the coffee cups, in buses on the way to work. And the dialogue that counts is that which takes place among people who do not understand variable functions; averages, medians, and means; and regressive analysis. To discuss a social topic, they must have it presented to them in a personalized form. This is precisely what the press did in the Peaches Browning case. The principals were symbols which people could use to talk about something that was really on their minds.

NEW BREED OF JOURNALISTS

The era of the twenties has passed into history. It came to an end partially because a consensus on public morality was ultimately reached, and partially because the Great Depression more than blotted out the concerns of the time. With plants closing daily, with banks going bust like firecrackers, with soup lines lengthening, who cared about "Terrible John" Torrio or "Machine Gun" Jack McGurn? As far as the Fourth Estate was concerned, they vanished into limbo and with them went the boozy reporters who were so dramatically depicted in the Hecht-McArthur play *Front Page.* A new breed of journalist was required—men (with a trickle of women) who had enough education to understand economics and social crises. Unfortunately, a lingering impression remained that the press was still in the "hot scoop" days. Many of the criticisms that I now hear daily assume a type of newspaper that virtually disappeared nearly half a century ago.

The new breed which came in with the depression included people with a conscience. They were determined to present "significant" facts and to probe beneath the surface of events. They were literate, socially conscious, educated, and possessed of political ideas—sometimes liberal and sometimes conservative (the latter much more than is generally believed). Above all, they regarded themselves as practicing a profession which had a mission to give the public the facts so the American people could make intelligent judgments on the course the society should take. They were intent on making an "objective" presentation of the news that would satisfy reasonable people about the good faith of the American press. Their failure is worth studying because it affords insights into the nature of journalism itself.

The transition did not take place overnight. Newspapers such as the *Chicago Tribune* and the *New York Post* in the 1930s, 1940s, and early 1950s had a very distinctive point of view, and it was expressed in the news columns just as strongly—and probably more effectively—as on the editorial page. But such newspapers were looked upon by most of the profession as quirky and somewhat disreputable, an attitude that did not exist during my father's era when they were the norm. I entered the field with a very brief stint on a police beat in Philadelphia and then a transition to Congressional correspondent for the United Press. It was in the latter role that I encountered the difficulties which accompany any effort to give a "straight" account of what is happening. There also was laid the foundation for my present belief that objectivity is a myth, a concept which was defined by Ortega y Gasset as the delusion that we can see the world as it would be if we were not there to look at it.

Certainly, if anyone struggled to attain objectivity it was the United Press. This did not reflect virtue on the part of its managers but simply the fact that we were selling our service to all comers. The slightest dereliction from the straight and narrow path of impartiality could mean the loss of a client. What we put on our wires had to be inoffensive to both the "liberal" *Chicago Sun-Times* and the "conservative" *Indianapolis News*. Furthermore, we could not get by on "brighteners"—feature stories about children, dogs, and ceremonies which held the flag in due reverence. We had to cover hard, fast-breaking news in areas where the public was torn by emotional controversies. Before the war, this meant the fervid clashes between isolationists and interventionists; after the war, the communist spy investigations which culminated in the era of the late Senator Joseph McCarthy.

Walking this tightrope meant strict adherence to a system of rules. They were not codified but they were understood by everyone in the office, and any violation evoked the wrath of our top editors. Facts could be reported only when we had seen them ourselves or could clearly identify the person who gave them to us and explain the authority of our informant. (There was an occasional exception to this rule, but the only time I ever ignored it was when I had been given the story by a cabinet member.) We would accept anonymous information but use it only as a lead for finding facts that could be cited from a record. We were obligated to track down anyone who had been accused of wrongdoing and present "their side," and we had to be scrupulous in distinguishing between a charge made during a debate and a formal accusation which had consequences. Finally, the major canon was a flat prohibition of any value judgment other than the amount of space which an item deserved. That, of course, was modified somewhat by the amount of wire traffic on any given day. On Thursday, a news blockbuster was fortunate if it received four paragraphs; on Sunday the same item could command two columns of solid type.

As a set of rules, these appear at first glance to be unexceptional. Of course, they were not always followed rigidly. Human nature varies from person to person and there were always a few backsliders who would try to run a "fast one" in order to score a scoop over the Associated Press. In addition, it was impossible to handle all the traffic on a "hot news day" without a foot slipping from time to time. But on the whole we could claim without blushing that we were basing our reporting on the fundamentals above. And most of us discovered sooner or later that every single one of our canons would frequently operate to distort the facts, or to give unfair emphasis to one side of an argument, or to favor an unfounded claim on the part of a government bureaucrat. Let me run over a few examples.

The rule against accepting anonymous information (except announcements) was made-to-order for administrative heads who wanted to pull a fast one. It was far too easy for them to make announcements that could easily be refuted by a few conversations with their subordinates, who would, in turn, lose their jobs were it known that they had talked. Occasionally it was possible to pick up enough information to lead to facts and figures that would place the original announcement in perspective. But this was an exhaustive reportorial process which rarely bore fruit in time for the reader to associate it with the administrator's original claim. It was frustrating to put on the wire news items which we knew to be questionable but whose flaws could not be documented.

During World War II the rule against accepting anonymous sources was modified—primarily because the U.S. was dealing with other nations that were not as open in dealing with the press. The result was a continuing flow of "background" information from the war agencies—a practice which was apparently acceptable to our allies as long as it was not identified as "official" U.S. policy and could be kissed off by our Secretary of State (often with tongue in cheek) as "press speculation." The practice continued after the war ended with one additional modification—that there be an indication of the bureaucratic level of the source. Thus a "reliable source" meant someone who had been consistently dependable in the past; a "highly placed" source meant someone who attended important meetings; and an "unimpeachable source" meant a cabinet officer, the National Security Council Advisor, or the President himself. I have never known an instance in which the classifications were misused, despite the number of Washington correspondents who resent the necessity for using them. It is galling to hear a government official who has been leaking stories all over the city express surprise when those stories appear, and then to castigate the press for speculation. Some efforts have been made to kill the practice altogether, but they have been abortive. Too many important facts are available on no other basis.

The situation becomes even more delicate where accusations are involved. Most such stories can be suspended until there is clear-cut identification of some record which can be examined by other people. But occasionally a story comes along where an anonymous source must be taken very seriously. The outstanding exception is the "Deep Throat" source used by Woodward and Bernstein of the *Washington Post* in their exposé of the Watergate scandal.[5] Ben Bradlee, the *Post* editor, laid down a flat rule that anything coming from Deep Throat had to be confirmed by two other sources. Furthermore, this source was used largely to corroborate or kill suspicions aroused in the minds of the two reporters by examining evidence already on the record. Even so, the practice is still regarded as dangerous by most journalists with whom I have spoken.

The rule of tracking down the victim of an accusation and carrying his side of the story usually turns out to be a futility. The rule is still observed, but it does the person on the receiving end little good. A denial is never as strong as an accusation, as we discovered during the reign of Joe McCarthy. It serves its purpose only when the journalist is able to give some value judgments in the original story. I have a very burning memory of how McCarthy used this principle in his campaign to brand Owen Lattimore, a Johns Hopkins professor, as communist spy.

This happened during a hearing by a select committee set up to examine the McCarthy charges. The Wisconsin senator appeared before the group early one morning and announced that he was holding in his hand a letter written to the chief of the East Coast branch of the World War II Office of War Information by Lattimore, who was then chief of the West Coast OWI branch. This letter, according to the senator, ordered the East Coast branch to place its reliance for information about China on a group of Chinese who McCarthy alleged to be communists. We had become very skeptical of McCarthy's changes, but we could not get our hands on the letter. Finally, we wrote stories based solely on the McCarthy testimony, asking our desks to get hold of Lattimore as rapidly as possible.[6]

5. See Woodward and Bernstein, *All the President's Men.*
6. McCarthy's relationship with the press is well covered in Bayley, *Joe McCarthy and the Press.*

Eventually, McCarthy allowed us to get our hands on the letter, and we all raced for the press room where we made copies as fast as we could (this was before the photocopy era and they all had to be typed). When we sat down to study the letter, however, we could find no substantial evidence to back up the charge. The best that could be said was that Lattimore had recommended attention to a Chinese newspaper. This placed us in a genuine quandary. We could not say that ten or twelve journalists had looked at the letter and found virtually nothing in it. That would have been a value judgment. The alternative was to put it on the wire so newspapers could print it and the readers could judge for themselves. But the letter consisted of many more pages than could be printed by any newspaper at the time—a period when newsprint was at a premium. The result was a rash of stories which conveyed to the reader the impression that the McCarthy charge had a solid foundation. We could not present the simple fact that McCarthy's knowledge of communism was nil and this, like his other charges, involved little but rhetoric.

I had run into the same problems when I covered the House Unamerican Activities Committee hearings on Alger Hiss and Elizabeth Bentley. Here facts were presented, and the overwhelming probabilities are, that the people involved were guilty as charged. But those of us who sweated through the experience found it to be an ordeal, because the guilt was blown out of all proportion. This could have been handled easily had we been able to make a simple point. The committee was composed of Republicans and anti-New Deal Southern Democrats, and the hearings were held in an election year. To have pointed this out would have involved the use of value judgment and would have called into question our objectivity. Of course, there were "liberal" political magazines that made the point in editorials, but the only result was to find themselves branded as pro-communist. It was a period when things seemed to be out of control, and when it became perfectly apparent to me that the so-called standard of objectivity was a delusion—as Kierkegaard pointed out, an assumption that there could be thought without a thinker.

PLACING FACTS IN PERSPECTIVE

In the aftermath of the McCarthy era, the rules were changed by thoughtful journalists appalled at the confusion that had been created by so-called objectivity. This does not mean that journalists were granted a green light to shade the facts by pure opinion. But the modern-day correspondent does surround his facts with an effort to place them in perspective. This is not a simple matter, and it does open the temptation to substitute editorialization for factual presentation. But this, in my judgment, is still preferable to the situation that existed when I was a working journalist. Furthermore, a number of factors have entered into play which have resulted in a different type of newspaper. The high degree of partisanship which existed during the McCarthy era has been virtually abandoned. One can now read through the *Chicago Tribune* or the *Chicago Sun-Times* without forming any impression of their political leanings. The reign of such political giants as William Randolph Hearst, Colonel Robert R. McCormick, E. W. Scripps, and Roy Howard is over. Journalism today is a business proposition with only minor exceptions. The press has just about abdicated its role of political leadership.

There are a number of reasons for this development. First should be cited the inexorable laws of economics which have made it unprofitable in most cities to have more than two—and sometimes more than one— newspapers. Second is the rise of home delivery, with very few newspapers being sold on the streets outside of New York. I have not heard a newsboy shouting "extry" in more than forty years. Third is the advent of radio and television, which are both far superior to the printed press in feeding the public "spot" news. This means that in order to survive, print journalism must supply its readers with some perspective—something at which electronic journalist is not very successful.

When these factors are put together, it becomes obvious that newspapers cannot be overly partisan. The type of journalism which characterized the *Chicago Tribune* or the *New York Port* of thirty years ago would mean an offense to readers and a possible loss in circulation. There is no point in hanging a scoop on an opposition paper, as the opposition paper does not exist. The overall result is a bland impartiality leavened only by some distinctiveness in the few newspapers that are still individually owned—such as the *New York Times* or the *Washington Post*.

Unquestionably, the current situation has led to a tremendous improvement in the reporting of the news. The modern American press is unexcelled in its presentation of factual material. It can be criticized legitimately for its selection of the facts to be reported; for the emphasis it places upon some facts at the expense of the others; for its frequent failure to notice important social developments until they take a violent form. But an actual misstatement of fact that can be attributed to the journalist or the journalist's editor is a rarity. When such a misstatement does occur, it can usually be traced to a typographical error or to overly quick judgments made under incredible deadline pressures.

This is a difficult point for many Americans to swallow. The few instances of outright fraud that have occurred loom very large on the public horizon, and they always leave behind them the lingering feeling that if one such incident has been exposed there must be many others that have been successfully concealed. There is, of course, no answer to such an argument, as it is a classic instance of the double negative. An example is the case of Janet Cooke, a *Washington Post* reporter who won a Pulitzer prize in 1981 for a series of stories on the "dope scene" in the District of Columbia. Generally speaking, her work deserved the prize. But she included one fictitious story of an eight-year-old boy, identified only as "Jimmy," receiving a shot from his mother's boyfriend. The *Post* itself exposed the swindle and returned the Pulitzer prize.[7] This led to a re-examination by a large number of newspaper editors. A *New York Times* correspondent was forced to resign because he had fabricated an account of an atrocity in Northern Ireland, and the *New York Times* admitted that it had been duped by a free-lance writer who peddled a phony account of a trip to Cambodia with Khmer Rouge rebels.[8]

In each of these instances, the facts were made known by the same newspapers that had printed the original stories. In each instance, it was also obvious that the fraud had been due to careless editorial supervision rather than a belief that the newspaper itself would benefit. Procedures were tightened all over the country, and it is now highly unlikely (although obviously not impossible) that anything similar could happen again on any significant scale. At the very least, it should be apparent that fraudulent presentations are not a common practice. Nevertheless, a deeper distrust of the American press is revealed in every poll. Why? Why is it that the steps taken by journalism to clean up its act have been met with increasing skepticism? When we ask that question, the usefulness of my brief historical review will become apparent.

First, we must define the word "journalism" with somewhat greater precision than is normally used in casual conversation. For our purposes we shall consider it to be the daily presentation of factual accounts in an organized fashion by professionals who gather, process, and commit to print or to the airwaves what they regard as the significant events that have happened since the last presentation. Generally speaking, this is how most of the men and women who regard themselves as professional journalists think of their role. It is not, however, what most of the public regards as journalism in discussing the subject. The common understanding is that anything printed in a newspaper—other than the ads—is journalism, as is anything they see on television that is not clearly labelled entertainment. In other words, a political reporter such as Dave Broder, whose function is to tell his readers *what* is happening, is lumped together with William

7. The Janet Cooke incident is analyzed in Broder, *Behind the Front Page,* 309–12.
8. Broder, *Behind the Front Page,* 313.

Buckley, the columnist, whose function is to tell his readers *how* they should think. Most newspapers attempt to distinguish between the two functions, but the distinctions rarely sink in. As far as John Q. Citizen is concerned, "I read it in the *Milwaukee Journal* and you can't tell me that is not the press." In their divestiture of the trappings of political leadership, many newspapers have reduced their editorializing to approving endorsements of mothers, children, and dogs. What "red meat" they do feed to their audience is carried in the form of syndicated columns placed on what has come to be known as the "op ed" page. As a rule, they try to balance liberal and conservative writers, but for some reason the liberal readers seem to notice only the conservative columnists and vice versa.

Another clue to public distrust of the press can be found in a review of the state of journalism from my childhood. In those days, there were newspapers which were not only distrusted but absolutely hated. However, there was always at least one—and sometimes two—which were trusted absolutely. I was far too young to draw any conclusions from this phenomenon, but even then I noted with some bewilderment that the hatreds and the trusts varied from person to person. In the very Irish section in which I grew up, the *Chicago Tribune* was read as a form of gospel, but the *Daily News* was looked upon as production of the devil. It was many decades before I understood why. Colonel Robert McCormick, publisher of the *Tribune*, was an obsessive and rabid anglophobe, and his thinking matched perfectly the Gaelic prejudices of my playmates and their families. In my area of the city he was telling the truth, whereas the *Daily News* was covering up the machinations of King George to dominate the U.S. This, of course, was a grotesquely exaggerated viewpoint fed by the then-recent attainment of nationhood in Ireland. I have not encountered anything quite like it since. (One of my grammar school teachers actually opened every one of her classes with a recital of the tortures endured by her brother at the hands of the Sassenachs in a Dublin prison and closed by telling us that we could not trust our textbooks "because they are written by King George.") But I have found that the basic mental process which made the exaggeration possible is universal. To all of us, truth lies in our ideological commitments. The only definition of objectivity that I can find as valid is the publication of any set of biases that agrees with my set of biases.

The basic point, however, is that in the 1920s and the 1930s there was such a wide variety of newspapers available that every citizen could find at least one that was "objective" and "told the truth." In light of present-day publication, the range was tremendous. At one end of the spectrum in Chicago was the *Tribune*—so conservative that it consistently labelled even moderate Democrats as radical. (This was a question of the style sheet, not just editorialization; for instance, it would refer to "Senator Tom Walsh, Radical, Montana.") At the other end was the *Chicago Sun-Times* which regarded Franklin Delano Roosevelt as a fit candidate for canonization. In between were several newspapers occupying different quadrants—the *Chicago Daily New*, the *Evening Post*, the *American*, and the *Chicago Herald-Examiner*. For a while the city even boasted (or perhaps apologized for) the *Midwest Daily Record*, an official publication of the Communist Party.

Most of those newspapers are now gone and the survivors have very little partisan coloration. They have adopted neutral techniques which they hope will stave off criticism. Instead, the criticism has increased. Readers find themselves unable to find an organ that "tells the truth" simply because they see nothing that fits the truth as they know it. There is no such thing as a point of view that is neutral for the observer.

This reality was brought sharply to my attention in the early 1970s when President Nixon was embroiled in the Watergate scandal. Upon the request of the Associated Press, I wrote an article on the history of impeachment and the steps that would be necessary to carry it out. It was *not*, in my judgment, a particularly partisan piece (if it had been, I do not believe it would have been carried by AP). My relations with Mr. Nixon had always been good despite the fact that I was not one of his admirers. My attitude was not shared by a lady in Little Rock, who wrote a letter ripping me from stem to stern for my "left wing views." She added that she was particularly incensed by the conduct of the *Arkansas Gazette* in carrying my words as part of its scheme to brainwash the people of the city. She explained that she had escaped the brainwashing because she had a subscription to the *Omaha World-Herald*, which she admitted possessed a Republican orientation but which "told the truth in its news columns."

Since that experience, I have made a conscientious effort to keep my own biases in the forefront of my mind whenever I read a news story. I doubt whether it has done much good, but I do, at times, recognize that what I had first thought was a deviation from factual presentation was merely a viewpoint that disagreed with my viewpoint. The basic reality is that we must take into account the bias of the reader as well as the author when judging a presentation.

Does this mean that meaningful communication to a general audience is impossible? Obviously not. As Americans we have many disagreements, but we are still held together by a common body of belief. We have been quite cohesive as a nation, and in a democracy that means there must be some form of communication. How do we achieve this in a society where the lady from Little Rock believes that the *Gazette* is a left-wing rag and the *World-Herald* is a harbinger of the truth? I find the answer in a college experience which I did not understand at the time but which took on more meaning as the years went by.

There was a period when I roomed with a Russian who had been born and raised in Harbin, Manchuria, where his parents had fled from the Bolshevik Revolution. I was fascinated by his stories of life in the Soviet Union, although I realized they were all second-hand and had to be judged in the light of his parents' trials. He had one account which stuck with me. It involved the two major Soviet newspapers, *Pravda* (Truth) and *Izvestia* (News). According to my friend, one would occasionally find on the front page of either or both an article extolling cabbage. This lowly vegetable would be presented as the perfect nutrient, building body and sometimes even increasing sexual virility. In such cases, the reaction of the reader would be "Aha! The wheat crop's failed again!"

At first, I regarded the story as merely comic. But the realization came to me finally that it also demonstrated the difficulties involved in brainwashing people on a large scale. During World War II, I had an excellent illustration myself of how propaganda really works. I was stationed on Guam in the Pacific, and we spent quite a bit of time listening to the Tokyo Rose propaganda broadcasts from Japan. We were not greatly impressed by the propaganda, but she had some recordings of American music that were superior to those of the Armed Forces radio station. Her so-called newscasts were ridiculous. On Monday, the Japanese fleet would sink the American fleet off the Philippines; on Tuesday off Formosa (now Taiwan); on Wednesday off the Mariannas; on Thursday off the Bonins; and on Friday off Okinawa. It was grotesque, as the war had reached a stage where the Japanese could barely put a canoe out on the ocean, let alone a fleet. We pitied them for thinking they were winning the war when it was already lost. When we actually got into Japan, however, we discovered that they had not been fooled in the slightest. They had realized that every one of those "victories" was bringing the action a thousand miles or so closer to Japan.

In short, what had happened was that both the Russians and the Japanese had become sophisticated concerning their own propaganda. It always followed a pattern and they recognized the pattern. Extrapolating on that point it seems to me that the basis for useful journalism is a recognition for fundamental rules that are *always* followed. The audience will interpret what is written in accordance with the biases of its individual members. But the common base makes it possible to use newspaper accounts in the public dialogue. None of the discussants may be happy with the accounts they read but they can at least agree on what they are and go on from there.

THE PERILS OF ADHERING TO RULES

Again, there is a danger in strict adherence to the rules. It lies in the tendency of people working by strict standards to disregard anything that does not fit into those standards. A genuinely new set of circumstances is usually not handled well by experienced professionals and may wind up being ignored altogether. What this means in terms of journalism can be illustrated by two major events within recent memory, the black liberation movement and the women's movement. The press completely failed to prepare us for the advent of either one, and we did not know they were there until they had exploded physically.

What happened to the black liberation movement can be easily traced. It was sparked by the invention of the Rust cotton picker which displaced the huge gangs of pickers from the southern plantations. They headed for cities, where it was possible for totally uneducated and largely unskilled people to make a living by scrounging. But the movement was not the kind which fit into the classic patterns of the journalism of the 1920s and the 1930s. Ten or twelve blacks in Yazoo, Mississippi, boarding a bus for Chicago was not the substance of headlines. The few became a steady trickle and the steady trickle became a torrent. But journalists were caught up in the old philosophical conundrum, How many hairs make a beard? Neither the northern nor the southern papers had any writers with the expertise or the background to interpret the movement, and when the huge numbers could no longer be ignored, the stories that were written tended to segregate the blacks in the papers just as they were segregated in society. I can still recall the black man who slipped into the side door of the *Chicago Tribune* once a week to write a column of social notes which were printed in a section that was distributed only in the black area of the city.

The results were predictable. Total segregation is possible in a plantation economy where complete control can be exercised over the personal lives of the workers. Similar control encounters grave difficulties in a large city, where mobility is essential for a normal life. Explosive forces build up among the people so confined, and eventually they locate an outlet. In Chicago a riot occurred when a black boy was stoned by whites for swimming across an imaginary line that had, up to that point, effectively segregated the people using the beach. This is the first time I can recall that the "race issue" actually broke into print—thus reinforcing the belief among some black leaders that the only way to get Whitey's attention was to throw a brick through Whitey's window. Of course, quite a bit had been written at one time about the black heavyweight boxing champion Jack Johnson, but most of it was an account of the unsuccessful search for a "white hope" that could defeat him.

The women's movement is another example of a social trend that was completely missed by the press until it broke upon us. The physical violence did not match that brought on by the black revolution. But it is possible that the psychological shock might have been eased by earlier and sensible discussion. Again, the press was totally unprepared—partly because most reporters outside of the society page were male but also because it offered a new perspective for which editors were not prepared.

At first, the movement was treated as a joke. Humorous columns were written speculating on whether women named Goldman would change to Goldperson and presenting mythical accounts of the dean of a girls' school who told her pupils to "pray to God and she will answer you." Occasionally there would be a piece about "bra burning ceremonies" (I have never seen evidence that any such thing ever took place) or hinting at the influence of lesbianism in the "movement." The writers had a field day when one group formed WITCHES (Women's International Terrorist Conspiracy from Hell). That at least attracted some attention. But overall, it was the kind of treatment that tended to work against rational discussion of an important social problem. The economic patterns of society had changed, and we had to work out a new relationship between the sexes. It was not helped by the kind of reporting that took place.

Before closing, it would be well to take a look at the impact of television on the press. As I have stated earlier, the most important effect stems from the superiority of "the tube" in reporting spot news. For a newspaper, an event must be written, set up in type, printed and distributed by somewhat clumsy mechanisms. The television newscaster is not tied by the same bonds. He or she can interrupt at any feasible time and, if a story warrants it, all of the airwaves can be dedicated to the event—which happened in the aftermath of the assassination of President Kennedy and the attempted assassination of President Reagan. This, of course, can be a two-edged sword. Television is superb at covering live action. It is not so superb when it comes to long, drawn-out episodes in which there are few events. Television was guilty of a number of gaffes in both instances simply because anchormen found themselves on the air with little to say.

Regardless of the gaffes, however, the ability of television to cut in at any time of the day has forced a new style of print journalism. The modern press attempts to put stories in perspective; to explain, as well as relate, what is happening; and to pick up long-range social trends. Here they have spotted the major weaknesses of electronics and are playing to it.

What I have done in this article is to try to give the reader some feel of what goes into news production. The questions that are usually raised can be answered simply.

Can we rely on the accuracy of the factual presentations in the American press? Yes—but we must remember that journalists are as human as their readers and are subject to mistakes as all of us are.

Can we rely on a fair and balanced account when we read the American press? Here the answer must be qualified somewhat. We can usually count upon what a reporter regards as a fair and balanced account, but we must always ask ourselves if we are capable of reading what he has written with a fair and balanced eye.

Can we rely on the press to be objective? Only to the extent that we can rely upon ourselves to be "objective."

Can we rely upon the press to give us a full account of an event? No. The best for which we can hope—and which we usually get—is an account of those elements of an event which the reporter considers significant.

Can we rely upon the press to expand our horizons and educate the population at large? No. The press is not an educational institution. It operates on the theory that the reading public is already educated and that the role of the press is to present facts which the educated person can use in solving problems of society.

Can we rely upon the press to alert us to long-range social trends? No, although journalists are aware of this problem and are trying to do something about it. They are held in the same trap that catches us all: a tendency to regard the world which we know as the only real world and to ignore the new facts with which we are not familiar.

To sum this up, the press is a useful and reliable instrument as long as we realize it is fundamentally a means of carrying on the public dialogue in a mass society. It cannot rise above that dialogue and survive, but it is not very likely to fall below it either. It never gives us enough information to make up our minds on a public question, but it does give us enough that we can go and get further facts on subjects in which we are interested. In one sense, the press is a public reference service.

Above all, however, we must remember that the press exists to give us a *daily* account of *daily* events. It is not an effort to write history, but an effort to keep us alert to the world we live in. It will never be satisfying unless we reach a stage of evolution in which all human beings are cast in the same mold. But without it, we would not be able to manage a mass society, because we would have no way of talking with each other.

BIBLIOGRAPHY

Allen, Frederick Lewis, *Only Yesterday: An Informal History of the 1920s.* New York: Harper & Brothers Publishers, 1957.

Bayley, Edwin R., *Joe McCarthy and the Press.* Madison: University of Wisconsin Press, 1981.

Bleyer, Willard Grosvenor, *Main Currents in the History of American Journalism.* New York: Houghton Mifflin Co., 1927.

Broder, David, *Behind the Front Page: A Candid Look at How the News is Made.* New York: Simon & Schuster, 1987.

Gay, Peter, *The Enlightenment: An Interpretation.* New York: Alfred K. Knopf, 1966.

Kobre, Sidney, *The Development of the Colonial Newspaper.* Pittsburgh: Colonial Press, 1944.

Mankowitz, Wolf, *The Extraordinary Mr. Poe: A Biography of Edgar Allan Poe.* New York: Summit Books, 1978.

Mott, Frank Luther, *American Journalism: A History, 1690–1960.* New York: Macmillan, 1962.

Sinclair, David, *Edgar Allan Poe.* Totowa, NJ: Rowman and Littlefield, 1977.

Woodward, Bob and Carl Bernstein, *All the President's Men.* New York: Simon and Schuster, 1974.

SUGGESTIONS FOR FURTHER READING

Gans, Herbert J., *Deciding What's News.* New York: Vintage Books, 1980.

12

Religious Bigotry and the Press: The Treatment of Gerald L. K. Smith

Glen Jeansonne

Religious bigots raise an important question for a free but ethical press: What is more important, the public's right to know or the protection of society from the lunatic fringe which feasts upon attention? Bigots unfortunately profit by publicity, yet their actions are legitimate news. If they are sufficiently bizarre, a group of only a few hundred misguided fanatics may capture media coverage. The Aryan Nation, the Identity Churches, the Neo-Nazis, and the followers of Lyndon Larouche have made national headlines and won notoriety, earning for them the scorn of responsible citizens but also bringing some emotionally disturbed people ready to join any cause which promises notoriety.

The growth of satellite communications and the increasing popularity of national newspapers such as *USA Today* have complicated the old problem of ethics versus popularity. What makes the problem particularly difficult is that the public demonstrably wants to know about these groups; articles about them sell papers. Yet the power of suggestion is strong, and copycat groups spring up as a result of publicity. Just as an episode of Rod Serling's "Twilight Zone" featured an airplane hijacking, thus inspiring the first actual hijacking, in more recent years the lacing of Tylenol capsules with cyanide spawned terrorists who mimicked the incident after it was given widespread publicity. Another example is hostage-taking. Some argue that Soviet citizens are seldom the target of terrorists because Soviet authorities refuse to publicize incidents. Is the press responsible? Or is it irresponsible?

In the 1930s and 1940s the American press faced a similar dilemma concerning the treatment of religious bigots whose popularity was inspired by the Great Depression. Father Charles E. Coughlin, Rev. Gerald Winrod, and Gerald L. K. Smith were depression-era religious leaders who won millions of followers through media coverage of their demagogic appeals. Coughlin won attention as a radio speaker and publisher of the journal Social Justice. Winrod gained converts to his political and religious movement by delivering sermons and speeches and publishing *The Defender.*

Gerald Smith, however, was the most notable bigot. He outlasted Coughlin and Winrod and remained active until his death in 1976. However, the press deliberately limited coverage of Smith after the early 1940s, something it was never able to accomplish with Coughlin because of his access to radio, or with Winrod because of his church audiences. Moreover, fueled by high-powered oratory, Smith combined religion with politics in a manner which blurred the distinction between religious and secular crusades. An examination of the case of Gerald Smith may reveal much about the problems and possibilities of a disciplined press and its coverage of a demagogue who protected himself with the doctrines of religious liberty and free speech.

SMITH'S CAREER

Who was Gerald Smith? Persons born after the Second World War may not remember him. Or if they do, they might identify him as the architect of a seven-story statue of Jesus and producer of a religious passion play in the small Arkansas Ozark community of Eureka Springs. But Smith was much more. He was a renowned orator, a controversial political figure, a popular writer, and a religious leader with a mass following. As a speaker and writer he addressed more Americans personally than anyone of his generation. He published a religious monthly, *The Cross and the Flag,* ran for the presidency three times, and received more than one hundred thousand votes when he ran for the U.S. Senate in Michigan in 1942.

Smith was born to Danish and English parents on the frigid Wisconsin prairies in 1898. He came from four generations of preachers and became a preacher himself in the Disciples of Christ church. Educated at small rural schools and at Valparaiso University, he pastored several churches in rural Wisconsin before he obtained a large church in Indianapolis. From there he moved to the prestigious Kings Highway Christian Church in Shreveport, Louisiana. Smith arrived in Louisiana when the Great Depression was tightening its grip on the nation, a time when Huey P. Long already held a tight grip on the Bayou State. Long, Louisiana's governor from 1929–32 and subsequent U.S. Senator, was an ambitious enemy of Franklin D. Roosevelt and advocated sharing the wealth of millionaires with common people to make "Every Man a King" and alleviate the economic misery of the times.[1]

After Long intervened to save some of Smith's parishioners from foreclosure on their homes, Smith left the ministry and joined Long's movement. He never pastored another church, but for the remainder of his life he combined religion and politics with a zealotry which won him the title "Savonarola of the Swamps." Smith became a handsomely-paid organizer for Long's Share-Our-Wealth Society, a loose organization based upon a plan to redistribute wealth and establish a national organization which would promote Long for president in 1936. An assassin's bullet thwarted Long's ambition, but Smith's association with Long and his eloquent preaching at Long's funeral propelled him to national prominence.[2]

Smith next joined the old-age pension movement of Dr. Francis E. Townsend. Townsend, like Long, advocated a panacea to end the Depression; his plan was to stimulate spending by giving generous pensions to the elderly. In 1936 Smith, Townsend, and Coughlin joined forces in a new third party to support North Dakota Congressman William Lemke for president against Roosevelt. Smith hated Roosevelt venomously and invoked the memory of Huey Long to attempt to defeat the aristocratic New Yorker. He developed oratorical gimmicks to cloak himself in Long's glory and appropriate some of his popularity. Campaigning for the Long machine in 1936, Smith summoned the voice of Long from the heavens— and a record player in a treetop blared forth the Kingfish's voice. He denounced Roosevelt and the anti-Long faction in Louisiana for having shed the blood of the martyred Long, then dipped his hands in red dye and lifted them up for the audience.[3]

Father Coughlin was confident of his own speaking ability, but Smith overshadowed him in their joint campaign for Lemke in 1936. One reporter who had listened to Smith and Coughlin wrote that "before a live audience he makes Father Coughlin seem less articulate than a waxworks."[4] Journalist H.L. Mencken, who had heard the best speakers in America, wrote:

> Gerald L. K. Smith is the greatest orator of them all, not the greatest by an inch or a foot or a yard or a mile, but the greatest by at least two light years.

1. Jeansonne, "Preacher, Populist, Propagandist, 303.
2. Jeansonne, "Preacher, Populist, Propagandist," 314–15.
3. Bennett, *Demagogues in the Depression*, 132; *Detroit Free Press*, 20 Sept. 1936.
4. Harris, "That Third Party," 85.

He begins where the next best leaves off. He is the master of masters, the champion boob-bumper of all epochs, the Aristotle and Johann Sebastian Bach of all known earsplitters, dead or alive.[5]

Still another journalist wrote of Smith: "The man has the passion of Billy Sunday. He has the fire of Adolf Hitler. He is the stuff of which Fuehrers are made."[6] The comparison with Hitler was apt, because Smith, influenced by the anti-Semitic books and articles published by Henry Ford, became a vicious anti-Semite. He read Ford's *The International Jew* and claims that Ford introduced him to *The Protocols of the Learned Elders of Zion*. Angry because he thought the assassin of Long was a Jew (he was not) and bitter because he thought the Jewish press libeled Father Coughlin and him, Smith began to employ his oratorical and journalistic talents in the cause of anti-Semitism. He came to believe that Roosevelt was a Jew and that Jews were behind Communism. He charged that World War II had been fought to save the Jews and that the Holocaust was a hoax. Quoting the Bible, praising the Constitution, and denouncing Jews and Communists, he whipped crowds to hysteria. His talks resembled Klan cross-burnings and high school pep rallies. Smith attacked a cast of stock villains: Karl Marx, Nikolai Lenin, Franklin Roosevelt, and the entire Jewish people. He said that Jews had murdered Jesus and now plotted to destroy democracy in America and enslave the gentile population.

ATTEMPTS TO STIFLE SMITH

Smith's sensational charges, expressed in a mellifluous speaking voice and with a facile pen, captured front-page headlines frequently in the national press in the 1930s and early 1940s. Smith held mass rallies in football stadiums and auditoriums. His eloquent demagogy seemed to threaten the safety of Jews and leftists, but what could be done if he violated no laws?

One option was militant opposition. Jewish, labor, and liberal organizations began to picket Smith's meetings, to heckle him, and to deny him the opportunity to rent places to speak.[7] In Los Angeles ten thousand pickets opposed his speech at Embassy Auditorium. In Saint Louis veterans took over his meeting and turned off the microphones; in Chicago he

5. Mencken, "Why Not Gerald?" Baltimore *Evening Sun*, 1936.
6. Huie, "Gerald Smith's Bid for Power," 145.
7. I discuss these incidents and the subsequent attempt of Jewish and liberal groups to quarantine Smith in detail in chap. 10, "From Courtroom to Quarantine," of *Gerald L. K. Smith*.

was pelted with stones and eggs, and once was arrested for incendiary oratory. Mammoth anti-Smith rallies were held. Articles denouncing Smith appeared in national publications. He was sued by libelled parties and investigated for income tax evasion. He found it difficult to move around the country and to rent halls to speak or hotels to stay in.[8]

Nonetheless, Smith's crowds grew and so did his income. By the mid-1940s he was receiving over $100,000 yearly from collection plates passed at his rallies and money enclosed in letters from supporters. When shouted down he became a martyr; when allowed to speak he became a celebrity. He collected libel settlements from *Time, Newsweek,* the *Wichita Beacon,* and former U.S. Attorney General Francis Biddle. He thrived on publicity, good or bad, and relished journalistic combat. He was the subject of investigative reporting, but this only stirred increased interest in his speeches and articles.[9]

The media attention was clearly counterproductive to amicable group relations, but how could Smith be stopped? People wanted to read about Smith and journalists found him entertaining. Every article that excoriated Smith made curious people want to hear him speak and to read his magazines. He cooperated with the journalists covering him by issuing press releases, posing for photographs, and agreeing to interviews. He covertly encouraged pickets and hecklers because they made his rallies newsworthy and colorful.

The content of Smith's speeches and articles seemed less important than the reactions they provoked and the crowds he attracted. When Smith and his followers created political parties, staged conventions, and ran candidates for office, they were considered newsworthy because they were provocative and controversial. They demanded equal time on radio and television, and federal authorities could find no grounds on which to deny them. Moreover, the press had traditionally reported on third party crusades such as Populists, Socialists, and Dixiecrats. Was Smith any different? In principle, Smith was entitled to be heard. In practice, by encouraging bigotry he was dividing the country.

Ministers and rabbis, like journalists, had problems in dealing with Smith. Smith was a religious figure as well as a political demagogue, and many Christians believed that he was a sincere man who preached the

8. Smith, *Besieged Patriot,* 104, 316.
9. McClusky, "Huckster of Hatred," 65; Smith to Martin Dies, 2 Aug. 1943, Box 8, Folder 1943, Dies Committee, Smith Papers, Bentley Historical Library, University of Michigan; Walter P. Reese to Phil W. Davis, Jr., 6 Dec. 1954, Box 43, Folder Davis, Phil. W., Jr.; Phil W. Davis, Jr., to Smith, 26 Jan. 1955, Box 43, Folder 1955, David, Phil W., Jr.; Smith to *Time* Magazine, 7 Sept. 1960, Box 56, Folder 1962, *Time* Magazine (libel suit), all in Smith Papers.

gospel. He lashed out at sinners, and if among his targets were Jews and Communists, the fault lay with them. Some ministers asked Smith not to attend their churches, but public ostracism was also news and made the dailies. Moreover, unscrupulous ministers could obtain large crowds, increased donations, and free publicity by hosting Smith. Finally, there was the question of free speech. Smith had just as much right to speak in churches and to appear in newspaper articles as anyone else. Freedom of speech included freedom to preach hatred, some ministers and journalists argued. Besides, in the free marketplace of ideas, the best ideas would triumph. If Smith were permitted to speak and if what he said was reported accurately, he would make a fool of himself. The average person could distinguish truth from falsehood, Christian love from racist hatred.

But did the best ideas inevitably win out? What about the Crusades, the Inquisition, the burning of witches, or, more recently, Hitler's tyranny? People could be duped, confused, and persuaded to commit atrocities. And before they could be stopped great evil could be done. Further, America professed to tolerate minorities while Smith promoted hatred of them. Was not a concern for minority rights a legitimate argument in favor of silencing Smith?

Even if moderates could agree that silencing Smith would be a good idea, how could it be done? Some believed that turning the glare of publicity on Smith would discredit him. Smith could not fool the American people indefinitely. Furthermore, picketing Smith, while it might bring him attention, would also bring attention to the goals of those picketing him. Active opposition to racism would also galvanize Smith's critics, unite the forces of tolerance, and raise the morale of Smith's intended scapegoats.[10]

A NEW STRATEGY: SILENCE

Rabbi S. A. Fineberg, one of the nation's foremost opponents of anti-Semitism, decided to experiment with a different weapon against Smith— silence. Instead of denouncing Smith, the Jewish community would ignore him and attempt to persuade the press not to cover his activities. They would not picket or heckle him, or prevent him from renting auditoriums. They would smother him with silence.[11]

The best argument against militance was that it was counterproductive. An FBI agent who had followed Smith commented: "There is little doubt that publicity, even though bad as to his character and reputation,

---

10. Glaustein and Howe, "How Fight Rabble-Rousers?", 460–64.
11. Fineberg, "Checkmate for Rabble-Rousers," 223.

aided Smith. Without question, some of the people came purely to see and hear the man who had gained so much notoriety in the press."[12] Fineberg remarked, "If the opponents of Smith are going to provide the advertising, it merely saves Smith a lot of money."[13]

Militancy was also hazardous because minorities risked inciting a reaction against their own group of harassing Smith,[14] and alliances with Communist and Socialist opponents of Smith damaged the credibility of moderates.[15] Besides, the goals of the militants were not well conceived. What did they hope to accomplish? They probably could not physically stop Smith from speaking, and force would not change the minds of many Americans who were not already convinced that Smith was a menace.[16]

There were both principled and practical reasons for turning away from physical opposition at Smith's meetings. After a mob had broken up a Smith meeting in Minneapolis in 1946 the *Minneapolis Star* editorialized, "A mob is a mob whether the target of its abuse is Gerald L. K. Smith or an Alabama Negro."[17] Militant opposition added excitement to Smith's meetings and increased the interest in him by the community. After veterans had broken up a Smith meeting in Saint Louis in 1946, a reader wrote the Saint Louis *Globe-Democrat*, "I have never heard what Smith had to say nor what he upholds, but now I am very curious, as no doubt at least half of those who attend Gerald L. K. Smith rallies are attracted out of curiosity resulting from all the publicity."[18]

Fineberg believed that Smith deliberately provoked his opponents in order to goad them into activities that would be covered by the press. Fineberg explained, "When Smith comes to a community he wants all the publicity he can get. Adverse publicity is almost as good as favorable publicity if only it reaches the masses and if only they feel impelled to hear this very important gentleman, who is so very important that all the important people are worrying about him."[19] Militant opposition inflamed those who already supported Smith and inspired them to contribute more to his cause; it also gratified his massive ego.

If unfavorable publicity could defeat Smith, Fineberg argued, he

12. FBI Report on Gerald L. K. Smith, 21 June 1945, F 62-43818-754, 3. Obtained under the Freedom of Information Act.

13. S. A. Fineberg to David Jacobson, 26 Dec. 1945, American Jewish Committee Archives.

14. Ed., *Los Angeles Today*, 10 Nov. 1945.

15. Anton Lourie to Ira M. Younger, 30 July 1945, American Jewish Committee Archives.

16. Fineberg, "How Fight Rabble-Rousers?", 466.

17. Quoted in Fineberg, "Checkmate for Rabble-Rousers," 223.

18. A. W. Olsen to Editor, 31 May 1946.

19. S. A. Fineberg to David Jacobson, 26 Dec. 1945, American Jewish Committee Archives.

would have fallen long ago into obscurity. Jewish and liberal organizations had spent millions of dollars fighting Smith and yet their efforts had been futile. In cities where militant opposition incited violence, and where newspapers covered the conflicts widely, thousands of people went to hear Smith, perhaps excited by the prospect of a confrontation. Because Smith's arguments were not logical, he could not be refuted by logic; nor could he be deterred by force. Fineberg explained, "If all that would be needed to stop persecution is the protest of the victim, no people would ever have been persecuted."[20] It would be just as foolish, Fineberg wrote, to fight illiteracy by picketing the homes of illiterates.[21] Fineberg clinched his argument: "A rabble-rouser can no more be blown out with blasts against him, than an electric light can be blown out by one's breath. The one thing rabble-rousers cannot overcome is that which would close any show on Broadway—a complete lack of publicity in the general press."[22]

Fineberg's policy, which he called a "quarantine" or "dynamic silence," was not unanimously accepted, nor was it easy to implement. By 1947, however, Fineberg had persuaded the major Jewish organizations to experiment with a quarantine. It remained for them to convince the media. The deliberate neglect of a figure as notorious and newsworthy as Gerald Smith was difficult to engineer. Representatives from Jewish groups approached newspaper publishers, radio and television station owners, and religious leaders and urged them to ignore Smith—to permit him to speak but to prevent him from exploiting the media. They appealed to the consciences of media leaders concerned with bigotry; but sometimes they threatened boycotts of publications, programs, and advertisers.[23]

The media slowly began to comply. The blackout of Smith was never universal, nor was it immediately adopted, but by the end of the 1940s it had become remarkably successful. Stories about Smith were removed from the front to the back pages. As attendance at his meetings dwindled he became less newsworthy, and stories about him disappeared entirely. One who examines the clipping files of major dailies cannot help being struck by the decline in coverage between the end of World War II and the beginning of the 1950s. William F. Buckley told an interviewer that Smith was a good example of the deliberate social isolation of an extremist. "As an example of the social sanctions," he said, "I give you what has hap-

20. Fineberg, *Overcoming Anti-Semitism*, 108.
21. Fineberg, "Checkmate for Rabble-Rousers," 226.
22. S. A. Fineberg to Editor, *National Jewish Post*, 25 April 1947.
23. George Kellman to Isaiah Termin, "An Appraisal of the Silent Treatment," 27 May 1947, American Jewish Committee Archives; Ed., Boston *Jewish Advocate*, 17 July 1947; Denver *Post*, 11 Aug. 1949; Ed., Milwaukee *Journal*, 12 Oct. 1949.

pened to Gerald L. K. Smith, the fierce anti-Semite. Would Smith be invited to join the sponsoring group of the Lincoln Center? If he gave a $1,000 contribution to the President's Club, would he be admitted as a member? No. Gerald L. K. Smith has been effectively isolated in America and I'm glad that he has been."[24]

On the one hand it is satisfying to witness a sharp curtailment of Smith's influence and his hate-mongering. On the other, it is astonishing to realize that a program to deliberately deny coverage to so prominent a speaker and journalist could have succeeded on such a scale. True, there were no limitations on Smith's speaking or writing, but one wishing to learn about Smith could not read about him in major newspapers, periodicals, or scholarly journals. Imposition of the quarantine demonstrated the degree of influence of Jewish organizations on the national media—and their determination. There was no conspiracy in the sense that Smith employed the term, and Jewish groups had only influence, not control, of the media, and their actual ownership of media outlets was extremely limited. Yet there was some truth in Smith's assertion that there was a conspiracy of silence to deprive him of a forum: "If I am so wrong, then why am I denied the right to express my opinion? Wouldn't it seem that the fallacy of my doctrine, if expressed freely, would so quickly expose itself that I would no longer be a threat?" Smith wrote a Harvard student that he was not getting all sides of the issues at Harvard. "It occurred to me," he wrote, "that you must live in an environment where the uniformity of viewpoints concerning these matters could become a bit monotonous. It is possible for men to become narrowminded in their determination to be broadminded."[25]

The question of the point at which free speech becomes dangerous is ancient, complicated, and fraught with potential inconsistencies. Did American liberals violate their own principles in quarantining Smith? Were they willing to accept dissent from the left but not from the right? Was it a matter of "whose ox is gored"? Perhaps. But Smith was a dangerous man, and the fact that he directly provoked no violence against minorities is no guarantee that he could not have done so, given the opportunity. Moreover, in the context of the period encompassing World War II and the immediate postwar period, he may have used the exercise of free speech to threaten the foundations of democracy and ultimately deny free speech to others. In retrospect Smith appears an irritant rather than an immediate threat, but that was not so apparent at the time.

24. Buckley, *Inveighing We Will Go*, 50.
25. This and previous quotations are from Smith to William G. Dakin, 23 March 1954, Box 41, Folder 1954, Ha-Hi (misc.), Bentley Historical Library.

Smith's decline as a mass orator was not entirely due to the quarantine. His emotional, long-winded, simplistic style was becoming unappealing to more educated audiences, and he could not compete with television. Besides, he was growing older. He no longer had the fire and stamina he had had in the 1930s and 1940s. His major enemies were dead. It was one thing to call Franklin Roosevelt a communist; it was another to apply the term to Dwight D. Eisenhower. Smith had competition in the 1950s and 1960s from McCarthyites and the John Birch Society. Anti-Communism was more marketable than anti-Semitism, but Smith remained primarily an anti-Semite.

Smith did not become entirely irrelevant, however. He merely changed his tactics. He felt he could reach more people by writing than by speaking, and he became a prolific writer and publisher of right-wing extremist literature. He had founded his monthly, *The Cross and the Flag*, in 1942, and in the 1960s and early 1970s his circulation reached twenty-five thousand. He issued so many tracts that his collective output fills more volumes than the *Encyclopedia Britannica*.

Smith's writing style was as simplistic and direct as his oratory, and for those reasons he enjoyed some success. His tracts were cheap and easily obtainable. He established his own printing plant and worked feverishly, fourteen hours a day, to write copy to keep the presses busy. He received more money through the mail for his written financial appeals than he had received from speaking. He bought several Victorian mansions and began to collect art, jewelry, and Bibles. He bought Lincoln Continental automobiles and was chauffeured everywhere he traveled.

SMITH'S "SACRED PROJECTS"

Then, in 1966, he began to attract the attention of the press again, this time not as an orator but as the architect of Christian shrines. Smith bought a tract of land in the small mountain community of Eureka Springs, Arkansas, and brought the somnolent tourist industry to life there by the construction of what he called his "Sacred Projects." First he built a gigantic statue of Jesus on a mountaintop, naming it "The Christ of the Ozarks." It could be seen from four states. Religious music played at the site, and spotlights bathed it in color at night. Devout people came to see the statue, and Smith's name began to appear in the national news. Journalists wrote that he had mellowed; the local newspaper and the Eureka Springs chamber of commerce recognized the Smiths as model citizens.

The Christ of the Ozarks was only the beginning. In the next decade Smith added a passion play, a Bible museum, and an art gallery. He bought and restored an old home, Penn Castle, and divided his time between living in Eureka Springs and in Los Angeles. Tourists began to flock to the Sacred Projects. Motels and restaurants were built by local people to capitalize on the tourist trade. Business boomed and Smith became a local hero. He was responsible for making the town of less than two thousand inhabitants the leading tourist attraction in Arkansas.

Although most Arkansans approved of Smith's Sacred Projects because of their economic benefits, some did not. Elderly residents disliked the increased traffic and rising property taxes. Those living in communal colonies in the area resented the commercialization of Eureka Springs. But very few local residents knew anything about Smith as an anti-Semite. He did not publish any books or tracts there and did not mail *The Cross and the Flag* to local people. A few of the better-educated people realized that Smith was anti-Semitic, but Smith rarely issued controversial statements from Penn Castle.

There was one major exception to the uncritical acceptance of Smith in Arkansas—the state's largest daily, the Little Rock *Arkansas Gazette*. From the time Smith bought property in Eureka Springs and began to erect the Christ of the Ozarks, the *Gazette* attempted to persuade him that Arkansans were not hospitable to anti-Semites. Investigative journalists writing for the *Gazette* revealed that Smith was mixing money from his anti-Semitic Christian Nationalist Crusade with money from the Elna M. Smith Foundation, named for his wife and incorporated to operate the Sacred Projects. The *Gazette* wrote that Smith was still publishing anti-Semitic literature in California and that he would taint the good name of Arkansas by moving to Eureka Springs.

The *Gazette*'s crusade against Smith broke the grip of the quarantine on coverage of Smith's activities. However, most of the stories in papers outside of Arkansas were devoted primarily to the Sacred Projects. To some journalists Smith seemed to have mellowed; the title of one article was "Twilight Years of a Kindly Old Hatesmith."[26] Jewish groups attempted vainly to preserve the quarantine, then decided to abandon it themselves when they learned that federal money was to be used to finance a project that would provide better access to Smith's Sacred Projects.

At issue was the repaving of a road leading to the site of the Christ of the Ozarks and the passion play. In 1970 syndicated columnist Jack Anderson revealed that the Department of Commerce planned to spend $182,000 on the road. Previously the grant had been routinely approved, but a national outcry arose when it was learned that the project would benefit a notorious anti-Semite. The Anti-Defamation League demanded

26. See Ryan, "Twilight Years of a Kindly Old Hatesmith," 88–91.

that the Department of Commerce cancel "an outrageous expenditure of taxpayers' money" and argued that the federal government "should not be a partner to a man who business has been spreading racial and religious bigotry for more than 30 years."[27]

Initially most Arkansas politicians supported the road project because they believed it would benefit the tourist industry. In a letter to the editor of the *Arkansas Gazette*, Governor Winthrop Rockefeller stated that "when government gets into the business of approving or disapproving of projects on the basis of whether it agrees with every enterprise that might benefit, then the kind of government I believe in and I hope the kind of government you believe in is on the road to ruin."[28]

Despite support in Arkansas, in the context of national politics the road became an embarrassment to the Nixon administration. The Department of Commerce admitted that when it had approved the grant for construction it had not realized that the Elna M. Smith Foundation mentioned in the application was named for the wife of Gerald L. K. Smith and was operated by him. Congressman Ed Koch of New York led a crusade by liberals against the road.[29]

The American Civil Liberties Union of Arkansas joined the fight against the road. The Arkansas branch of the ACLU denounced the road as a public works project designed to promote a sectarian cause and filed suit to prevent the use of federal money. Smith, on the other hand, claimed that opposition to the road was based on religious prejudice directed against him and filed suit against the Anti-Defamation League, threatened to deliver a speech on the floor of Congress, and bought advertisements in Arkansas newspapers (including the *Gazette*) to denounce those opposed to the project. He blamed opposition on "the lethal enemies of Jesus Christ" who were engaged in a "vicious attempt to destroy us." He also filed a lawsuit in which he demanded an investigation of the Jewish "conspiracy." On 20 July 1970, Commerce Secretary John Volpe cancelled the project. His official reason was that the road was "a marginal project at best," but it was clear that the incident was more of an exercise in power politics than an attempt to ensure that the work was cost-effective.[30]

Smith was outraged. He argued that the Nixon administration was

27. Forster and Epstein, *New Anti-Semitism*, 29.
28. Forster and Epstein, *New Anti-Semitism*, 29–30.
29. Extension of remarks by Mr. Edward I. Koch of New York, "More on Gerald L. K. Smith," *Congressional Record—House*, 91st Cong., Sess., v. 116, pt. 1, Jan. 19–27, 1970, 236–37.
30. Forster and Epstein, *New Anti-Semitism*, 35–36.

making ideology a test for receiving federal aid. Certainly many private and parochial schools and other non-profit projects had received aid even though their ideology might not be acceptable to everyone. The Jewish organizations themselves had promoted federal aid to such groups. Civil rights advocates and federal anti-poverty aid recipients had not been subject to any test of belief in return for money. Smith maintained that the government was applying a double standard against him which might not have been acceptable had it been applied to groups and organizations of which they approved.[31]

Smith claimed that he was denied access to public development because of the unpopularity of his beliefs. He asked: "What would be the judgment of the *Gazette* and other critics of mine if I were to organize a program to prevent the improvement of a street in front of a synagogue, or a tabernacle, or a church, or a temple, or a cathedral, or a college, black or white, merely because I did not agree doctrinally or politically with the people or the institution past which the street or the road was to be built?"[32] Despite technical arguments about other matters, Smith argued, the issue was clearly that one group was using a religious standard against a group of which they disapproved, and that the media was serving as an ally and a spokesman against a specific minority. "It's a sin to be a hate-monger," he wrote. "It's a sin to hate a man for his race. It's a sin to hate a man for his religion. But there's one thing people don't realize. It's also a sin to hate Gerald L. K. Smith. I'm people."[33]

If it is a sin to hate Smith, it is a sin difficult to avoid. And yet on the broader issue of free speech and freedom of religion, was the press fair to Smith? Should it have been? Does Smith's type of anti-Semitism clothed in Christian phrases constitute genuine religious beliefs? Does Smith have a point when he argues that, if any criticism of Jews can be suppressed as anti-Semitism, we have created a privileged minority? How do we distinguish anti-Semitism from responsible criticism?

The relations of the press toward religious bigots and their organizations pose difficult questions for the press. Does the press have a right not to cover news? Does this constitute managed news? Can the press, or persecuted groups, decide that some newsworthy events are too disreputable to cover? On the other hand, can the press be entirely passive in news stories, divorcing itself from the consequences of what it covers? What is the greater evil—to afford bigots such as Smith unrestricted access to free society, or to use the forces of society to isolate and ostracize them? Given

31. Forster and Epstein, *New Anti-Semitism*, 34–36.
32. Gerald L. K. Smith to *Arkansas Gazette*, 13 June 1970.
33. *Arkansas Democrat*, 22 May 1970.

that Smith was a disruptive influence, could we quarantine him without harming free speech in general? Is the press playing God by making or unmaking men and women and their movements?

That Smith was a dangerous religious bigot is inescapable. but how do we apply the "clear and present danger" doctrine to determine whether he was a legitimate threat, a potential fuerher rather than a mere crackpot? And who is to apply the doctrine? Surely we cannot await court rulings on every incident. The press itself will have to decide what to cover and how to cover it.

Some individuals and groups have been around long enough to be categorized as either threatening or harmless. But many groups fall into a fuzzier category, groups such as the Unification Church and the Larouchites. These are matters of judgment, not legalities. At the very least, these groups ought to be permitted to speak for themselves in their own publications. If they are to be reported in mainstream newspapers and periodicals, some element of balance should apply. Their activities should be described in their complexity, and the potential dangers they pose should be discussed realistically.

In the case of Gerald Smith, a religious bigot was successfully muzzled by the press, and he never became more than an annoyance. But what was possible in the 1940s and 1950s may no longer be practical in the 1980s. Religious leaders, bigoted or not, can buy time on television. Some newspapers are dominated by fringe groups, which assures that they will receive publicity. As to whether bigots are best defeated by the glare of publicity or the void of ostracism, there is no simple answer. In a heterogenous setting they will receive attention. But responsible reporters will try to avoid sensationalization.

Finally, what stand should historians take on writing about bigotry? Here the answer is clearer. Historians write about the past, and are on firmer ground in criticizing the errors of the past than in condemning the foibles of the present. The results of bigoted activities are more certain and can be discussed more temperately. One thing is clear to the historian. He or she cannot write the history of an era without the raw material furnished by contemporary reporting. For the historical record if nothing else, the activities of bigots should be reported.

BIBLIOGRAPHY

Bennett, David H., *Demagogues in the Depression: American Radicals and the Union Party, 1932–1936.* New Brunswick, NJ: Rutgers University Press, 1969.

Buckley, William F., Jr. *Inveighing We Will Go*. New York: Putnam, 1972.

Fineberg, Solomon Andhil, *Overcoming Anti-Semitism*. New York and London: Harper & Brothers, 1943.

_____, "Checkmate to Rabble-Rousers: What to Do When the Demagogue Comes." *Commentary* 2 (Sept. 1946): 220–26.

_____, "Fight on the Real Battle-Line" (Part 3 of "How Fight Rabble-Rousers?"). *Commentary* 2 (Nov. 1946): 460–66.

Forster, Arnold and Benjamin R. Epstein, *The New Anti-Semitism*. New York: McGraw-Hill, 1974.

Glaustein, Irwin Lee, "Against 'Silent Treatment'" (Part 1 of "How Fight Rabble-Rousers?"). *Commentary* 2 (Nov. 1946): 460–66.

Harris, Herbert, "That Third Party." *Current History* 45 (1936): 85.

Howe, Irving, "The Value of Mass Action" (Part 2 of "How Fight Rabble-Rousers?"). *Commentary* 2 (Nov. 1946): 460–64.

Huie, William Bradford, "Gerald Smith's Bid for Power." *American Mercury* 55 (1942): 145.

Jeansonne, Glen, "Preacher, Populist, Propagandist: The Early Career of Gerald L. K. Smith." *Biography* 2,4 (1979): 303–27.

_____, *Gerald L. K. Smith: Minister of Hate*. New Haven: Yale University Press, 1988.

McClusky, Thorp, "Huckster of Hatred." *Christian Herald* 73 (1950): 65.

Ryan, John Fergus, "Twilight Years of a Kindly Old Hatesmith." *Esquire* 70 (1968): 88–91.

Smith, Elna M. and Charles F. Robertson, eds., *Beseiged Patriot: Autobiographical Episodes Exposing Communism, Traitorism and Zionism from the Life of Gerald L. K. Smith*. Eureka Springs, AR: Elna M. Smith Foundation, 1978.

SUGGESTIONS FOR FURTHER READING

Ribuffo, Leo P., *The Old Christian Right: The Protestant Far Right from the Depression to the Cold War* (Philadelphia: Temple University Press, 1983) has an excellent chapter on Smith, emphasizing his career in the 1930s and 1940s. Ribuffo writes with insight about attempts to minimize publicity about Smith.

Smith, Gerald L. K., *The Cross and the Flag*.

Notes on Contributors

Charles M. Austin, an ordained Lutheran pastor, is a free-lance writer in Teaneck, N.J. and a former religion reporter for the *New York Times* and *The Record* (Hackensack, N.J.). He has also been a staff writer for the Religious News Service, English editor for the Lutheran World Federation in Geneva, and director of news for the Lutheran Church in America. He is the author of two books and numerous articles and reviews.

Kenneth A. Briggs, an ordained United Methodist elder, was religion editor of the *New York Times* from 1974–85. Since then he has been a free-lance writer, an adjunct professor at the Columbia University Graduate School of Journalism (1985–87), and a regular television commentator for United Methodist Communications. Briggs is also a senior editor for the Gallup Poll and is working on a book about Catholic America.

Herb Brin, publisher of the California-based Heritage chain of Jewish newspapers, has won several awards for Jewish journalism, including the Communications Award of the Anti-Defamation League of B'nai B'rith. A former feature writer for the *Los Angeles Times*, he opened the *Times*'s Middle East bureau and covered the Eichmann trial in Jerusalem. Brin is the author of four books of poetry and *Ich Bin Ein Jude*, about his travels in Europe and visits to the Nazi death camps.

George W. Cornell, religion writer since 1951 for the Associated Press, is the author of six books about religion, including *The Untamed God*. An Episcopal layman, he is the recipient of numerous awards for religion reporting, including the Supple Memorial Award and the 1987 Reporter of the Year Award from the Religion Newswriters Association.

John Dart has covered religion for the *Los Angeles Times* since 1967 and is currently first vice president of the Religion Newswriters Association. His distinctions include the Supple Memorial Award for religion writing and a National Endowment for the Humanities fellowship for journalists at Stanford University. His 1976 book *The Laughing Savior*, about the discovery and significance of the Nag Hammadi Gnostic library, was reissued by Harper & Row in 1988 under a new title, *The Jesus of Heresy and History*.

Peter Elvy, a Church of England priest, is vicar of Great Burstead in Essex and a former journalist. Editor of the British religious quarterly *The Sower*, he broadcasts regularly on radio and television and was for six years religious programs organizer for a local radio station. Elvy has contributed to publications in the U.S. and Great Britain and is the author of *Buying Time: The Foundations of the Electronic Church.*

Benjamin J. Hubbard is associate professor and chair, Department of Religious Studies, California State University, Fullerton, Calif., where he teaches a course on religion and the mass media. The author of a book and several scholarly and popular articles, he has also taught at Marquette University and the University of Waterloo, Ontario. He was associate editor of the *Wisconsin Jewish Chronicle* in 1981–82.

Glen Jeansonne is professor, Department of History, University of Wisconsin—Milwaukee, where he specializes in American political history and southern history. He has also taught at the University of Southwestern Louisiana and Williams College. Jeansonne is the author of numerous articles and four books, including the recently-released *Gerald L.K. Smith: Minister of Hate* which was selected as best non-fiction book of 1988 by the Wisconsin Council of Writers.

Martin E. Marty, Fairfax M. Cone Distinguished Service Professor of the History of Modern Christianity at the University of Chicago, is a leading authority on religion in America, including press coverage of religion, and a former president of the American Academy of Religion. Marty is the author of forty books, including, most recently, *Modern American Religion, Vol. I: 1893–1919, The Irony of It All*; and *Religion and Republic: The American Circumstance.* Marty is a recipient of the National Book Award and twenty-nine honorary doctorates.

George E. Reedy is Nieman Professor of Journalism at Marquette University, where he teaches journalistic ethics, and political communications and the mass media. His books include *The Twilight of the Presidency, The U.S. Senate: Paralysis or Search for Consensus?, and Lyndon B. Johnson: A Memoir.* A former United Press International congressional reporter, Reedy was a longtime aid to President Johnson and served as his press secretary from 1964–66.

Ira Rifkin, a free-lance writer in Los Angeles, specializes in articles on religion and ethics and is a regular contributor to *Media & Values* magazine. He is a former religion reporter for the *Los Angeles Daily News.* Rifkin has worked for several other news organizations, including United Press International and the *Andean Times*, Lima, Peru. In 1973–74 he taught environmental journalism at the State University of New York, New Paltz, N.Y.

Elizabeth Thoman, a Catholic sister in the Congregation of the Humility of Mary, is the founding editor of *Media & Values* magazine and a leader in the emerging field of media awareness education. Co-author of the *Guide to Teleconferencing for Churches and Religious Organizations*, Thoman received the 1983 Faith and Freedom award from the Religious Heritage of America for her leadership in creating a values approach to media issues. She serves on the Standards and Practices Committee of the new VISN-TV interfaith cable television network.

William Thorn is associate professor and chair of the Department of Journalism at Marquette University, where he teaches religious journalism and media history and directs the Institute for Catholic Media. The current president of the Teachers and Researchers Federation of the International Catholic Union of the Press, he has authored five books, including *Models of Diocesan Communication* (with Frances Trampiets SC).

Index